INDONESIA

From Sabang to Merauke

John Keay

B🍃XTREE

For
Julia
without whom I will not go again

and with special thanks to her and
Anna for the maps and to Nell for
the drawings.

Published in Great Britain in 1996 by
Boxtree Ltd, Broadwall House, 21 Broadwall, London, SE1 9PL

First published in Great Britain in hardback in 1995 by Boxtree Ltd

1 3 5 7 9 10 8 6 4 2

ISBN 0 7522 0551 X

Cover designed by Roger Updegraff
Front and back cover photographs © Michael Freeman
Typeset by SX Composing, Rayleigh, Essex
Printed and bound in Great Britain by The Bath Press, Avon

A CIP catalogue entry for this book is available from the British Library

By the same author:

Into India
When Men and Mountains Meet
The Gilgit Game
India Discovered
Eccentric Travellers
Explorers Extraordinary
Highland Drove
The Honourable Company

The Robinson Book of Exploration (editor)
The Royal Geographical Society's History of World Exploration (general editor)
Collins Encyclopaedia of Scotland (co-editor)

Contents

	Introduction	1
1.	Troubles in Aceh	11
2.	Tip Top times	29
3.	Of brigadiers and bishops	45
4.	Isle of dreams	61
5.	Why is West Sumatra?	79
6.	Raffles country	95
7.	Dire straits	115
8.	Living dangerously, dying horribly	135
9.	Every little breeze	153
10.	All is palace	171
11.	Surabaya Sue	191
12.	Paradise lost	209
13.	Ours The Land and The Water	229
14.	Islands of exile	249
	Epilogue	271
	Further Reading	279
	Index	280

Drawings by Nell Keay

Banda Aceh Mosque	11
Food barrow, Medan	29
Batak house, Toba	45
Big house, Bawomataluo, Nias	61
Bukittinggi clock	79
Rafflesia	95
Krakatau, Strait of Sunda	115
Sukarno	135
Dutch colonial Town Hall	153
Stupa, Borobudur	171
Becak, Surabaya	191
Pagoda, Bali	209
Bugis *pinisi*, Lombok strait	229
Lamp post, Banda Naira	249

Maps

The Indonesian Archipelago	iv
Sumatra	9
Java	125
Bali, Sulawesi and Nusa-tengara	211
The Moluccas and Irian Jaya	256

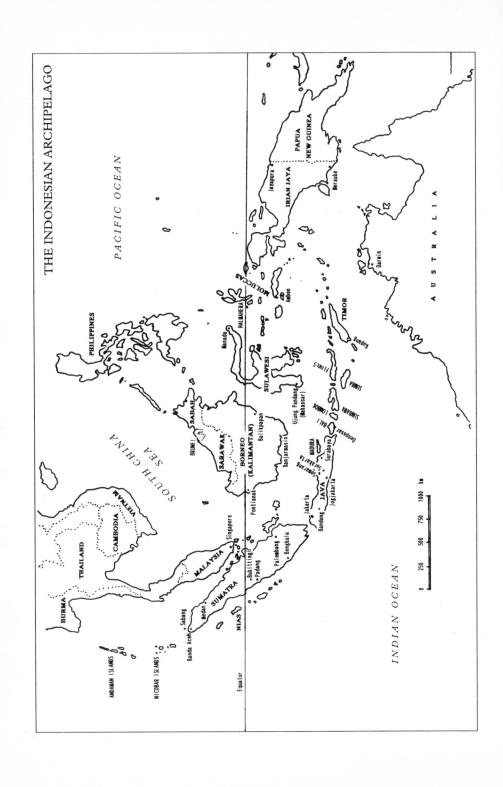

THE INDONESIAN ARCHIPELAGO

Introduction

After fifty years of nationhood, to foreigners there is still something slightly unconvincing about Indonesia. It sounds arti-
ficial. A scientific term perhaps; or possibly some mandated
speckle of islands in mid-Pacific? Nigeria or Pakistan – smaller
nations of more recent provenance – sound much more substantial. And so indeed do some of Indonesia's constituent parts. To
Java, Bali or Sumatra can be confidently ascribed an image –
temples, beaches, jungle – and even the appropriate shape on a
map. But Indonesia? It could be anywhere. The very word, a
hybrid of mainland Asia (Indo-) with island Pacific (-nesia), lacks
precision. One grapples with the idea of Gandhi in a grass skirt,
Gauguin at the Taj.

It doesn't help that the country is almost devoid of land borders.
Indonesia is unique among major nations in that most of its territory is water and the rest is islands. The sea has a special relevance
to Indonesians who declare theirs a 'pelagic state'; but it leaves the
country with no readily recognisable shape while the whole concept of pelagic territory seems to imply precarious fluidity. There
are said to be about 14,000 islands, but the number varies with the
rise and fall of the tides and even, this being a region of intense
seismic and volcanic activity, of the land. In 1883 an island in the
Sunda Strait became three islands overnight. Later, with the
emergence of Anak Krakatau, they became four.

Cataclysms apart, the country rarely makes the headlines. A
foreign correspondent's graveyard, its politics are deemed im-

penetrable, its regimes hostile, and its news value minimal. Most people would be pushed to name a single event in Indonesia's recent history and, starved of newsreel footage, know of its politics only from a much-screened feature film. This was 'The Year of Living Dangerously', in which a young and sweat-soaked Mel Gibson played an Australian journalist confronting an exceedingly hostile Jakarta. A dwarf photographer (Linda Hunt) becomes his local informant. Together they expose the iniquities of Sukarno's corrupted dictatorship before Gibson makes a hair-breadth escape as the country goes up in gun-smoke and massacre.

The film, a minor classic, conveys an overwhelming sense of menace, without clouding the issue with the obscurities of Indonesian politics. It was curiosity about those politics and the events of 1965, the dangerous year in question, which prompted my first visit. I myself experienced no journalistic nightmares in Jakarta, but evidently they still haunt the world's newsrooms; in 1993 the fortunes of this nation with the fourth largest population in the world were 'covered' by just three resident correspondents of British nationality, four Americans and three Australians. Their attentions, in a not uncongenial posting, were directed almost exclusively to minority issues – human rights abuses in East Timor, land settlement in Irian Jaya, the desecration of tribal societies there and in Borneo, and ecological depredation just about everywhere. Indonesia, in short, gets little press, nearly all of it bad.

In striking contrast to that of Bali or Java, the image of the country as a whole is decidedly negative, one of a dour and corrupt military dictatorship periodically rocked by social tremors, but generally stabilized by international recognition of its stranglehold on the nation's vast natural resources. A recent BBC programme went so far as to caution its listeners about visiting Indonesia lest their travellers' cheques help to sustain such a pariah regime. Yet, apparently unaware of the contradiction, a week later the same programme commended a package holiday to Bali's Sanur Beach. Bali, of course, is an earthly paradise. Its currency, according to the Glasgow *Herald*, is the Thai baht and its ambience, according to Rodgers and Hammerstein, South Pacific.

Indonesia, on the other hand, is a police state where Indian importunity meets Malay torpor and where multi-nationals make free with the environment while troops gun down dissidents.

For such contradictions history, especially colonial history, bears some responsibility. India got the British *imperium*, Indo-China the French *mission civilisatrice*, and the Philippines got both Spanish Catholicism and American consumerism. But Indonesia got the little Netherlands whose colonial posture was essentially parochial and whose best intentions could never convince their Indonesian subjects that they had been co-opted into a glorious family of nations. The Dutch language had limited use as an international medium and no glittering prizes awaited the Indonesian intellectual who assimilated Dutch culture. Holland's low international profile, not helped by two world wars, ensured that Indonesia's was even lower. The indignity of having been colonized by such a global nonentity still rankles and may account for something close to a national inferiority complex.

Other colonial powers made a habit of patronizing the Dutch and criticizing their colonial management. It was the British who restored Dutch rule after the Napoleonic Wars and they and their allies did so again after the Second World War. This bred a profound contempt which still influences British attitudes to the extent that many, if pressed, would characterize Indonesia as a basket entity into which were scooped all those bits of South-east Asia that were left over after the successor states in Malaysia, Singapore and Australia had taken their share.

The idea of a freak nation appears confirmed by its vital statistics. From Sumatran nose to Irian tail Indonesia's 5,000 kilometres make it the second longest country in the world, broader than the USA or Australia and shorter only than Russia. The journey – my journey – from one end to the other is equivalent to travelling from London to Tehran.

Straddling both hemispheres and spanning three time zones, this linear construction also links two oceans and two continents. Less a bridge than a line of stepping stones, its terrain ranges from the South-east Asian rain forest of Sumatra and Borneo to the Australian scrub of Timor and the Pacific atolls of Kei and

Tanimbar. Malay at one end, Indonesians become Melanesian at the other, with an estimated 366 ethnic groups speaking at least 250 distinct languages in between; Islam yields to Hindu-Buddhist syncretism in the middle, and to innumerable animist and Christian variations at the extremities; monkeys give way to marsupials and the banyan to the gum tree. Travelling through Indonesia you change continents without crossing a frontier and move from old world to new without noticing the difference. It is a country less of contrasts than of constant gradation.

Just where Asia becomes Australasia or Oceania is still debatable. Naturalists used to propose lines, most notably the Wallace Line between Bali and Lombok but, as Wallace himself found, even quadrupeds had a habit of leap-frogging such geological and climatic boundaries; he blamed the archipelago's seafaring Noahs and their indiscriminate distribution of species. Instead of lines, natural scientists now talk of transitional zones.

It was this sense of a linear gradation and transition that commended the idea of travelling from one end to the other. Some countries lend themselves to radial forays; you start at the centre, the capital, and explore outwards. Javanese, who make up the country's largest ethnic group, tend to see Indonesia in this way; with its centres of excellence, decorum and antiquity, Java becomes a Middle Kingdom, the epitome of Indonesian identity whence radiate concentric zones of declining civilization until one reaches the still savage extremities.

A conceit, but not without some substance, I wanted to test this Middle Kingdom theory against another image of Indonesia, that of a Mediterranean-type trading area in which ancient maritime links had created and diffused a common heritage – as well as a lot of animals. Today's *bahasa Indonesia*, the country's official language, is not Javanese but the Malay of these trading and commercial classes. And for every rice-and-ritual dynasty that has left its mark on inland Java, history reveals a tantalizing glimpse of another maritime kingdom silted up in the swamps of Sumatra or remembered only in some obscure Sulawesi chronicle. Neither to miss nor marginalize such clues, mine had to be an end-to-end progress.

*

A foreshore of soupy mud from which protruded the blackened piers of a long-forsaken jetty welcomed the visitor to Pulau Batam. Cormorants hung out their wings to dry and a rusty freighter lay beached like a whale at the entrance to the bay; the *merah-putih*, Indonesia's red and white flag, hung limp from a bent flagstaff. Lord Jim, I thought, would have liked it here. It was the sort of place where questions went unasked and dark secrets quietly festered. I hailed the contrast between Singapore's perspex skyline, still just visible across the Straits, and this low mangrove-fringed tangle of greenery. The smells were of diesel, creosote and old fish plus that sweet aroma, as evocative as the plangent gamelan, of smouldering cloves. To the land of the *kretek* cigarette (so called because as the cloves burn their crackle sounds like 'kretek'), illuminated hoardings for the most popular brands – Bentoel and Gudang Garum – added their welcome. Indonesia may be an amorphous construction and a political enigma, but nowhere has a more distinctive sensory profile. A whiff of *kretek*, a note of gamelan, and the brain swoons.

It had seemed appropriate to arrive in this pelagic world by sea, although half an hour in a pink-upholstered hydrofoil slaloming through the world's busiest shipping lane scarcely counted as a voyage. As well as the Malacca Strait, I had crossed the divide between mainland Asia and the archipelago; it was also, supposedly, the economic equator between prosperous North and destitute South; and to one susceptible to exotic imagery and clove smoke, it could pass for the twilight zone between reality and romance – or even this world and the next.

Indeed, anyone anticipating an eventual stopover in Purgatory is strongly advised to try Singapore first. Raffles' creation was conceived as a place of passage and purchase between east and west. But in so far as social benefits, toy-town planning and draconian laws have since removed most of life's great uncertainties, it now closely resembles an ethereal trading post between the here and the hereafter. For minor transgressions, one meekly atones by being minutely regulated, mentally atrophied and heavily overcharged – but carry on shopping and it'll soon be over. The two terminals at Changi airport, Asia's most efficient, were designed as retail malls and, but for the taxi ride, downtown easily passes for a third. When leaden skies unburdened themselves on my few essential purchases – sticky brown parcel tape, Vick's Vapo-Rub, Callard and Bowser's Nougat – I complained to the umbrella salesgirl about the exuberant sprinkler system; she managed only the tired smile of someone who had heard that one before.

Departure had been such a model of soulless Singaporean efficiency that it passed unnoticed. Seranaded through a further shopping mall, here designated the Singapore Cruise Centre, passengers glided from check-in to gate number. Only when the kung fu movie came on and the floor tipped backwards did it become apparent that the departure lounge was actually a boat.

Arrival was a different matter. Out of the air-conditioning and into the equatorial reality we staggered, up a gang plank and along a timber jetty to the ramshackle customs office. Queues snaked across its unswept floor; taxi touts scaled the barricades. It was hot, hellishly so; but with Purgatory a distant glimmer on the horizon, I was expecting great things.

It was my fourth visit. In the mid-1980s the then generous BBC had financed two forays into Indonesia. With the most congenial of producers I had overflown the archipelago, swooping down on the great and the good to canvass opinions on batik motifs, archaeological priorities, political dissent, Islamic rock music and other subjects worthy of Radio Three's small but discerning audience. In the course of this work I had met many whom I hoped to meet again, academics and columnists for the most part, but also a few celebrities like Pramoedya Ananta Toer, Indonesia's outstanding novelist, Abdul Haris Nasution, the man who might have been president, and Dr Soekmono, the archaeologist who was responsible for the restoration of Borobudur.

I had also acquired new travelling habits. Radio Three presenters disclaim the hairy-kneed bravado associated with travel in remote-ish places. Experience suggests that few places are as remote or primitive as the adventurer would make out and, where there is the prospect of even minimal comforts, the R3 man experiences no qualms about taking advantage of them. Conversely, where there is none, he moves on. Now as an independent, I was set on travelling entirely by public transport, mostly bus and boat. This should not be taken as evidence of intrepid resolve, merely of necessity, there being no viable alternative for one of limited means; air travel would be a last resort to be reserved for the later stages where weeks might otherwise be wasted waiting for ships. And though noble motives suggested themselves, it would be dishonest to suggest that travel in so congenial and intriguing a country could be other than an unadulterated indulgence.

Outside the Batam harbour terminal, smooth tarmac swept up into the forest. A colourful wall-map declared this particular bit of jungle a country club and nine-hole golf course. So did the roadside billboards. It wasn't yet evident. As the taxi sped down empty boulevards we passed more billboards and more maps. Here, they said, was the Hi-Tech Business Park, there the Batam Centre, the Tiara Trade Centre and the Nagoya Centre Business District, 'the bursting heart of Batam' where 'branded lighters and designer leatherware' were among the 'bargains galore'. Somehow I missed them all. There's a lot to miss in Pulau Batam. Perhaps the 'Waterfront City' and the 'Asia Port' would have proved more substantial.

Batam is billed as the second Singapore. Along with Singapore and Malaysia's neighbouring Johore it forms one of Asia's vaunted 'growth triangles'. Multi-national investors, seduced by the generous incentives on offer, are reportedly falling over themselves to cover the island with production facilities and leisure centres. As Singapore, like Hong Kong, transforms itself from a low-cost sweatshop into a marbled service centre, Johore and Batam must accommodate the smokestack manufacturing and processing industries of the newly industrialized triangle. For their cheap land, labour and energy, they get infrastructural investment, technological spin-offs and a lot of hype. Thanks to all those trade centres, plazas and business parks, Batam already apes Singapore; all it lacks is a city and people.

A traffic cop, cast in concrete and convincingly painted even down to his serial number and rank, presided over the main intersection. His arms were raised in a typically ambiguous signal, not helped by the loss of one hand, and his crash helmet was the bomber variety invariably worn by German troops in war movies. Still popular with Indonesia's older generation, it can make provincial rush-hours recall occupied Paris.

Hard hats were all the rage in Batam. Construction workers climbed into the cabs of big yellow caterpillars which then crawled abreast over a puddled wasteland of red mud that looked big enough for an Olympic venue. It was a race against time. As they disappeared into the west, weeds and seedlings and saplings were encroaching fast from the east.

At Hang Nadim International Airport the twin runways of Changi's future rival for the world's jumbo traffic had been quickly asphalted, and the skeleton of a gigantic precast terminal building now bristled with steel rods. It is to replace the row of single storey sheds where I checked in for Sempati's flight to Sumatra. As the sun achieved an astonishing intensity, my fellow passengers stood three deep in the shade of the shed's eaves. The check-in was a window in the wall and the only concourse was the car park. Cool lofty lounges with coffee shops and travelators took on a devastating appeal. At the third attempt I found the hole in the perimeter hedge whence led a path to the airport restaurant. It too was a hut and the patrons all wore hard hats. Over the first of many beers I studied the map.

The trouble with a linear journey is that, like a fast bowler heading for the end of his run-up, you have first to turn your back on the pitch and wander off into the outfield. Indonesia's western extremity, and so my immediate destination and starting point, is Banda Aceh (pronounced 'Atchay'), the capital of Aceh province at the tip of Sumatra. This tip points into the Bay of Bengal and logically one would approach it from India's Andaman and Nicobar Islands. That was how James Lancaster, commander of the English East India Company's first voyage to the East, came in 1601. Like a nervous guest heading straight for the gents' cloakroom, he stopped at Great Nicobar, less than 200km away, for fresh water and the hoisting of ensigns and pennants before presenting himself at Aceh.

But today Banda Aceh is not a recognised port of entry. It would like to be and has decidedly better credentials than, say,

SUMATRA

Batam. But Jakarta doesn't trust the Acehnese. It prefers that their province remain a distant dead end. The ancient gateway to the archipelago is closed and forgotten.

'Banda Aceh?' queried the Chinese lady sitting next to me on the plane. 'Banda Aceh!' she told everyone, 'Banda Aceh! Banda Aceh!'. Then, scooping my uneaten lunch pack into her capacious bag, she confided, 'Banda Aceh, yuk.' It was actually more dismissive than 'yuk', a sort of 'tut-tut, what-will-these-foreigners-think-of-next' laced with metropolitan contempt. At Medan she and most of the other passengers got off. For the last leg of the flight there was no packed meal.

When Indonesians want to evoke the 5,000km spread of their country, their equivalent of 'Land's End to John o'Groats' is not 'Aceh to Irian', but 'Sabang to Merauke'. Merauke is hard by the Papua New Guinea border on the south coast of Irian Jaya; Sabang is the tiny township on the little island of Weh which was just visible to the north of Aceh as we came into land. Its harbour once rivalled Singapore's, and here Mountbatten's South-east Asia Command set up shop when the Allies reclaimed the archipelago in 1945. In the 1970s it was actually threatened, briefly, with 'growth triangle' status. Then Singapore urged Batam's greater convenience and the funds and hype were duly redirected. Sabang reverted to being just another coral-and-coconut paradise glinting in a turquoise sea; only the name has any national relevance. It was actually a Dutchman who coined the 'Sabang-Merauke' tag, but Sukarno eagerly appropriated it for independent Indonesia. Both had good reason to prefer the phrase, any phrase, so long as it contained no unnecessary mention of troublesome Aceh.

1. Troubles in Aceh

Iqbal had borrowed a camera; I bought the film. Without pictures the day would hardly qualify as an occasion. We studied the map over breakfast and bought oranges for the bus while Iqbal divulged his dream of one day becoming a tourist guide. Opportunities for displaying his undoubted talent for handling foreigners were few and far between in Banda Aceh; so he currently cleaned rooms in my hotel. But employees of the Hotel Sultan got little time off. The day for him was therefore precious and not to be marred by any lack of forward planning. For me it was by way of a trial run-up. Having reached the western extremity of Sumatra, I welcomed the idea of a short excursion on public transport before tackling the long haul ahead.

In the back of the *bemo* (public mini-bus), as yellow light flooded across the façades bordering the Aceh river and slipped under the palms to gild the town's white-washed mosque, we lurched off to the bus station. Sure enough, there was the bus for Meulaboh, engine running. '*Jam delapan*,' said the ticket collector; 'Eight o'clock', said Iqbal, beaming with satisfaction.

Parked beside the stream-lined *bis bis malam* – plush 'night buses' which had thundered up the notorious Trans-Sumatra Highway from Medan – the Meulaboh bus looked small and bad-tempered. A Japanese automotive expert had once hit upon the idea of maximizing the carrying capacity of twisty mountain roads by designing a 40-seater on a short wheel base. Engine, front seats including the driver's, and front door had accordingly been positioned forward of the front wheel and this whole projection had then been given a shark-like profile which ended in a broad gnashing grille. Cornering high in the hills, the barracuda's snout could explore the abyss while the wheels still safely crunched the dirt.

'Back is best,' said Iqbal; more leg room, thought I, as we bagged the middle seats on the bench behind the rear door. The bus slowly filled and the air thickened. Gentle activity inside my shirt turned out to be runnels of sweat feeding a small navel lake.

'Not *pedas*,' corrected Iqbal; that was 'pepper-hot'; *panas* was 'heat-hot'. Watched with awe by our fellow passengers he began deftly loading the camera with film.

Half an hour later and filled to capacity, the bus unexpectedly set off across the rubble forecourt. Sluggishly, like chocolate melting, the air within stirred while upfront a screen flickered and a wall of sound (which proved to be music) rushed through the bus. It was good to be moving, albeit fitfully as we stopped for more passengers and then lumbered into a petrol station. We left it the way we had come. Several stops later the bus was back on its old stand at the bus station, marooned in the heat. My navel reservoir refilled, then overflowed to incontinent effect.

To pass the time I told Iqbal about James Lancaster and about his stopping in the Nicobar Islands in 1601 to prepare for his, and England's, commercial debut in the East. 'Acheen' as Master Lancaster called it, was then the great western entrepôt of the archipelago. The voyage, and so the whole future of the infant East India Company, hinged on his reception. In the event it proved a resounding success and when the king of Aceh, surprisingly well-informed, asked whether Lancaster's royal mistress was not the Queen Elizabeth who was said to have lately routed an entire Spanish Armada, Lancaster positively blushed with pride.

'Queen Elizabeth?' Iqbal, also well informed, had almost leapt to his feet at the name.

'Yes'.

'Ah, you have seen the newspaper?' He produced yesterday's *Kompass* and indicated a headline. My *bahasa Indonesia* was not up to it.

'Charless, Prince of Wireless, yes? Son of Queen Elizabeth, yes?

He say very good things.' Apparently the Prince of Wales had been speaking about Islam. His audience, I later learnt, had been Oxford luminaries but the speech must have been widely reported and was now causing a sensation in Indonesia. Bits about Christians and Muslims sharing the same values and working together for a new world order went down especially well. The story would follow me down the archipelago as if the 'Prince of Wireless' were snapping at my heels. For once, being a subject of Her Britannic Majesty carried Islamic kudos. I knew how Lancaster must have felt.

It was now all of nine and bus loading had begun in earnest. The leg room disappeared under a white polystyrene crate which oozed a brownish mucus and the smell of bad fish. On top was placed an elegant wickerwork cage containing six speckled pullets. 'Now we go,' shouted Iqbal as the bus suddenly darted again across the rubble and a gang of bony lads burst through the rear door. Two came to roost beside the pullets, forcing our knees into the vertical.

'Not more than three hours. Most beautiful. You see.'

I couldn't much. But after dazzling breakers, beneath an armpit, had doubtless rolled onto the beach of pristine sand which was framed by two identical pink head-veils, we seemed to be climbing. 'One of the prettiest roads in the world', says Dalton's *Indonesia Handbook*, through 'one of the most untouched areas of Indonesia where tigers come down from the mountains to steal livestock'. Shattering convulsions as the suspension disdained a succession of craters levelled the luggage and lowered incautious heads. Something on the end of a string was being passed down the bus. Behind the video screen I could see the driver panning the snout of his bus through a cliff of vegetation as we ground round another hairpin. One pink veil was vomiting freely out the window while the other, who couldn't reach, shouted through the music for 'plastiques' – sick bags.

The first serious halt came courtesy of a landslide. From out of a tangle of trees obliterating the road the arm of a digger waved and jerked like a drowning swimmer. Lithe brown figures with bandanas and chainsaws swarmed through the branches or waded in the now crusty slick of clay beneath. In the immensity of the

forest the whine of saws and the clanking of the digger were profoundly reassuring; they would become an abiding memory of
Sumatra. In the hills, never far away, it rains most days; the rain is
always a deluge; and every deluge launches seawards another
sloop, fully-rigged, of soft Sumatran mountain. After petrochemicals and plantations, landslip clearance may be the island's
major industry.

Iqbal got out and took the opportunity to try different angles for
a shot of the bus and me, then of the bus and him. Most stayed on
board. As the music blared forth louder than ever to challenge the
chainsaws, a deadpan gentleman in a fez climbed on to his seat
with one eye on the video screen. Gingerly, as if he had been
passed a hand-grenade, he raised what I now recognised as a
microphone and, without the smallest concession to stagecraft,
lugubriously sang along with the raunchy coquette on the video.
He was followed by an Acehnese matron in a cotton print who
cheerfully crowed, to the accompaniment of Hawaiian guitars,
through what sounded like 'Auld Lang Syne'. Then it was the turn
of the two pink veils. One still had her head in the 'plastique', and
the other was wiping the window sill. They were not pressed
further. Instead the entire bus faced about and stared towards
Iqbal and me as we regained our seats. Unconcern, diffidence,
even a frank declaration of impaired vocal chords failed to staunch
their demands. The bus lurched forwards through the partially
cleared undergrowth and still there were sixty expectant faces. I
was contemplating the open door when one of the bony lads sitting on the fish crate took pity on a stranger. The microphone
extension, he seemed to be saying, reached only as far as the pink
veils. Overcome with gratitude, I disentangled a segment of
orange and passed it to my first good Sumatran.

In-bus karaoke apart, the journey was proving discouraging.
Between Aceh and the ferry to Java lay 1,500km of Sumatran bus
travel. They say that on the big *bis bis malam* (night buses) you can
reach Jakarta, conditions permitting, in about three days. But I
cherished the idea of a more leisurely, less nocturnal progress, and
one which allowed for sights other than landslips and 'plastiques'.
Yet, as we bobbed down to the coastline once again, a rapid calcu-

lation suggested that 60km on the day-bus had just taken three hours. That meant seventy-five bus-hours to Java – six days, say, of unrelieved discomfort. And with another roughly 5,000 km beyond to journey's end in Irian Jaya.

Today's destination was what Iqbal referred to rather mysteriously as 'the German's hotel where we have lunch'. Whether he had actually been there was unclear but at least the bus driver seemed to have heard of it. He dropped us off where the road regained a stretch of empty beach. We watched as the barracuda cruised its length and then nosed back into the forest.

The solitude would have disconcerted Man Friday. Except for the exploding surf, no sound disturbed the high noon stillness and no structure interrupted the perfect perspective of beach and road and trees.

Standing on tiptoe, for he was short even for an Acehnese, Iqbal sniffed the air, puckering his moustache in the process. Schnitzel? Satay?

'Lunch no smell'.

The sun hammered down puddling the tarmac and transfixing each smudge of shade with the trunk of a palm tree. In search of something more climbable from which to spy for cooking smoke, we stumbled on a sandy track winding back up the coast between the road and the Indian Ocean. Along it we slogged for what seemed miles.

'Look, German hotel, yes?'

I thought congratulations might be premature; yet it couldn't be every north Sumatran coconut grove that boasted a white flagstaff with the blue flag with gold stars of the European Union limply looped over an adjacent branch. Nor a rusty bedstead masquerading as a gate with a board announcing 'Eurocamp, M. Erfurt'.

'Hotel, yes, hotel?'

Iqbal was now pointing triumphantly into the forest canopy. We had emerged onto a sun-drenched cove where Salvador Dali tree stumps projected from the smooth sand. Beyond, slender trunks leant out from the encircling promontory like strings mooring their distant fronds to the rocks. I was fantasizing about paradise as two beachcombing sirens, long-haired and long-limbed, drifted into the shade and began scaling a bamboo ladder. Iqbal was right. The hotel was in the canopy, an elaborate structure of walkways, verandahs and rope ladders in the rigging of a giant *ficus*.

The proprietor evidently preferred a dank terrestrial abode of more substantial construction which backed on to the uncleared forest. No Tarzan, he trundled from this bunker like a panzer on alert.

'Lunch? Naturally. Fruit salad, ya?' A plastic vacuum tub half filled with papaya chunks was produced and from another with a tap he drew off a glass of tea.

'Two,' I said.

'Nein, nein. Here no Indonesians. Tell him to wait over there. Your boy, he must wait, ya?'

The German manoeuvred between us, grunting. His mousey stubble barely camouflaged the pockmarks which riveted his nose in place; sweat wetted the hair behind his flange-like ears.

'No, we're together. This is Iqbal, my friend from Banda Aceh. He has brought me.'

'Friend, guide, boy. So. He is Indonesian, no? Here no Indonesians. You understand, ya?'

Giving ground with the grace of a subject race, Iqbal proffered the camera and asked politely if he might take photographs. Impossible. According to Erfurt the *bupati* (local governor) had made it a condition of his business that no Indonesians would be allowed in Eurocamp. I didn't believe a word of it; and surely the ravaged lady who appeared to be Mrs Erfurt was herself Indonesian.

'You like this place? You want tree house?' He flapped an arm more blotched than freckled towards a leafy balcony where the sirens, now naked, were applying sun cream.

'Just lunch. For both of us. No apartheid.'

'No, no. No apartheid. Just security, yes? You like Indonesia? Beach ya? What is this apartheid? You want peace and quiet. No trouble, no overcharging. Isn't that right?'

I said I'd rather be ripped off than segregated. How could a bit of South-east Asian coastline possibly be a European preserve?

This was 1993. Where did he think he was?

'Where? Ya, where, I tell you. My English friend in Penang. He says back end of Asia is like back end of cow. You look at the map. See, China is the rump, ya, backside? India? India is the udder. And in between, Malaya; Malaya is the back leg, ya? So what is Indonesia? I tell you. Indonesia is what the cow leaves behind it. Shit, ya? A trail of shit. These islands just a trail of shit. Shit is good for mushrooms. So this place? Mushroom farm, ya?'

A Dutch official once described Indonesians as 'a nation of coolies and a coolie amongst nations'. Pramoedya Ananta Toer, the country's outstanding novelist, talks of 'frogs cooking in the oven of their own isolation' and even President Sukarno goaded his people as 'a bean-curd nation', i.e. fit only to be trampled and pummelled from beans into curd. Frogs, mushrooms etc. all reinforce the stereotype of a soft and pliant people cowed by culture and climate into a ready acceptance of hard labour and rough justice.

Lunchless, yet mindful of mushrooms and bean curd, Iqbal and I trudged back, crestfallen, through the coconut groves. I apologised for the German, he for the fruit salad.

Yet this was Aceh, proud, unruly and fanatical Aceh, the last bastion of resistance to colonial rule, the first focus for pan-Indonesian nationalism, and still a no-go area for the heavy-handed centralism of the Jakarta government. Ironically it was precisely here – I suspect on Eurocamp's rocky reefs – that on a stormy November night in 1883 the Sunderland-built *SS Nisero*, Suez-bound with a cargo of Javanese sugar, ran aground and, in so doing, pitched the incomprehensible politics of this Sumatran extremity back into the international arena.

The *Nisero*'s crew, 29 men commanded by Captain Wood-house, came ashore bedraggled and wondering where on earth they were. They were promptly rounded up by a local raja and declared hostages. Some died of cholera and Woodhouse absconded by breaking the terms of a safe-conduct. But the rest, though tolerably treated for most of the following year, became helpless pawns in an affair which found their own government upholding the grievances of their captor while the Dutch invaders turned to a local adventurer who would later become Aceh's greatest freedom fighter.

Matters had not always been so complicated. When Europeans like Lancaster first reached the East they found in Aceh a powerful and independent maritime kingdom ruled by a forceful and opportunistic sultan. In the 16th century Aceh contested supremacy of the vital Malacca Straits with the Portuguese and in the 17th century the Dutch and English resorted to Aceh as an agreeable place for loading Sumatran pepper. The Sultan's entertainments, often held waist-deep in the cool waters of the Aceh river, would long be remembered for their conviviality and for the charming accompaniment of an all-female orchestra.

In the 1620s Sultan Iskander Muda, the successor of Lancaster's well-informed host, sought a closer alliance and asked merchants of the East India Company to find him an English bride. In fact he wanted two. But the temptation of thus doubling its chances of an Anglo-Acehnese succession could not reconcile the Company's conscience to bigamy. Nor in the end were scruples about marriage to a Muslim overcome, although a candidate 'of excellent partes for music, her needle and good discourse, also very beautiful and personable' was readying her trousseau for the next voyage.

The reign of Iskander Muda (1607-36) marked Aceh's zenith. His rule extended over more than half of Sumatra and his fleet exacted tribute from many of the Malay states on the mainland. But in 1629 this fleet was destroyed by the Portuguese and his oppressive rule became vulnerable to internal opposition. After his death the throne was disputed. Under a succession of elderly queens Acehnese territory shrunk while quarrelsome local rajas, known as *uleebalang*, asserted their rights to choose the sovereign and to manage their own affairs. The commercial value of pepper, the region's main cash crop, also dwindled and increasingly benefited only the *uleebalang*.

In 1783 William Marsden could still describe Aceh as the only Sumatran kingdom to have acquired political consequence in European eyes; and a century later, when the *Nisero* grounded on the coast north of Meulaboh, this consequence still counted.

Dutch encroachment along both coasts of Sumatra during the 19th century had come to look like a pincer movement aimed at Aceh. But the Acehnese placed their confidence in a succession of pacts made with the British whose commerce at Penang and Singapore still accounted for much of Aceh's pepper. It was these very treaties, giving the British a say in Sumatran affairs, that incited Dutch anxieties about their exclusive rights in the archipelago. When the British eventually signified that pepper, and so Aceh, might not actually be worth fighting for, the Dutch began to turn the screw.

Meanwhile the Acehnese turned to Turkey, long revered as the guarantor of their Islamic orthodoxy, then France, and even the United States. News of a Turkish warship heading for Eastern waters excited wild speculation in Aceh while a draft treaty ceding to the US, in exchange for a defensive alliance, the little island of Sabang (off Banda Aceh) was actually drawn up but never signed. Perhaps it never reached General Grant in Washington; perhaps the Land of the Free wasn't yet ready for a South-east Asian commitment. Anyway it was too late.

For this was in 1873, the year in which the Dutch, after fruitless blockades and intrigues, finally launched their invasion. Near Banda Aceh, the home of the Sultan as well as the main town, a force of 3,000 landed, advanced, attacked – and within three weeks had been convincingly defeated. It was Holland's first rout at the hands of an Eastern kingdom and it sent shock waves through the archipelago. Unlike the British in India, the Dutch in Indonesia had seldom had to fight to acquire their empire. European military superiority had simply been taken for granted by both sides. For the Dutch it was therefore imperative that defeat be immediately avenged and the myth of their invincibility decisively reinstated. A second expedition of 10,000, the largest force they had ever assembled, returned within the year, sacked Banda Aceh, and then again ran into difficulties.

Aceh's influential *ulama*, or religious leadership, now turned resistance into a *jihad* against the infidel; the secular *uleebalang* achieved a fragile sense of common purpose in resisting a new Dutch blockade of their ports; and the Dutch deposition of the

Sultan served only to enhance his otherwise tarnished credentials as a focus of defiance. Meanwhile Dutch casualties were more than doubled by an outbreak of cholera; plans to overrun the whole sultanate were abandoned for want of adequate reinforcements; and when in August 1883 Krakatau erupted to devastating effect, opinion united in seeing the disaster as a judgement of the gods on the wickedness of Dutch policy in Aceh.

Such was the situation when three months later the crew of the *Nisero* unwittingly blundered on to the scene. The Dutch demanded their immediate release; but their captor, raja Teuku Imam, had other plans. He wanted a lifting of the Dutch blockade which was interfering with his pepper exports and, more to the point, he wanted a lasting undertaking that it would not be reimposed. The Dutch, he reckoned, could not be entirely trusted in this respect and, resurrecting their worst nightmares, he therefore demanded that only a guarantee by the British government, Aceh's erstwhile ally and conveniently an interested party in the fate of his captives, would be acceptable.

There followed a flurry of diplomatic activity as Banda Aceh, Batavia and The Hague protested their competence to Penang, Singapore and Whitehall. Questions and debates in the House of Commons revealed ancient sympathies for the Acehnese, plus a lofty contempt for a colonial power incapable of managing its own affairs. Intervention seemed inevitable and promised to be ambitious as British military intelligence argued for a landing at Pidie, on the north coast, and a cross-country advance which would probably enjoy Acehnese support. The alternative was a simple gunboat raid on the west coast, but here a succession of abortive peace missions were already trailing through Eurocamp's coconut groves and up into the forest to plead with Teuku Imam and to deliver supplies to the captives.

Two such British missions did little more than spy out the ground and encourage Teuku Imam's growing interest in cricket. The Dutch tried threats and bribes, then enlisted the help of the raja's neighbour and rival, Teuku Umar. With arms and money by way of payment for the hostages, Umar was put ashore on his native soil and promptly murdered the Dutch crew which had brought him, appropriated the ship and the treasure and raised his own banner of defiance. It was the last straw; once again the Acehnese had won. In August 1884 a joint Anglo-Dutch mission arrived at Teuku Imam's mountain base. In return for the release of the hostages and a nominal submission, Imam got a substantial payment plus a guarantee of free trade endorsed by the British.

After twelve years and two wars aimed at establishing their exclusive authority the Dutch controlled only a few square miles round Banda Aceh and had been obliged to concede the British interest which they had come to eradicate. They were now assailed by an increasingly confident and motivated enemy. Near Banda Aceh – renamed by the Dutch 'Kutaraja' – Acehnese *mujahedin* under the inspirational guidance of a sheikh known as Cik di Tiro stole their weapons, assailed their defences, and sabotaged their communications. Further south the turncoat Teuku Umar and his equally resourceful wife, Cut Nyak Dien, lorded it over the pepper ports of the west coast. Such was Umar's power and such his extraordinary plausibility that in the 1890s he was again entertained by the Dutch as their ally-cum-agent against the *ulama*. But in 1896, having taken delivery of the guns and cash deemed necessary for a new offensive, Umar yet again changed sides and laid siege to his paymasters in Banda Aceh.

'He took their guns, you see, and then he pointed them at the Dutch. Ah Teuku Umar, he was very clever.'

Iqbal loved this story and I now knew it well. Immortalised in verse epics and subsequently popularised in song and film, the exploits of Teuku Umar and the lovely Dien, of Sheikh Cik di Tiro, Teuku Imam and a host of other heroes have become the focus of Acehnese identity and culture. Along with the great sultan Iskander Muda, theirs are the names conferred on streets, buildings, boats, even buses throughout Aceh. And because their defiance was directed at the colonial power they have also been co-opted into the national mythology. Jakarta too has streets named after Umar and Dien and so do the distant provincial capitals of Kalimantan and eastern Indonesia.

Teuku Umar was finally ambushed and killed here on his old stamping ground north of Meulaboh in 1899. A sustained offensive, begun in the previous year and relentlessly pursued until 1904, drew only the feeblest of protests from British Penang and eventually quelled all overt resistance. Simultaneously an enlightened policy, devised by that great Dutch Islamicist with the unforgettable name of Snouck Hurgronje, seduced the disaffected with investment and respect for their religion.

But it was not the end of Acehnese nationalism. In 1942 after less than forty years of colonial rule, a mere caesura in the three centuries of turmoil, the Japanese replaced the Dutch. Aceh welcomed them. A new generation of freedom fighters and *ulama* militants learnt about self-discipline and ballistics in the Japanese militia; then, recalling Teuku Umar, they relieved the Japanese of their weapons and turned them against them after Hiroshima. The Japanese surrender brought the allied forces to Sabang, then still an important dockyard, but the Dutch, more than busy elsewhere in Indonesia, wisely steered clear of Aceh. Unlike the rest of Indonesia, Aceh was never reoccupied after the war.

This meant that the Acehnese played no part in Indonesia's final independence struggle. Instead they contrived their own even bloodier revolution. At the time it was seen as a civil war between the *uleebalang,* the commercial aristocracy who were tainted with having eventually collaborated with the Dutch, and the *ulama*, the religious establishment. Marxists of Sukarno's era would prefer to emphasize its class war credentials, the *uleebalang* being equated with feudal landowners and the *ulama* with the rural proletariat who slaughtered them. But it was also an Islamic revolution in which the Acehnese proclaimed their preference for the kind of theocratic consensus and penal rigour now demonised as 'Muslim Fundamentalism'.

This became clear in 1950 when, the *ulama* triumphant, Aceh endeavoured to foist its religious orthodoxy on Jakarta. The Acehnese wanted to be part of an Islamic republic and it was not an unreasonable demand considering that Indonesia has the largest Muslim population in the world. But it would have meant alienating a substantial minority of Hindu and Christian Indonesians. The latter are well represented among the Batak peoples of North Sumatra and it was the threat of being incorporated into this part-Christian province that provoked the Acehnese revolt of 1953-9. Although ruthlessly suppressed by the Indonesian armed forces, Aceh thereby managed to preserve its reputation for sustained and ferocious dissent and was duly placated with recognition as a separate province with an exceptional degree of autonomy.

When I asked Iqbal why then there was still so much tension between Aceh and Jakarta he said nothing and deliberately left the table for the food bar and another mountain of rice. I had obviously been indiscreet. We were lunching in an open pavilion set back from the road and so smothered in bougainvillea that only weary walkers willing to credit any structure with dining facilities would have bothered to investigate it. In fact and rather mysteriously considering its isolation, it was a restaurant. A glass cabinet displayed a dozen bowls of well-turmeric-ed Padang curries. Tea and steaming rice came through a window from the hill behind and big green mangoes from a basket suspended from the roof. If there were staff they made a point of being invisible. But there was another table of diners. One, a large man in tailored shirt and tight trousers, had introduced himself as from the Department of Tourism. While I supplied the answers to an impromptu questionnaire which would be important for the Department's promotional plans, Iqbal was told to take photos of us.

'We are lucky. That was policeman, Batak.' Once out in the glaring equatorial afternoon, Iqbal was keen to talk. Tourism Department? What tourists? There weren't any.

I had to agree. Apart from Eurocamp I hadn't seen a foreigner in three days. And for a market researcher the man did seem to have an unnecessarily assertive presence.

'These people no good. And so many. Everywhere, everywhere. You have read what happened last year in Banda Aceh? Two killed, just like him, plain clothes; policemen, informers, I don't know. And big, big demonstrations.'

Although not always reported, 'troubles in Aceh' are such a constant of Indonesian politics as to have become an attribute of

Acehnese identity, like 'floods in Bangladesh'. To pride in their religious orthodoxy and in their remarkable history is now added a strong sense of economic grievance because the province contributes, largely from offshore oil and gas, far more to the national economy than it receives. The Meulaboh road, for instance, the only west coast route and the one on which we seemed doomed to spend the rest of the day waiting for transport, had been surfaced only in the last year. It was still not finished and was served only by the ancient barracuda bus. Big bold plans to commence my stepping-stones progress down the archipelago by following Sumatra's least frequented coastline were being hastily revised.

Between frantic efforts to stop anything that passed on wheels, we lolled by the roadside and swapped vocabularies. I was still on the days of the week but Iqbal, who attended Aceh's university in between his housekeeping shifts at the hotel, hankered for idiom and fluency. Tenses bored him and so did parts of the body. Female body parts, although seemingly the same in both *bahasa Indonesia* and English, kindled a new enthusiasm. From his wallet he extracted a small creased photograph in which a girl in a head-veil was just visible amongst a lot of floral upholstery.

'This is my fiancée, yes? She has agreed to marry me'.

'Congratulations. She looks lovely. You are very lucky.'

'Not lucky. I write to her but she never write to me. Maybe she not love me any more.'

The veil suggested a conservative family. I presumed that it was an arranged marriage and that declarations of love might have to wait on a better acquaintance.

'Not arranged. I ask her and she say yes. She love me I know. We have slept together.'

The driver of a truck with a chassis so twisted that it appeared to be approaching crab-wise waved cheerily as he lumbered past, brushing our open palms. Thumbs are bad manners but everyone, I was told, stops for an open palm. It was just that on the Meulaboh road hitching was a novelty; they didn't yet know the conventions.

'What is this meaning in English – "sleep with"? I sleep with my fiancée, yes? You understand? We sleep together, yes? Is this meaning sexual intercourse?'

I said that that was my impression. What did he think it meant?

He looked hard at the photo and frowned.

'Yes, I think you are right. I sleep with her, alone, in the same bed, together. We take off clothes. But no sexual intercourse. I think she was afraid of pregnancy.'

He actually said 'pricknancy' and then, with the disinterested diagnosis hitherto reserved for shutter speeds and Acehnese history, went into intimate detail about this and other sexual encounters. There was, it appeared, a problem other than his fiancée's caution. Counselling seemed the obvious solution but such treatment was not available in Banda Aceh and he preferred the hotel's in-house movie programme. It so happened that room cleaning often coincided with a sequence in which Michael Douglas and Sharon Stone claimed to be enjoying 'the fuck of the century'. Had I seen it? Was this not 'sleeping together'? And how could he convey the news to his fiancée?

Acehnese Islam is not bigoted and the wearing of veils is not obligatory. When the 'Prince of Wireless' had deplored Islamic extremism it was thought that he was referring to Iranians rather than Acehnese. No friendlier and more gracious people are to be found in Sumatra. But it is an orthodox society in which religion is taken more seriously, and infringements punished more severely, than anywhere else in Indonesia. Many Acehnese have Arab blood; it was to Aceh that Islam came sometime in the 8th century; and it was via Aceh that Indonesian Muslims departed on *haj* to Arabia. Visitors are invariably reminded more of the Gulf or of Jedda than of the gamelan and Java. The Acehnese *ulama* consider themselves pillars of Qur'ānic righteousness amongst fickle fellow-travellers on this frontier of *Dar-ul-Islam*; indeed it was in the name of *Dar-ul-Islam*, 'the world of Islam', that Aceh defied Jakarta in the 1950s. In this tight and often tense society where demurely veiled girls sit amongst floral upholstery and the men pray five times a day, Iqbal's prospects of penetration – he called it 'penistration' – could not be good.

Yet I was touched by his tale. His frown had less to do with any mystification than with a natural solemnity plus the cramping of features inevitable in a face scaled down to his diminutive stature. Like a map with too much detail for the space available, it radiated earnestness. There is a widespread misunderstanding among Asian peoples that any solitary male Caucasian who strays from the tourist lounges must be in search of some stimulant. If it isn't dope it must be sex; 'fuck or fix?'. Tirelessly importuned by what sounds like a Hallowe'en greeting, one becomes intensely grateful to anyone prepared to credit you with understanding as well as appetite. When at last a smart new minibus scooped us from the roadside we boarded companionably, each with a new vocabulary and food for thought.

The day done, the sun slipped unceremoniously into the ocean like an end of party cliché. Five miles later, as we climbed into the hills, bats big as buzzards dropped on to webbed wings and began to beat purposefully along the face of the cliffs below us. Pipistrelles manoeuvred erratically above the road but it was the big flying foxes of bomber command, winging across the sea on some deadly night mission, that presaged equatorial pyrotechnics.

Quite suddenly the hills, whose tousled vegetation had offered no contrast all day, softened in a golden haze and took on the varied patina of an old master. Leafy bowers hinted at casual rustic dalliance, and a glimpse of sward merited an ivory-limbed Aphrodite. But this was Indonesia and on the ocean's horizon a rim of grey cloud composed itself into the sharp shapes of Javanese shadow puppets.

Overhead, dazzling oases of cumulus became the islands of the Golden Chersonese. They swam in a sea of princely pink and royal scarlet which shaded to imperial purple. The ocean below was a sheet of blue-grey velvet from which the breakers now rolled and foamed with the creamy opacity of churned milk. The palms glittered with gold. As we swept round the hairpins every turn revealed a new vista of tear-jerking splendour. Throughout the 'bat hour' between sunset and black night it was indeed 'one of the most beautiful roads in the world'.

The finale of the day's programme was to be a visit to the Qur'ānic recitation contest at the Great Mosque. We rode back into town past the blanched walls, ghostly in the moonlight, of the Dutch cemetery. Here lie the cornets and colonels of the Indies Army who succumbed to Aceh's deadly dose of small arms and cholera during the thirty years war. Through a fine gabled gateway where the roll call of the fallen fills every available surface I could see the gravestones impeccably whitewashed and standing to attention in grassy parterres like a regiment on parade. 'Hier rust Theodore Kist' read more like an order than an epitaph. At least half the dead were not Dutch at all but Christianized Jacobuses and Johannes from Ambon and Manado in the eastern archipelago, colonial mercenaries whose only friends in Islamic Aceh would have been the Fatimas who now rested among them.

All of twenty acres, the cemetery adjoins a cheerier garden centred on an enigmatic structure something like a squat wedding cake. This is Aceh's *gunongan*, literally 'mini-mountain', a mythic symbol of Hindu-Buddhist provenance more often associated with Java and Bali. But this one is credited to the great sultan Iskander Muda and was supposedly a discreet retreat for his womenfolk. Next day I climbed up inside it to emerge on the upper parapet through a small circular hole quite unsuitable for plump sultanas. It was midday. The whitewash dazzled and the heat struck like a scimitar blow. Not for Aceh the dripping humidity of most of Sumatra. Its air is the clearest, its light the brightest, its spirit the fiercest.

No less enigmatic was the bell-shaped monument beside the mosque. 'Teuku Umar's hat', said Iqbal. 'He was very clever. He took the Dutch guns and then turned them against them'.

The Islamic taboo on representational art prohibits an actual statue of the patriot and it may account for numerous other monumental curiosities in Banda Aceh. The lump of wrought concrete on the riverside could well be a memorial to Umar's spirited wife.

Oddly the Great Mosque, one of Indonesia's finest with black and shapely domes crowning its white and arched façades, proclaims not Aceh's orthodoxy but its opponents' efforts at conciliation. The main structure was built by the Dutch after their second invasion to compensate for having razed the sultan's palace which once adjoined the *gunongan*; additional domes came courtesy of Jakarta at the height of the 1950s rebellion.

Tonight in the glare of floodlighting a glass kiosk had been erected at the top of the broad flight of steps to serve as a studio for contestants in the All-Aceh Qur'ānic Recitation Contest. Loudspeakers slung in the crowns of the royal palms relayed their efforts to the townsfolk, most of whom were gathered on the grass beneath picnicking on boiled peanuts and iced cartons of lychee and pineapple juice. White shirts and black skirts were in evidence; decorum reigned. The contestants, all male, all moustached and all wearing the *peci* or fez, were called to the kiosk one at a time. Over a lectern and a battery of microphones they faced the panel of judges whose steel-rimmed spectacles glinted behind a long table at the foot of the steps. Preliminary rustlings in the kiosk were so amplified from the palm tops as to make one think that at last the Sumatran tiger was coming down for his supper.

As soon as the first verses were intoned the crowd settled and the traffic fell silent. The Qur'ān is never sung but neither could this be called reading. Perhaps it was chant but more virile and staccato than plain chant, an utterance from the chest which wheeled and swooped among the syllables like a dervish. If the Arabic calligraphy which adorned the Mosque could come to life, this is how it would sound. I fancied that I was hearing the voice of Aceh's restless and tenacious spirit battering on the walls of Dutch conformity and Indonesian compromise. Then, as another contestant climbed stiffly to the microphones, I ruined it all with a silly crack about Qur'ānic karaoke. Iqbal winced and we trailed home, he to the Housekeeping Dormitory and me to Douglas and Stone.

2. *Tip Top times*

You need a reason for loitering in Medan. Just recovering from the Banda Aceh *bis malam*, the Penang hydrofoil or the Singapore flight is not enough. For Sumatra's largest city is by general consent its unloveliest. Outside the old colonial Tip Top Restaurant a pavement cafe offered 'beefstuk compleet' and 'Hollandse Poffertjes'. Ice creams seemed more appropriate as, ensconced in a wicker-work chair before a glass-topped table, I watched the other side of the street loom in and out of the exhaust fumes. The heat was exceeded only by the humidity which bore down on the carbon fog, trapping and compressing it between the grime-streaked office blocks. A cold glass wetted itself with condensation in a matter of seconds; cigarette smoke required emphatic exhalation if it was not to be reinhaled.

'OH GOD HELP / THEM WHO / HELP THE / BLIN PUPLE / THAN YOU' said a sign on the collection box by the door. Why was it in English? Inside, the ferocious air-conditioning and Stygian darkness competed with the sizzling of escalopes as a four-man combo played 'Michael Rowed the Boat Ashore'. Identical in white trousers, crimson shirts, yellow bow ties and jackets of lovat tweed, they should have belonged to a circus; Batam's concrete cop had showed more animation. In the gents a chestnut cockroach, big as a mouse and showroom shiny, watched and waved its antennae. When I returned the Medan Maestros were begging Bill Bailey to please come home. Fat chance.

Unlovely and ungainly, Medan is also unhistoric. The earliest reference to the place seems to be that in John Anderson's report of *A Mission to the East Coast of Sumatra.* Anderson was a Scot and so am I. In fact, I had just edited an encyclopaedia of Scotland. Castles and clans still lingered in the mind, like the after-taste of a memorable meal, and it was clan business which was my reason for stopping in Medan. But not clan Anderson. The importance of the Anderson mission was the date, 1823.

This was the critical period for Sumatra. Following Napoleon's defeat, Holland's possessions in the East, briefly occupied by the British to deny them to the French, had just been returned to the Dutch. They included Java, the Moluccas or Spice Islands, and the port of Malacca on the Malayan peninsula. Other islands, like Bali and Sumatra, remained as yet largely outside the Dutch ambit and were considered fair game by the other colonial powers. Americans had cornered the pepper produce of Sumatra's west coast south of Meulaboh, and the British still clung to their own pepper ports around Bengkulu in the extreme south-west.

Pepper was also exported from the east coast and, with the British established at Penang (since 1786) and now Singapore (1819), trade with the petty sultanates just across the Malacca straits began to prosper. Anderson, a British official from Penang, was to secure favourable commercial arrangements and to encourage the sultanates to resist interference either from the Acehnese, who still claimed a vague overlordship dating from the days of Sultan Iskander Muda, or from the Dutch who were now anxious to resume their efforts to monopolize the production of the whole archipelago.

His first port of call was the sultanate of Deli, sometimes confusingly spelled 'Delhi'. Like the other east coast sultanates – Siak, Asahan, Serdang, Langkat – Deli was more a river than a chunk of territory. A sultan's authority depended on his control of the produce coming down his river which was typically the only means of communication in a region where what wasn't impenetrable swamp was impenetrable jungle. Deli had two rivers, the biggest being the Belawan at whose mouth now stands a major port and industrial complex; from what has been called 'the harbour of death' visitors return with fonder feelings for Medan. The lesser river was the Deli and it was up this one that Anderson went looking for the Sultan. He found him at a place then called Kota Java where the Sultan was bombarding a rival. The rival held the next stretch of the river, reported Anderson, including 'Meidan, a village containing 200 inhabitants'. The village also had a mosque but was otherwise unworthy of comment.

Anderson patched up the quarrel and was rewarded with a treaty giving the British exclusive commercial rights in Deli. He was thinking of pepper from upriver but he felt duty bound also to draw attention to the extraordinary fertility of Deli itself. The rice grew tall and strong as a forest; 'I never saw any paddy equal to it'. It stood three feet higher than a man and was extremely tiresome to walk through. Tobacco and sugar cane were equally impressive; so was the variety of timber. In fact 'I do not know so productive a country as Deli, nor is there perhaps one on the face of the globe, possessing so many natural advantages'.

Anderson's plea for a more assertive attitude towards this bountiful sultanate went unheeded and in the following year the British and Dutch redefined their spheres of political influence. The British got Malacca and a free hand in the Malay peninsula; the Dutch got Bengkulu and a free hand in the archipelago, including Sumatra. They were already gobbling up the Minang-kabau country of West Sumatra and now quickly snapped up Palembang, then Siak and, in the 1860s, Deli. The sultan protested to the British but he had in fact already granted to a Dutchman called Jacobus Nienhuys '1000 bouws' of land on the banks of his river near 'Meidan'. It is not recorded whether Nienhuys had read Anderson; but he was growing tobacco.

Over the next thirty years, at the rate of a million acres a decade, tobacco, and then rubber, coffee, cacao and oil palms turned the coastal plains north and south of the Deli river into one of the most productive plantation economies in the world. It was the nearest thing to a gold rush ever seen in South-east Asia. Speculators poured into the area from Penang and Malacca, from Java, from Holland, and from all over Europe. 'Intrepid adventurers, out-lawed Russian counts, German officers discharged because of some shady affair [and] anyone with a good voice for shouting at coolies' could either buy in or find work as an overseer. Amongst them was a young Hungarian, Laszlo Szekely, who heard the news of Deli's incredible soil in Budapest and gambled all on a voyage. 'Tropic Fever' he called it and that was the title of his book. The Sultan grew prodigiously rich as he leased out ever remoter tracts of forest, little of it his; Medan just grew prodigiously.

Prodigious, too, was the human cost. To turn virgin forest into virginia tobacco necessitated the sort of clearance programme for which the New World sanctioned the slave trade. Slavery was outlawed by the Dutch; instead they relied on indentured labour which amounted to much the same thing. 'Prime quality labourers, carefully selected, sturdy, young, physically sound and strong' were advertised by the shipload. In the 19th century they were principally Chinese recruited from Penang, Malacca and south China, later Javanese from east and central Java. They arrived, with nothing but the clothes on their backs and the thatched cones on their heads, at the rate of about 20,000 a year; and they were expended nearly as fast. 'Men died like flies', wrote Szekely. 'The fit ones cleared away the dead and continued the life-and-death struggle.' Malaria, tigers and other perils of the Sumatran forest accounted for many; others fell beneath falling trees, were roasted in the forest fires, drowned in the swamps or flayed alive in draconian beatings; most just succumbed to a lethal mixture of exhaustion and despair.

And all the while the forest burned and smoke filled the air. Ash mingled with sweat and entered the pores of the skin. Tender consciences were troubled. But the work went on and the bright green tobacco grew tall and strong in the rich brown soil. Connoisseurs marvelled at its quality; it was 'thinner than cigarette paper and softer than silk'; buyers bid high to secure the best cigar wrapping-leaf in the world.

For the planters and overseers the work too was hard but nothing like as fatal as the climate. Szekely vividly evokes 'the stupefying heat' and the evil menace that seemed to lurk in every fetid pool and every stinking ditch. Crocodiles thrashed amid the mosquitoes and hideous creatures crawled from their crevices for nocturnal feasts on human flesh. Dysentery and 'red dog' struck as soon as the newcomer set foot on shore. Black water fever, yellow fever, malaria and cholera queued up to follow.

Yet in the boom towns of Siantar, Tebingtinggi and Tanjung Balai the bars and verandahs of the planters' clubs provided some creature comforts. From the outlying estates the Europeans converged in their carts, red and raw from distant labours with the whip, to slake mighty thirsts and renew casual friendships. In Medan, where hotels like DeBoers and The Grand Medan competed with the smartest of planters' clubs, they came in traps and carriages with white linen suits buttoned to the chin. On *hari besar* (holidays) a band played on the *padang* (square) outside. Inside, between the potted palms and the orchestra, dancers waltzed and quadrilled across the French polish before dining on *beefstuks* and *koekjes*. Tip-top times indeed.

Outside DeBoer's Hotel, now renamed the Dharma Deli, there stands a fountain commemorating Jacobus Nienhuys; not far away is the erstwhile Vereenigde Deli Maatschappij built by him in 1869; and behind the London Sumatra building, also on the *pedang*, a plaque commemorates Baron Mackay, the first mayor of Medan. I would like to have known more about the Medan Mackays. Mackays, eased out of Sutherland by their pushy Gordon neighbours, had served and then settled in the Netherlands in the 17th century; as mayor of Medan in the second decade of the 20th century this baron was presumably the grandson of Aeneas, 2nd baron, who had actually succeeded to the chiefship of the clan as the 10th Lord Reay. In due course the mayor must have become the 12th but it was not until the 13th that the clan chief resumed British citizenship. My business, though, was not with the Medan Mackays but the Medan MacLeods, in particular Captain and Mrs Rudolph MacLeod and their two small children, Norman and Jeanne-Louise.

Ask a writer for an introduction and you are invariably given the name of someone deceased. 'Check out Captain Cook while you're there. Says he lost 30 crewmen in Batavia. Fever or something.' The MacLeods lost one, little Norman, but it ruined their marriage and broke up their family. It also ended their colonial interlude and launched Mrs MacLeod on a career of startling notoriety for which she adopted a new name, Mata Hari. In Malay and in modern *bahasa Indonesia* 'mata' is 'eye' and 'hari' is 'day'; 'the eye of the day', i.e. sunrise – precisely the hour when, eighteen years later in the Bois de Vincennes outside Paris, Margarethe MacLeod faced a firing squad.

Her biographer (who is also my wife) traces the transformation of dutiful *mevrouw* into scandalous *demi-mondaine* to two events. One was in Java. Returning to the East with his young bride, Rudolph MacLeod, whose Scottish ancestors had also settled in Holland in the 17th century, was posted to Tumpang near Malang in east Java. There Margarethe, with time hanging heavily on her manicured hands, explored the famous group of Hindu-Buddhist temples of the 13th century Singosari kingdom. She visited them repeatedly and usually alone. She was nineteen years old and delightfully impressionable. In the tumbled towers of stone she found a romance and exoticism that was lacking in an officer's quarters; and to the statuary and reliefs – swaying figures of curvaceous nymphs and fleshy deities – she responded with an awareness more physical than aesthetic. A wayward sensuality which the Captain, corpulent, bald and twenty years her senior, had failed to arouse, let alone gratify, suffused soft limbs and gnawed at a fickle heart.

In 1899 Rudolph was posted to Medan as garrison commander. Promotion for him, it was purgatory for her. Fresh from the highlands of Tumpang, Margarethe with five-year-old Norman and one-year-old Jeanne-Louise, relished neither Medan's steamy miasma nor Deli's 'tropic fever'. Rudolph salved his conscience with an obsessive concern for the health of his children which, though touching, proved irritatingly prescient. Within three months both were fighting for their lives. The little girl lived; the boy died; and amid fearful recriminations the marriage collapsed. The question, a seemingly superfluous one given Deli's reputation as a living dictionary of mortal disorders, was whether he had been poisoned; and if so, why.

★

'So where now, tuan?' asked the *becak* driver. A *becak* (pronounced 'betchak', 'c' being always 'ch' and the 'k' scarcely sounded) is a cycle rickshaw. In Java the passenger travels feet first through the traffic with the pedaller/driver grunting behind his back. But in Medan *becak* are so designed that the driver is abreast of the passenger. It makes for easier conversation.

'St Elizabeth Hospital.'

'He not dead then?'

'He dead, but maybe hospital people know where the grave is'.

So far we had drawn a blank. A knowledgeable old retainer in the Dharma Deli had remembered the Dutch cemetery. It had been in Polonia, the colonial garden city, so named because a Pole had had the first concession there. But sometime in the 1980s it had been bulldozed to make way for the Istana Shopping Plaza. The Plaza's car park could have covered several graveyards. Entering into the spirit of the thing, my *becak* driver had insisted on quizzing the attendant, sundry shop-keepers and the entire staff of Dunkin' Donuts. They hadn't even heard of the hospital although, according to the old boy in the hotel, it was to the hospital that some of the gravestones had been moved.

Once again we wheeled past the Maimoon Palace where in 1888 the Sultan of Deli had commissioned an Italian architect to contrive a setting worthy of his new-found wealth. Finished in propitious yellow, the pillared halls rose forlornly from gracious lawns while, in the shade of a *porte cochère* where elephants once disembarked their passengers, a ragged figure tinkered with a Toyota.

Misunderstandings came thick and fast at the hospital. First I was rushed to the head of a queue for the dispensary. The dispensing sister was all for immediate admission. A doctor then cleverly diagnosed that the patient was actually a visitor. His relief gave way to condolences, and the condolences to mystification, as I explained that young MacLeod was long dead and that I sought neither his bed nor his effects but his gravestone. Obviously it was a case for the registrar, and there at last a glimmer of comprehension entered the proceedings. The man I wanted was 'Pastor Wiro'; he lived across the road.

A tall bespectacled Dutchman with lank hair answered the door. From the dark interior came strong smells of boiled cabbage and Palmolive soap. Wiro, of the Dutch Reformed Church, knew all about the graveyard. It hadn't been at the Istana Plaza but a bit further south along the road to Deli Tua – 'Old Deli' where ruined walls mark the site of a pre-Nienhuys, pre-Anderson fortification. Wiro drew a map and laboriously annotated it in copperplate worthy of a medieval manuscript; Palmolive, or clerical immunity, seemed to spare him the attentions of the mosquitoes. Apparently the graveyard had been cleared; only remains known to be those of missionaries had been dug up and reinterred in the churchyard. Somewhere there was a list of the names. The gravestones had been appropriated by the adjacent *waqf* to cover Muslim tombs. Any inscriptions would have been erased. It was a pity MacLeod had not been based in Siantar or Tebingtinggi because less development meant that there the cemeteries were still intact.

I retired, itching and beaten. No hard won crumb of Mata Hariana would drop on to the biographer's desk; the mystery of young Norman's death would remain. The inquest had said poison and the finger had been pointed at the children's nurse-maid whose lover is supposed to have had some grudge against the Captain. No doubt a lot of people had a grudge against the commandant of Medan. But equally, without chloroquine or malo-prim, the children could simply have fallen foul of a mosquito well charged with malarial plasmodium. Either way, Rudolph never got over the loss while Margarethe never had a chance to confront it. Bullied and abused, she trailed back to Holland bent only on escape.

In 1903 she did escape – to Paris. Two years later 'Lady MacLeod, a native of Java, wife of an officer' was reported to be graciously introducing 'the richness of Oriental colour and life' to a 'satiated city'. As well as perfumes and jewels, her particular contribution was a solo performance of sacred dance into which she had been initiated in Java. Isadora Duncan fans flocked to see it. The postures could have been erotic if they were not so sacred and the gestures suggestive if they were not so poetic. Ancient Indian choreography as miraculously preserved in exotic rural Java recognised no such distinctions; why should Paris? Jewellery, especially elaborate headpieces, comprised the most striking costume element; the drapery was plausibly minimal, all of it diaphanous and progressively dispensable.

For a stage name 'Lady MacLeod' adopted 'Mata Hari'; it served her famously. But her 'oriental' looks, notoriously short-lived, faded fast. With them went her more fashionable paramours. By way of compensation she added to her repertoire an air of mystery and intrigue not unsuited to the times. When war broke out it too served her famously. 'Mata Hari', reported the *Daily Express* of 16 October 1917, 'the beautiful dancer spy, was shot at Vincennes at six o'clock this morning . . . She fell dead at the first volley and was buried in the prison precincts.'

The *becak* driver seemed to enjoy the tale. There were a lot of Mata Haris in Indonesia, he said. I agreed. High on my agenda for Java and Bali was an enigmatic figure usually known to Indonesians as 'Miss Manx'. She had featured prominently in the independence struggle and, for all I knew, might still be manoeuvring behind the scenes of power. Comprehensively eclipsing Margarethe MacLeod as a mistress of many identities, she might even be here in Medan passing herself off, perhaps, as the plantation-owning daughter of one of Szekely's 'outlawed Russian counts'. But it was not her, and not spies, that the *becak* driver had in mind.

'Here in Medan, many, many.'

He pointed out a garden of regimental splendour in which stood a pagoda-like structure of grand proportions and tall black pillars.

'This Medan Club. Generals come here for Mata Haris. Very, very beautiful. But no good. Bad place. Very bad place.'

According to Dalton's *Handbook*, the Club was built during the war by Allied POWs to serve the Japanese as a Shinto temple and a venue for Sumo wrestling. They built it well, like the bridge over the River Kwai; the timber pillars were turned by hand and secured without benefit of nails. I imagined the skeletal figures in baggy shorts tottering among the roof tiles while ferocious Korean guards, legs apart, hands on hips, barked obscenities. 'The emphasis today is on sports', says Dalton.

The Japanese went and have now returned. The world's most dynamic industrial economy runs on Indonesian energy and it protects this supply by massive investment in Indonesian development. Up in the hills at the head of the Asahan valley near Lake Toba, the $2bn hydro-electric plant, the largest in Indonesia, is a Japanese venture. It employs 3,000 Indonesians but the electricity all goes for aluminium production and the aluminium all goes to Japan. This is pretty much what was happening during the war years. The 'Greater East Asia Co-Prosperity Sphere' has thus been realised under the guise of regional development. Indonesia and the other karaoke economies of South-east Asia posture and vocalize and make fools of themselves while Japan calls the tune, supplies the equipment, and reaps the profit.

How, I once asked in Tokyo, would Japan respond if the supply of energy and aluminium were interrupted? It was shortly after the Gulf War. At the time students were fighting troops on the streets of Bangkok and there was the usual conjecture about a looming succession crisis in Jakarta. There, in the 1970s, sensitivity to Japanese investment had also brought the students out on to the streets. So it seemed a relevant question; but the answers were unconvincing. The Japanese constitution, I was told, precluded the possibility of direct military intervention; well, if Japanese nationals as well as Japanese property were threatened, some form of regional initiative might be necessary; but in reality the situation simply could not arise. Why? Because Jakarta, whatever sort of regime held power, could not afford to go it alone. Karaoke rules OK. Without screen, music or microphone, there was no show.

In Medan the Japanese presence is not obtrusive and no claim has been lodged for the return of their temple. Like the descendants of all those Chinese and Javanese plantation labourers, they easily blend into what is probably the most cosmopolitan society in the whole archipelago.

Two blocks south of the Medan Club another ethnic presence announced itself with a strong smell of burning coconut oil followed by a sharp swerve of the *becak* as two turbaned Sikhs reeled on to the roadway. 'Kampung Keling', said the *becak* driver, rolling his eyes skywards. In the gutter lay strings of crushed marigolds; the shops all seemed to be selling saris; somewhere a temple bell was being rung with urgency.

In Sumatra and neighbouring Malaysia all those of Indian extraction were once known as 'Klings' (sometimes 'Kelings') or occasionally 'Chulias'. Both words can be traced to very respectable Indian pedigrees. The former seems to hark back to the Kalinga kingdom, which dates from at least the third century BC and which occupied the coastal regions of what are now Orissa and Andhra Pradesh; the latter, somewhat later and further south, relates to the Cholas who gloriously ruled the Tamil country below Madras from the ninth century AD. All of which bears out the antiquity of Indian contacts with the Malay world.

Indeed 'Sumatra' itself probably derives either from *Suvarna-dwipa*, a place mentioned in the Indian *Ramayana*, or from 'Samudra', a port between Aceh and Medan visited by Marco Polo in 1292. The first means 'the land of gold', an apt description as will be seen; the second means 'the sea', a downright perverse name for a port. But the point is that both words are pure Sanskrit – the classical language of ancient India and of the Hindu scriptures. More Sanskrit placenames are dotted all along this Sumatran coast while south-east of Medan and deep into the interior occasional inscriptions, sculptures and the ruins of stone temples testify to the existence of ancient Indic kingdoms.

Of these kingdoms the mightiest and most long lived was that known from an inscription as Srivijaya ('Lord of Victory' in Sanskrit). Though its site has not been positively identified, Srivijaya seems to have been located at or near Palembang, now Sumatra's second city on the lower reaches of the wide and wayward Musi river. Like the Deli, the Musi provided its rulers with a lucrative control over trade with the interior. But it is also evident from the reports of Chinese visitors and from the distribution of Srivijayan inscriptions as far north as Thailand that this was not just another Sumatran river kingdom. Srivijaya was a major Asian sea-power which controlled both the Malacca and Sunda straits and may therefore be considered the first significant Indonesian polity.

Its dates are still a little uncertain but from the mid-seventh century it supported important Buddhist establishments and it was still a power to reckon with in the eleventh century when, ironically, an inscription on the wall of the great temple at Tanjore (south of Madras) records that a Chola armada devastated the Srivijayan ports. Thereafter supremacy seems to have passed to Melayu, a port city in neighbouring Jambi which has also left extensive Indic remains.

Historians, not to mention nation-builders, would dearly like to know more about Srivijaya and Melayu. As it is, from the scanty materials available they may well have made too much. Maps which show a watery Srivijayan empire covering most of Southeast Asia serve a young nation's need for precedent and pedigree better than they do scholarship. And the notion that from Srivijaya and Melayu there passed to the Javanese kingdoms of Mataram, Kediri and Majapahit a tradition of Indonesian integrity and hegemony has to be discounted as wishful thinking.

One recurrent problem is that the familiar terminology of territorial authority – kingdoms, empires, states – does not easily translate into the realities of pelagic control. Unlike the land, the sea was not a major provider of either labour or produce. It yielded only ships which, like fish, soon disappeared if over-exploited. Trade had to be harboured and husbanded, not harried. Authority lay not in oppressing those who accepted it but in excluding or neutralising those who challenged it. Maritime rule has more of the loose give-and-take of corporate business than of the tight tax-and-grab of government.

'Not empires. I do not like this word. Spheres. Historical and commercial spheres. This is our experience.' I had once asked Dr Sartono, the venerable professor of history at Gajah Mada University in Jogjakarta, how it was that Indian culture had first come to Srivijaya. His point was that Srivijaya was not an empire but the regulating authority and cultural focus of a maritime sphere – essentially the Malacca Straits. Indonesia consisted of a number of such spheres and they could be regarded as geo-political constants in the archipelago's history. With the blind man's refreshing disregard for inessentials, the old professor then outlined the succession of paramount powers in this particular sphere – Melayu,

Malacca, Johore, Aceh, Malacca again, and now Singapore. So
Srivijaya could be considered the Singapore of its day, a cultural
and commercial capital wide open to new ideas. Sanskrit and Buddhism just blew in, like the mobile phone and the free market; and
because they were perceived to be superior and effective, they
found favour. In time, fertile minds and a following wind brought
other ideas. Sumatran inscriptions switch clumsily from Sanskrit
to Malay in the 14th century while Buddhism bows out to Islam
very slowly between the 13th and 15th centuries.

It was not, though, the end of Indian contacts. Islam came to
Indonesia from India and most of the so-called 'Arabs' who
brought the new faith to Sumatra are now thought to have been
Gujeratis and Malibaris from India's Islamicized west coast ports.
Even the sultans of Deli, often portrayed as the premier representatives of Indonesia's Malay population, actually claim descent
from an Indian who was installed as ruler of Deli by Aceh's all-
powerful Iskander Muda in the early seventeenth century.

Two centuries later Anderson found that the population of the
east Sumatran sultanates was still small and far from homogenous.
To the extent that Malay was the official language places like Deli
were as much Malay states as those, like Johore, on the Malayan
peninsula. But in both areas the Islamicized sea-faring people
usually described as ethnically Malay barely outnumbered other
indigenous peoples like, in Sumatra, the Batak.

Today's population is therefore predominantly the result of the
massive influx which accompanied the late 19th/early 20th
century plantation boom. Deli's 120,000 in 1880 became 420,000
in 1900 and over one million in 1920. Now it's probably ten times
that figure. The residents of Kampung Keling, like those of
Medan's Chinatown, are mostly second or third generation
Indonesians who poured into Deli with the Chinese and Javanese
coolies. Szekely had a Bengali baker but most 'Klings' were
Tamils from south of Madras. Noticeably darker, taller and more
bony than Medan's other residents, they preserve the faith and fes-
tivals of South India.

Back in Banda Aceh it had been noticeable that the ethnic *kampung* had succumbed to a recognised Acehnese identity which

transcended the Indian, Chinese, Malay, Vietnamese and Batak elements that make up Aceh's exotic pedigree. But then Aceh has had a century of turbulent history for Deli's every decade; and strife and adversity are powerful catalysts. In Medan ethnic integration has a way to go.

As I toyed with a menu in one of the Kling eating houses, the skies opened. It was as if someone had pulled the celestial flush. The road became a swirling vortex while I stood at the door pressing the *becak* driver to join me inside for a *thali*. Thinking South Indian might not be his preference, I added the possibility of *nasi goreng* (fried rice) and *nasi campur* (Padang-style hors d'oeuvres). He still declined. With a tattered polythene sheet as awning the *becak* had been converted into a frail greenhouse wherein he smoked a *kretek* and ducked the drips. In the street, racks of ready-mades were careering through the flood and preventing a sweet vendor from reaching his sodden display of *jelabis*. A motorbike created a bow wave which crashed aboard the *becak*. The driver went on smoking, a look of blissful disdain suffusing simian features.

'We Batak people. Rain no problem'. In fact it was good for *becak* business. No one walks in the rain; even an umbrella is no protection against the splash-back effect when pint size drops rattle on to solid pavement. But the driver seemed suddenly rather contemptuous, even aggressive. Was it because I had abandoned the MacLeod trail too readily? Or did he simply disapprove of Kling food? True to his race, he was proving something of an enigma.

Practically all Indonesian peoples may be considered as Malays to the extent that they belong to the great Malayo-Polynesian family of peoples who are supposed to have spread from China to South-east Asia, the archipelago, and the Pacific a long time ago. But this migration itself took place over such a long time, and the later migrants were comparatively so much more sophisticated as to tools and diet, that several distinct waves of migration are now presumed. The situation is further complicated by uncertainty about the distribution and skills of the indigenous Australids (related to Australia's native population) whom the Malayo-Polynesians marginalized and perhaps absorbed. The Batak are thus thought to be descendants of an earlier wave of immigrants than most Indonesians or the result of considerable intermarriage with a prior Australid people.

Like 'barbarian' the name 'Batak' was one wished upon them by neighbours who shuddered at their primitive customs and unspeakable languages. Europeans, from Marco Polo onwards, knew principally of their well-attested reputation as cannibals. Naturally consciences were untroubled when the Sultan of Deli, whose writ ran no further from his river than a bullet could carry, graciously dispensed leases on Batak lands for plantation development. Itinerant jungle-dwelling tribes with cannibalistic tendencies could not possibly have land rights. The Batak were, though, permitted to stay on as 'free' plantation workers. They worked when they felt like it, according to Szekely, but generally preferred the two guilders a head offered for recapturing, dead or alive, absconding coolies. The work won them few friends; but they were very good at tracking.

Rather surprisingly it was also rumoured that they were highly literate, indeed that they were the only cannibals who also possessed a literature. In his *History of Sumatra* published in 1783, William Marsden claimed that 'more Batak read and write than do not'. He knew of them only by hearsay but understood that they wrote on bark and that their script ran from left to right – not right to left like the Arabic used for Malay texts and not, as claimed by John Leiden, the other authority, from bottom to top. As Marsden saw it, top to bottom, like the Chinese, was conceivable but bottom to top was most implausible because they would be forever smudging what they had just written. Marsden was also interested in their religion which seemed to include a trinity – the lords of the heavens, the air and the earth – and a soul which at death made its escape through the deceased's nostrils. But he had not apparently heard of the polysyllabic Sisingamangaraja, the mystical priest-king of the Toba Batak.

'Si-singa-manga-raja' is the sort of name that makes dubious historical excursions worthwhile. It lodges in the mind and rolls deliciously round the tongue longing for its vocal debut. It also demands a lot of space on the street map. Medan's city fathers had conferred it on the longest and straightest of all Medan's unlovely thoroughfares, that which continues the Trans-Sumatran Highway south towards the hills and the Batak homeland. No one seemed to know whether it was named for the original Sisingamangaraja of unknown date or for Sisingamangaraja XII who put up a good fight against the Dutch until he was killed in 1907 but who ten years later figured again as the messianic leader of a short-lived independence movement.

A generation later those Batak who had taken to the hills rather than work on the plantations or tangle with the Dutch began returning to Medan. With them came other Batak who had never been away from the hills. They came, like my *becak* driver, for the jobs and the opportunities offered by a growing metropolis. But now, instead of forest trophies and grisly human heirlooms, many brought with them examination certificates, degrees and languages. Up among the clouds and volcanoes of the Bukit Barisan, Sumatra's mountain spine, something had transformed one of Indonesia's most 'primitive' peoples into a disciplined army of officials, teachers, constables and brigadiers.

Shedding no tears over Medan, the busload bound at last for the hills rolled down Jalan Sisingamangaraja. The driver donned a leather jacket, unthinkable in Deli's humidity, and switched on the music. A Batak Miss Marple with granny specs and a woolly cardigan dropped her knitting to hand-jive to Guns 'n' Roses. The excitement was intense. Like souls released from purgatory we craned forwards and upwards, panting for the first gulp of fresh air, confident of cool breezes and bracing encounters.

N.K

3. Of brigadiers and bishops

The plantations extended surprisingly far into the hills. On the flat the crops were lower than the road level and screened behind a roadside ribbon of hoardings and warehouses interspersed with *kampung* and *warung* (eating houses). But after Siantar, in Anderson's day a Batak stronghold but now a thriving market town, the road began to climb and the labours of all those Chinese and Javanese coolies could be appreciated. It was as if the slopes had been upholstered. A plush cushioning of oil palms interplanted with cacao dipped towards folds in the hills where a line of catch crops – coconut and cassava – ran like ribbing. Ranks of rubber trees, each at exactly twenty degrees from the perpendicular, receded in a shady Gothic perspective. Seen from a distance they formed a pleated valance round the base of the hills. Only up in the clouds did the patchwork of corduroys give way to forest as represented by the slab grey buttresses of mighty kapok trees; and even here the forest floor was choked with an undergrowth of coffee bushes.

No doubt in Szekely's day the firing of the forest had contributed to such wondrous fertility. But here, as elsewhere in Indonesia, exceptional growth, particularly of plantation crops, comes courtesy of greater conflagrations. As Anderson had observed, the Deli earth was rewarding its cultivators long before they were ousted by the forest-burning planters.

A sudden change of gear brought a flood of sunlight as the trees gave way to Alpine pasture. Before a backdrop of sky, small

buffalo with wispy grey or tan coats grazed among patches of
bracken. A tractor pulled a trailer piled high with cabbages and
carrots. It was like being whisked, in the course of a sentence,
from Amazonia to Austria. Almost unnoticed in this abrupt transformation, the road had breasted a sharp ridge and now descended
steeply through sun-swept dales. Far below small ships plied
choppy waters. But for a beach, the waters could have been sea;
but, too, for an empty horizon, for the bank of cloud in the distance now revealed itself as an encircling wall of mountain. This,
then, was Danau Toba, South-east Asia's largest lake.

Toba is many other things: the 'mystical heartland' of the
Batak, the geographical navel of Sumatra and, at over quarter of a
mile deep, the most capacious volcanic crater in the world. It's
also a long and exciting geological epic. Out of a smaller, higher
crater some 75,000 years ago, in what was probably the mightiest
eruption our planet has experienced, came the fall-out which so
enriched the Deli plains. Finer dust and gases spread from Toba
into the atmosphere and have recently been identified as the prime
cause of the last European ice age. In the process of the eruption
what remained of the volcano subsided into the empty magma
chamber and the hole then filled with water. Eventually this water
forged an escape route down the Asahan valley. The water level
fell to something like its current height, about 900m above sea
level, and a second eruption forced up a large segment of the lake's
bed. It broke the surface and is now Samosir island.

Lop-sided and filling nearly half the lake, Samosir takes five
days to walk round and proves to be not quite an island since a
corner just nudges the mainland. But few would quibble over such
geographical niceties. Housed in a Beatrix Potter cottage at a place
called Tuk-tuk, itself an appendage of Samosir, the improbability
of taking tea on the peninsula of an island in a lake in the middle
of another island, the lake being in fact the crater of a volcano,
1,000m up, a stone's throw from the Equator and the deepest
fresh water in the world – well, it seemed to be enough. And that
was without the Batak and their mysterious transformation from
cannibals into brigadiers.

So long as diffusionist theories held the floor, the Batak were assumed to have originally migrated to Sumatra from somewhere in the hills of Tonkin, Thailand or Burma. They seemed to have physical affinities to some of the Golden Triangle's exotic tribes and, as an upland people, when they reached Sumatra they naturally withdrew into the mountain recesses of the Bukit Barisan. There they revived, as best they could remember them, ancient skills in the working of timber and stone to fashion elaborate houses and megaliths. A similar history was created for the Niha whose greater isolation in Nias, an island off Sumatra (and my next excursion), afforded the only plausible explanation for such a profusion of monoliths that Nias was said to be still stuck in the Stone Age.

But the diffusionists are now on the defensive. If the idea of mass migrations by Indians and Arabs is no longer deemed necessary to explain the Hindu-Buddhist and Islamic influences in Indonesian history, why postulate a far less probable maritime migration for hill tribes from the South-east Asian interior? Greater credence is given to the possibility that isolated peoples could have developed similar characteristics and cultures independently of one another, or possibly in imitation of imported models. The language and theology of the Batak, for instance, betray clear evidence of that ubiquitous Sanskrit and Hindu influence.

Even those who assume the original Malayo-Polynesian dispersal to be proven now stress the Polynesian element in the equation as much as the Malay. This affords other clues. Ancestor cults, for instance, and clan-like social groupings based on genealogy, typically Polynesian, are found to underlie all cultural strata in Indonesia. And they are particularly evident among the Batak, the Niha and those other upland builders, the Toraja of Sulawesi. It's as if the higher a people's homeland, the more their prehistoric Polynesian or Oceanic culture protrudes from the Malay cultural matrix of the lowlands.

In the case of the Batak, clan consists of the exogamous and patrilinear *marga* (another Sanskrit word?), each of which has many thousand members and remains more important to a Batak even than his religious affiliation – which is saying something.

Hundreds of followers of the HKBP marched through the main streets of Medan on Thursday [reported the *Jakarta Post*]. They were protesting against what they alleged to be government meddling in their internal affairs.

The protest was held immediately after they attended the trial of their colleagues who were charged with criminal behaviour during a clash with rival camps for the right to use a HKBP church.

HKBP stands for *Huria Kristen Batak Protestan*, or the Batak Protestant Christian Church. It is said to have three million members and judging by the number of churches between Medan and Samosir this may be an understatement. It is certainly the largest Christian community in Sumatra, and probably, if one excludes the Philippines, in the whole of South-east Asia.

Rebuffed by staunch Muslims like the Acehnese, Christian missions first came among the Batak in the mid-19th century. Two Americans got themselves killed, and possibly eaten, in the 1830s but in 1860-90 conversions multiplied after the German Rheinische Mission sent Ludwig Nommensen with a Bible and violin to spread the word.

Cannibals often prove easy game for Christian missionaries, perhaps because they readily understand a faith that enjoins communion with the Almighty by consuming His flesh and blood. Although it is possible that any religion, so long as it was not that of their detested Muslim neighbours, would have been acceptable to the Batak, Nommensen's skill as a doctor, teacher and man of peace proved decisive. So did the fact that he was not Dutch.

Christianity gave the Batak educational opportunities which, combined with that improbable pre-Christian literary tradition, soon made them the most progressive ethnic group in Sumatra. It also gave them a more acceptable identity plus a taste for the work ethic. Ancient beliefs and loyalties were never abandoned but now constituted no barrier to advancement. Under the aegis of the HKBP, but with more than passing reference to Sisingamangaraja, the Bataks descended from the hills to make their mark as doughty fighters against the Dutch and then as officers and officials in the new Indonesia.

But as per the *Jakarta Post*, in 1993 all was not well with the HKBP. Somehow the Church had lumbered itself with two bishops-designate, each backed by a vociferous following of the faithful. When neither would give ground, orders, perhaps well-intentioned, came from Jakarta's ministry for religious affairs for the civil authorities to intervene. This might have been acceptable if the civil authority in question, the governor of North Sumatra, had not been a Muslim. Suddenly arbitration looked like mischievous interference. The original crisis was becoming overshadowed by sectarian sentiment; Christian-Muslim rivalry, recently reported in Java, now threatened Sumatra.

A short walk on Samosir suggested that it might have been better to let the schism run its course. Besides the HKBP, I counted two Pentecostal churches, two Catholic, and one Bethel. Additionally the Karo Batak at the north end of the lake have their own church; and Adventists, Jehovah's Witnesses and Mormons (to whom Batak genealogical awareness must be a blessing) are all well represented. Toba Bataks thrive on pluralism and it was no surprise to learn that religious allegiances tend to match *marga* membership. Doubtless ancient clan loyalties were also behind the warring bishops.

Outside Java and Bali, the Batak are the largest ethnic group in Indonesia. Population estimates vary from three million to six million, presumably because censuses tend to confuse ethnic origin with religious allegiance. For, although the Toba Batak are largely Christian and therefore easily quantifiable, they comprise only about half the total Batak population. Other Batak – notably the Simalungan from around Siantar, the Angkola and Mandailing to the south, and the Pakpak to the west – are predominantly Muslim. Neighbouring Acehnese, Minangkabau and Malays got to them before the Rhenish missionaries. They converted to Islam *en masse*, 'man being manifestly a gainer when he barters, for a paradise and eternal pleasures, so small a consideration as the flesh of his foreskin'. Marsden, in other words, doubted whether such conversions amounted to any more than an insurance policy lest the ancestors should withdraw their favours; and to this day a Batak Muslim is sometimes thought to represent a contradiction in terms.

Most distinguished of these Muslim Batak is the Mandailing general, Abdul Haris Nasution. 'Nas' is Indonesia's outstanding soldier and the man who almost succeeded Sukarno as head of state. Perhaps he would have done if his decidedly non-Muslim credentials, previously demonstrated in ruthless suppression of Islamic fanatics in West Java and Islamic separatists in West Sumatra, had not been so impeccable. But that was in 1965, 'the year of living dangerously'. It was quickly followed, for over a quarter of a million luckless Indonesians, by the year of dying horribly. Nasution's eight-year-old daughter was one of them; and he very nearly so. He has his own theories about the 'Indonesian holocaust' and about the abortive coup which triggered it. As the turning point in Indonesia's fifty years of independence both merit close examination.

The pogrom prompted those Batak who still clung to their ancient beliefs hastily to espouse either Islam or Christendom. Among the Karo Batak of Brastagi (north of Toba) a new church was born overnight to accommodate the new converts. As in Java and Bali, any parading of beliefs other than those sanctioned by the state was liable to be misconstrued as sedition. The general abhorred both the fanaticism and the lawlessness of the times. Living in an outdated seclusion in Jakarta, he still does. To age and anticipation of the 'eternal pleasures' awaiting the righteous Muslim he makes no devotional concessions whatsoever. Like many Batak 'converts', in death as so often in life he will doubtless return to the Batak hills to lie among his ancestors as a 20th century Sisingamangaraja.

It being Sunday, the country lanes of Samosir were alternately thronged with smartly dressed church-goers and then totally deserted as, from thickets among the rice fields, unseen choirs competed for the morning's favour like rival songbirds. I chose a muddy track on the outskirts of Tomok village down which a high corrugated roof pitched steeply from a tangle of bamboos and coconut palms. The service was already under way.

Although it turned out to be a Mass, the austerity of bare walls and concrete floor would have been agreeable to a Covenanter. All that distinguished the building as a place of worship rather than a barn was the large crucifix, with a strip light strapped to Christ's outstretched arms, which hung skew-whiff from the steel rafters. The altar was a trestle table with two large ledgers, a candlestick and a Heineken can filled with pink blossoms which clashed violently with the celebrant's tangerine chasuble. There was a strong smell of bat.

Of more interest was the congregation which was large, mostly female and wonderfully vocal. They sang to an electric organ with a gusto that threatened to lift the corrugated, every voice in tune, every line known by heart. Such fervour could trouble the ancestors. Yet the cadences recalled the South Seas and lent substance to 19th century reports of memorable paddling songs as the Batak took to the lake in their bark canoes. Now lauding the Virgin Most Pure, the hymns welled forth from a hundred heaving bosoms, each barely contained in a sturdy yellow bra which bunched dark and heaving flesh beneath tight blouses of transparent white lace. Hair of dazzling lustre, more porphyry than black, ballooned over bouffant back-combing or cascaded in heavy curls. Hats would have been an insult; but from every right shoulder hung the Batak lady's folded plaid, an intricately woven accessory which lends grace to the shuffling congas and formations of Batak dance. It's also useful as a sling for babies. Tough-looking toddlers slept in peace, their bullet heads a continuation of thick necks just like the log-carved idols of their ancestors.

The Lord's Prayer took approximately twice as long as it would in English and the collection plate netted about 10,000 rupiah (US$5). At last the congregation launched into a final hymn and the priest retired behind a screen. He emerged in fawn jacket, white trousers, and a beautifully tied silk tie. It was the first tie I had seen in Batak country. He looked like an off-duty croupier.

'Horas', I ventured as we filed past into the sunshine.

'Ah, you speak Batak?' I confessed that this all-purpose greeting was my only word; and lest he think up a suitable penance for the deception, I hastened to congratulate him on his congregation's singing. The compliment was dismissed with a wave of his prayer book.

'You see, most of our old music would be associated with the worship of ancestors or spirits. They would sing songs asking for blessings and also dance Batak dances. So they had to do all these dances and sing all these songs very carefully. If they make mistakes they would be cursed by the spirits of the dead.'

He picked his way cautiously up the muddy lane to the road, springing lightly from side to side to dodge a puddle or dislodge a piglet with his umbrella. It was not a question of avoiding offence to the ancestors but of preserving the Cherry Blossom shine of his brogues. His name was Father Robert.

Armed with these insights I struck off up the hill to investigate an *adat* village. Butterflies as big as bats swooped and danced, their wings like witch doctors' masks, matt black daubed with white spots and striations of electric blue. Distant thunder heightened the morning's stillness as down the lake a layer of puffy nimbus hid the hills. Above it an interval of blue sky ended with random gashes of thinner cloud behind which whole continents of high cumulus smudged with lead and ink rolled at random. And all the while, closer to hand, steamy white mist was stealing over the rim of the crater and sliding down its steep crevices. It was like a week's weather all at once. The sun still shone but from every quarter a downpour threatened. The lake lay calm and brooding, its beauty faintly sinister.

Thus far I had managed to stall thoughts of the Batak's reputation for eating people. Earlier visitors, Chinese as well as Europeans, had written of little else, the custom being guaranteed to exercise imaginations and sell books long before the word 'cannibalism' had entered the English language. But as in the Caribbean (whence came the name), Africa and New Zealand, I knew that there were very few reliable first-hand accounts of the practice. Obviously those best placed to spill the beans might have been boiled with them. It was equally plausible that the Batak exaggerated the practice, perhaps even invented it, to enhance their hostile reputation and discourage intruders.

Yet all this talk of ancient beliefs and surviving superstitions made one wonder. Marsden, Raffles and numerous later visitors and missionaries had gone to enormous lengths to verify their accounts; and the detail was particularly telling. Only criminals after due trial, plus some prisoners of war, were condemned as fit for consumption. They were eaten alive and they were eaten piecemeal, as if the Batak appreciated the 'nibble' in 'cannibal'. A fleshy nose, a choice cheek or a tender thumb-stick was always preferred to a haunch. Satay-size, each titbit could be devoured raw or lightly grilled but was always seasoned with a piquant chilli sauce. The blood was sometimes drunk. The victim, reduced to the shapelessness of a doner kebab, expired before the meal was over although much of him might remain untouched.

Raffles in particular had an enormous respect for the Batak (he called them 'Batta', the 'k' being scarcely sounded) as an intelligent and law-abiding people. He was at great pains to emphasise that though they professed to enjoy human meat, they never allowed appetite to get the better of them. Full-blooded accounts of the diners dispensing with knives and tearing the flesh from their victims with their teeth in a savage orgy of indulgence were nonsense. According to Batak *adat*, only those guilty of particularly heinous crimes – adultery, certain types of theft etc – could be eaten and there seemed to be a ritual significance to the punishment, as if mastication and digestion were the only sure way to dissipate the spirit of such an atrocious rascal. Otherwise, presumably, he would join the ranks of all the other ancestors and there wreak as much evil among the dead as he had among the living.

A ubiquitous word is *adat*. In the case of a house or village it translates easily enough as 'traditional'. Drawn up in a line, their sharp gables projecting over the village thoroughfare like schooners on the stocks, Tomok's houses proved the epitome of *adat* Batak architecture. Each stands on hefty timber piers where, below floors, buffalo and pigs are penned for the night and motor bikes may be garaged. Overhead the main structure, more hull than house, has long rakish lines and a barge-like bulge, all tucked beneath a steep and massive roof. Here in the Toba region, the ridge of the roof sags, saddleback-style, in a graceful arc which is continued beyond reason or necessity to gables which sail sky-wards, as high again as the house and half way across the street before they terminate. Only an expert in aerodynamics, or some-one with a financial interest in corrugated iron sheeting, could possibly have designed such profligate roofing.

It has often been asserted that these lateen shapes testify to some long-dimmed memory of sea-faring prowess. A few houses are still roofed with palm thatch and perhaps rattan sails did pro-vide the original inspiration. Lash a liana between two trees like a washing line, throw over it a heavy tarpaulin of woven palm frond, peg the two sides apart as for a tent, and something very like the profile of the *adat* Batak house must result. Shipbuilding expertise could also explain the neat and nail-less joinery; fanciful figure-heads may have inspired the intricately carved and painted under-side of the gables.

In a country with the most varied and exotic domestic architec-ture in the world, ship-houses, house-boats, water pavilions and other amphibious structures will recur. But already I was con-vinced that people like the Batak who could build such exquisite houses must, if given to eating people, have always been the most discriminating of cannibals.

Cannibalism apart, the Batak remain proud of their past and, whether Christian or Muslim, preserve many other features of their *adat* culture. But traditions in Indonesia as a whole are so elusive and diverse that the word *adat* has become loaded with all sorts of local and generic associations. As a political term, it evokes an ancient village ideal of consensus which is often por-trayed as an indigenous form of democracy more suited to local conditions than multi-party systems based on universal suffrage. As a legal term *adat* invariably means customary law as opposed to statute law or Islamic law (for instance in Aceh). And in a religious or social context it covers all those pre-Islamic beliefs, 'tribal' structures, and residual animist practices such as divination, ancestor worship, sorcery and astrology which permeate Indone-sian life to the bafflement of foreign observers. 'It's our *adat*,' says a press secretary when the President disappears into the wilds of West Java for a secret consultation with his *dukun* (roughly 'magician').

For the Batak, a people clearly full of surprises, mysterious figures like Sisingamangaraja are *adat*. So is that improbable pre-Christian literary tradition and the fastidious form of cannibalism; so too the houses like schooners, that meticulous regard for the ancestors, the Polynesian chant, Himalayan dance routines and even, it appeared, titanic chess battles.

'Horas, Mister John'.

Deafening cracks of thunder accompanied by great gobs of rain had sent me scurrying into the nearest shelter. A mere shack, definitely not an *adat* house, it opened on to a verandah facing the road. Beneath the deafening rattle of rain on corrugated I dripped past a couple of tables and, confident now that any roadside accommodation could rustle up refreshment, asked for coffee.

'Horas, horas, Mister John'.

A sudden rushing sound heralded a wind from nowhere which tore at the tin roof and scattered a scratching of hens. Stair-rods twisted in the gale and the ground, even the grass, erupted with knee-high fountains as the rain ricocheted against it. The grape-shot on the roof and the artillery in the clouds gave a fair impression of Waterloo.

'Mister John, yes? Horas'.

Without his trousers on, I hadn't recognized the barefoot pilgrim who had tripped in after me. Even a fawn jacket and silk tie make no impression when betrayed by bare legs and baggy boxer shorts printed with a tropical sunset. The white trousers, I now noticed, were neatly folded and roosting in the branches of his umbrella whence also dangled by their laces the polished brogues. Father Robert could have waded a river and still emerged with the sartorial wherewithal to confront a bishop.

Thinking of which, and by way of waiting out the elements, I invited his thoughts on the episcopal strife amongst his rivals of the HKBP. He pulled a chair into the shack to escape the encroaching deluge and sat down between the primus that was heating my coffee and two small boys squatting on the earth floor.

'See these boys? So it seems to me that they play chess. You know chess?'

A litter of small pigs with coats as fine as a mole's joined us in the dry. So did a large man in a singlet who had been sitting on one of the tables practising chords on his guitar. Huddled over their game, the two small boys were concentrating too hard to notice the invasion.

'See. Two bishops. Each boy has two bishops. Well no, I notice this boy has only one bishop. But my opinion is that he should have two.'

Actually he did have two but one was a replacement, fashioned from clay and bearing an uncanny resemblance to the log-headed idols of Batak ancestors in the graveyard in Tomok. A lot of other pieces were missing. Most of the pawns were bottle tops and one of the castles was a clever replica of an *adat* house.

At least they had a board. Szekely observed a Batak chess game where the players first drew the squares of a board with a stick in the dust and then collected cigarette butts for pawns and stones, beans, berries, pips etc for the other pieces. He also noted that, all things considered, they played a fair game. Of the current contestants neither can have been more than ten years old and I would have said they played with distinction.

'Once a Dutch grandmaster came to Medan. Perhaps it was in 1930 something. It seems on of our Batak players went to challenge him.'

Father Robert had made his point about two bishops being perfectly reasonable and was now savouring one of the great moments in recent Batak history.

'Personally I did not see the game. I was too young. I was not born. But people say that they played in the Grand Hotel in Medan.'

A thunder crack above our heads sounded like the great Toba eruption. The ground positively shook and the black queen toppled over.

'So who won?'

'Stalemate. Yes, it was stalemate. The world champion of the Dutch went away in disgrace, I think.'

On this triumphant note Father Robert unexpectedly took his leave, tucking his shirt back into the sunset shorts and ducking under his laden umbrella. The road was now a river in spate; the verandah was awash and the man in the singlet was hastily erecting shutters to keep out the flood. As the brollie, hung with white trousers and propelled by bare legs and a tropical sunset, disappeared over the brow of the hill. I thought of Noah. Faced with such a flood no wonder people built ship-houses.

The storm ended as abruptly as it had begun. The shutters were dismantled and the pigs, the chickens and the chess-players shooed outside. An Isuzu full of Chinese day-trippers from Siantar splashed past, Nintendos bleeping in the back seat.

Sallying forth into the sunshine I skirted lakes where there should have been parched terraces of stubble. Across the higher pastures streams explored the herbage and slithered anxiously among the thistles like nocturnal serpents overtaken by daybreak. Steam rose from the road; rivers raged through deep gorges; and high above, a 400ft cascade dived over the lip of the volcanic rim. Out on the lake the ferries pitched and tossed among the white horses. In the distant hills another landslide had cut the Trans-Sumatra Highway while down on the plains a mighty river was changing its course.

Sumatra must be a surveyor's nightmare. Stuck not in the Stone Age but in the dawn of creation, the land still quivers and pustulates with elemental forces. Eruptions and earthquakes work grumpily among the rocks; storms blast the forest, rains run off with the fields and rivers engulf the valleys. Yet climatic resilience makes good. Lava flows soon heal over, deserted river beds become stone-walled rice terraces. A graze in the forest instantly explodes with vegetation as if ploughed and sown with intent. In its sunlight the insects swarm, attracting new colonies of bat and bird. Strange vapours roam the new heath and one half expects to see herds of dinosaur chomping through the undergrowth.

Instead I breasted a hill and found myself surrounded by sarcophagi. Unlike the sombre megaliths of Tomok with their carved idols, these were concrete constructions, painted and in excellent repair, featuring miniature churches carefully inscribed with a cross and 'HKBP'. Others were built in *adat* style, mostly no bigger than dolls' houses but occasionally rivalling the dumpy rice barns which stand in front of the ship-houses in a traditional village.

Tucked away on its little plateau, the place was not so much a necropolis as a hamlet for pygmies. The wind had died, the sun was high, and all was quiet save for a distant flute and drums troubling the ether. One could imagine the big-headed idols of Batak ancestors emerging from their mini-churches, clubs at the ready, to visit *adat* relatives and revive old feuds.

If one excludes mavericks like the Parsees and Tibetans, the world roughly divides into those who bury their dead and those who burn them. A few, like the Balinese, do both; first the burial, later the burning. Marco Polo claimed that the Batak simply ate their dead, but this was nonsense. Some, notably among the Karo Batak, also both bury and burn but most just bury and re-bury.

For the first funeral a grave is used and no time is lost. The clan is summoned urgently from far and wide to give the deceased a royal induction into the ranks of his ancestors. Should he or she have had the misfortune to die childless, or to have been predeceased by his children, Toba rites allow for the presence of a *Si Gale Gale*, a stand-in doll appropriately dressed and ingeniously jointed to perform the expected gestures. One example, equipped with a sponge, even sheds tears. Feasting and dances accompany the ceremonies and it may have been the ritual killing and eating of vast numbers of pigs which was mistaken for consumption of the corpse itself.

Re-burials take place years, sometimes generations, later and, because of the expense, numerous related corpses may be reinterred together. Only the bones need be recovered and after careful cleaning and wrapping in accordance with custom they are eventually laid to rest in a smart new sarcophagus. Again large attendances are usual and the programme of festivities lasts for days.

I failed to witness either a burial or a reburial. But insight of a sort was provided by the conviction that my Beatrix Potter cabin was actually a sarcophagus. The proprietor insisted on calling it a 'Batak cottage' and had covered the floor boards with lino, hung a mirror on the wall, and somehow dragged a mattress up the access ladder and squeezed it through a door which allowed for admission only on all fours. Bare rafters afforded an appreciation of Batak joinery and of the considerable skill required to construct the sagging, pointed profile of an *adat* house, devoid of right angles, from rectangular sheets of corrugated. But perched on a secluded rock, its great winged gables reminding me of an eagle airing its plumage, it could never have been a rice barn. It was also much too small and dumpy for a house. I checked again. It was identical to the largest *adat* ossuaries.

Lying diagonally, with feet jammed into one corner and head pressed against one of the little floor-level windows, it was just possible to stretch out. The timbers provided handy shelves at convenient levels and from the cross-beams, where geckos mounted a constant patrol against mosquitoes, an extensive wardrobe could be hung.

But I grew to like it most for the view and the thunder storms. Each afternoon without fail towering columns of cloud built up over the rim of the volcano. Scarcely advancing, they seemed only to climb higher and higher, mushroom upon mushroom, until at last toppling inwards to smother the sky and smudge the lake. A sudden gust would tear at the roof as the first drops splattered on to the tin. The palms on the shore tossed their fronds like grief-stricken mourners; eddies of dust danced across the paddy fields and lasers of lighting conga-ed through the clouds. Effigies and funerals are all very well. They console the bereaved and bind the Batak together into societies that transcend the generations and suborn the tyranny of death. Sisingamanagaraja can come again as often as he is needed. But for an ancestor I was convinced that the essence of being a Batak is to be honoured by the elements as well.

N.C

4. Isle of dreams

The Batak lands succumbed to their first tourists soon after the
Dutch completed their annexation in 1908. To escape Deli's
intolerable climate, heat-crazed planters and emaciated officials
fanned out into the hills. From Medan some headed west up into
the Karo country around Brastagi, there to gulp pine-scented
breezes and encourage the production of such delicacies as French
beans and conference pears. Others went south for Toba territory
and the great lake where Parapat, on its eastern shore, became the
Batak roadhead and Sumatra's leading hill station.

All noise and no taste, Parapat is now a tawdry staging post on
what has since become one of the island's few cross roads. It is also
the main ferry terminal for all lakeside destinations. Colonial nostalgia lingers on only in the proliferation of guest houses and in the
stately gardens of the Parapat Hotel, founded in 1911. Day-
trippers, whose grandparents then toiled as coolie labour, now
have the run of the town. From a convoy of shiny landcruisers and
customized Hondas they bounce immaculate in stiff denim and
pneumatic trainers. Shutters click and camcorders whirr. The
afternoon rains pass in an animated lunch and sunset in shopping.
A mighty ignition and the sounding of klaxons heralds departure.
It's a busy life, being a conspicuous consumer.

Also conspicuous though less laundered, the descendants of
their grandparents' taskmasters, big blond MacLeods with Australian accents and Szekelys in singlets and sarongs, head for the
ferries through Parapat's accommodation touts and encroaching

souvenir stalls. For them the town is just a transit stop between Bukit Lawang, a forest rehabilitation centre for orphaned orang-utans and weary world travellers north of Medan, and the easy-going international enclaves on Samosir island.

Medan has its Hash House Harriers, a branch of the fun run movement which was started and so named in Kuala Lumpur. Samosir just has hash. 'Everyone sells and they're all unionized,' says Dalton's *Handbook*. 'On Mondays the police go round the *los-men* to collect their dues.' This was in the 1970s. Later editions of the book omit such period tips. 'For mushrooms head for the cow paddocks south of Tomok . . . One of the kitchens will make up an omelette and even turn out hash, or ganja, cookies (you supply).' But times have changed. Nowadays it's hard to find an omelette that isn't laced with doubtful fungi (they supply).

The hippies arrived in the Sixties and, as in those other pig and palm cultures in Goa and Bali, they easily slipped into the way of things. Like earlier colonists they also stamped the place with their own lifestyle. Signs for bike hire, bakeries and bucket shops sprang up along Samosir's lakeside trail; adjacent villages reached out to one another with a string of *losmen* (pensions), craft shops and cafes; Coke and Kodak supplied the awnings. Bamboo thickets were turned into cane furniture while avocados became something other than pig-food as guacamole joined gado-gado on snack menus. Pancakes and *pommes frites* added further international distinction. I was not ungrateful. Where the focus and substance of every meal is invariably a pyramid of rice or a bowl of squirm-ing noodles, one learns to appreciate the remarkable versatility of the potato and the ecstasy of a crusty baguette.

Since the hippies drifted home to Ballarat and Beaconsfield long-stay visitors have become the exception. A week or so is ample for Toba. Today's world traveller has an ambitious schedule and an onward reservation zipped into his money belt. Martine and Nathalie from Paris had taken a year for Nepal, Thai-land, the Philippines and Indonesia. It was their second trip. Travel was important. *Pour comprendre* of course. So now they were going to Pulau Nias. Not for the surfing. No, for the *culture*. The *culture* and the *fruits de mer*.

Martine's guidebook warned that there were 1,200 hairpins on the road down to Sibolga whence a ship, it said, sailed for Nias twice a week. I didn't doubt the ship but wondered how, in a country where quite basic information is often hard to come by, such precise details about the road alignment had been acquired. We shared a banquette, the aptly named seating that used to be provided for amorous couples in the back rows of provincial cinemas. This one was mounted upfront beside the bus driver on the cowling of his engine. It was quite warm, and the only place for legs was straight out in front, feet braced against the windscreen. A good view and agreeable company was otherwise marred only by having to work the brake pedal. The driver could depress it but, lacking a return mechanism, it was my job to tug on a short rope so as to restore it to position before the next hazard.

'No rabbits,' said Martine. I was hoping for tigers and Sumatran rhino. We were bowling across open grassland where elephants should have roamed and tapirs rootled. How could so much wilderness support so little life? Even the sky was birdless.

The hairpins began after Tarutung where roadside repairs and a long meal-stop meant a two-hour delay. The ship sailed at eight. Already the light was fading as we dropped through dense vegetation down the first hundred zig-zags. The tarmac ceased and on hairpin 306, busy now with the brake pedal, I lost count. It was seven-thirty and getting warmer. We had missed the celebrated sunset over Tapanuli Bay and were entering a succession of steep tunnels and rocky overhangs with no provision for oncoming traffic. 'Ooh la la' said Martine as we scraped the rock wall in backing up for a truck so rusted and battered it had nothing to lose. Rocks rained on to the roof and the dust hung in the feeble beam of the headlights like a yellow fog. My brake arm was aching.

Two hours later we were careering through the ill-lit streets of Sibolga in a fleet of *becak*. A fishy stench and dripping humidity augured ill for a three-day stopover; yet the urgency of the *becak* drivers gave ground for hope and, though the dockyard gates were locked, I could see the superstructure of a ship at the end of the jetty. For the fare plus 30 per cent and a lot of form filling the harbourmaster sold tickets. Another supplement persuaded the *becak* men to pedal the length of the jetty.

On board with seconds to spare, luggage intact and calm seas ahead, it would have been seemly to have subsided with a sigh of quiet satisfaction. There was no excuse for the row with the purser. He asked only the standard 4,000 rupiah for a cabin bunk; the sheets looked clean and the other occupants unobjectionable. Cutting things fine always means paying over the odds. But I was tired and another two dollars, on top of the others, was two dollars too much. The purser sympathised. If I wrote to the Harbour Board I might get a refund of the dock-gate supplement. The engineer brought a glass of water. The captain deserted his bridge to offer apologies.

I merely swore. 'Visit Indonesia Year' came in for harsh analysis. So did what is called the 'high cost economy', Indonesia-speak for official corruption. It didn't help. Trapped now by my own rhetoric, there was nothing for it but to stretch out on the bare deck. I spread a towel and stared hard at the stars. Later Martine appeared with cigarettes for her and a pillow for me. For some unfathomable reason she needed to confide about her relationship with the silent Nathalie. 'I love 'err. She love me. We are loverrs. You understand?'

I listened patiently to tales of unsympathetic mothers and the incorrigible sexism of the bourgeoisie as we slid past rocky atolls top-heavy with feathered foliage. The distant lights of invisible buoys pierced the darkness erratically. Ruffled spirits were calmed by the gentle roll of the sea.

It was Nias, next morning's enigmatic destination, that had been bothering me. It didn't fit in to what was supposed to be a straight run down the archipelago nor, like Sumatra's other forgotten satellites, could it be expected to yield any dazzling insights into Indonesian society. I should have been pressing on for the Minangkabau country and Sumatra's most influential history-makers. Pulau Nias shared little of the nation's past, contributed even less to its economy and was a total irrelevance. Worse still, I was not sure that I wanted to go.

Years ago I had somewhere read an account of the island that made it sound like the remotest place on earth. Sumatra then had seemed strange enough with its heady mix of cannibals and volcanoes smothered in forests of kapok and camphor. But Nias, which even Sumatrans evidently considered a god-forsaken place of irredeemable savagery, was straight out of Rider Haggard. Here heads were still being hunted and humans ritually sacrificed as late as the 1930s. While 12,000ft up cocktails and canapés were being served on Perth-bound turbo-props, down below a whole island with a population of quarter of a million was apparently still stuck in the Stone Age. In jungle clearings swarms of slaves manhandled outlandish megaliths and toiled at other Sisyphean labours. Grim samurai in leather masks and centurions' helmets strutted imperiously among them while, high on an adjacent hill, in an amphitheatre of stone, hooded patriarchs wearing robes of black and scarlet, their womenfolk demure and immaculate in trappings of gold, presided over heroic ceremonials and gargantuan pig feasts. To the thump of monstrous drums and the drone of bamboo buzzers maidens pirouetted atop tall basalt mushrooms, the slap of their feet exciting whirling warriors to vaults of suicidal athleticism. Fresh blood stained stone tables. Severed heads dangled by the hair from verandahs or stared pop-eyed from pikes.

Or so it appeared. It would be like visiting Stonehenge in its Druidical heyday, or mixing with the Hebridean beaker-folk to observe the solstice at Callanish. Perhaps. But of late big black doubts had been bubbling up like the rain clouds over Toba. The first deluge of disappointment had come when I made the mistake of trying to read up on Nias. Marsden, writing in 1780, had obviously never been there. He was mainly appalled at reports of slavery and reckoned that about a thousand Niha a year were bought by Minangkabau and Acehnese slavers. Though highly prized for their skills, they were 'always esteemed dangerous in that capacity' and were prone to suicide 'when disgusted with their situation'. They were racially quite distinct from Sumatra's peoples (fairer, flatter noses, smaller); they lived on pork and yams; and they were divided into fifty small kingdoms which were 'at perpetual variance with one another'. But there was no mention of megaliths, of a heroic society nor of any other prehistoric peculiarities.

Forty years later, in a letter to Marsden, Raffles had been delighted to add further details, not the least of which was that 'the Chiefs of Pulo Nias have ceded the sovereignty of that island to the [East India] Company'. This was news even to the Company which, not for the first time, would unhesitatingly disown Raffles' empire building. The Directors were having enough trouble reconciling the Dutch to his recent occupation of Singapore island. As with Singapore, Raffles had nothing but superlatives for Nias. 'The whole island is a sheet of the richest cultivation that can be imagined' and the people 'active, intelligent, rich and powerful'; nay 'fair, strong, athletic . . . industrious and ingenious'. More incredibly, 'what has most astonished me is the high degree (comparatively) of civilization to which they have attained, without communication from without'. Raffles claimed for himself the 'merit of first visiting and exploring its interior'. He was even considering a book 'to prove that they [the Niha] are the happiest and best people on earth.'

Needless to say, this picture of a productive and idyllic island echoing to the labours of cheery agriculturists and ingenious craftsmen had shattered my hopes. Again there was not a word about the Stone Age, no hint of human sacrifice, no suggestion of gruesome ritual splendours. Perhaps I had imagined it all. Too much Conan Doyle, too many Indiana Joneses. The only consolation lay in the discovery that, contrary to his assertion, Raffles had not actually explored the interior. In fact he had not set buckled foot on the island. All his information came from two agents, the botanist Dr William Jack and a Mr Prince who had spent six weeks in the south of the island in 1820. Their report contained some mention of stone staircases and paved streets, and it credited the Niha with only a reassuringly 'low state of civilization'. But, low or high, this civilization again failed to make any particular impression. It was no stranger than one would expect from any people, thought Jack, who had 'been separated at a very early period from their original stock and exempted by their singular situation from the influence of the various religions that have at different times pervaded the greater islands'.

This implied that at least the Niha must have been spared the devout monotony of Islam. Raffles took it to mean that they were therefore ripe for Christianity and urged the immediate despatch of missionaries. But in 1824 the British abandoned Sumatra and, as elsewhere, it fell to the Dutch to act on his initiative. Their troops arrived in 1825 and from a new fort at Lagundri in the south were soon winning the islanders' lasting hostility in a succession of vicious little campaigns. In the north German and Dutch Reformed missions also made steady progress. Neither found anything in Niha society worthy of publication in accessible form.

The next milestone in Nias studies thus came rather improbably from Milan where in 1890 Elio Modigliani produced his monumental *Un Viaggio a Nias*. Discovering this impressive volume had been almost as exciting as a parachute drop into the heartland of megalithic Nias. On the dust jacket a helmeted warrior with pike-size spear and ornate shield posed in front of massive cylindrical pillars, some vertical, others diagonally braced, which looked as if they might be the stocks in a shipyard. The warrior's helmet was especially fine with a superstructure of long steel spikelets splaying either side of a tall tiered arrangement, evidently made of gold and somewhat reminiscent of a gladiolus with all its blossoms in flower at once. Inside illustrations and even photographs revealed all that one could hope for in the way of primitive artefacts, enigmatic icons and frowning savages with even more outlandish head-dresses. The seven hundred pages of text must surely redress the century of Anglo-Dutch indifference and end history's mysterious conspiracy of silence.

But I can't read Italian and this discovery was almost immediately superceded by that of a reprint of F.M. Schnitger's *Forgotten Kingdoms in Sumatra* which turned out to contain the 1938 description of the island that had originally triggered my imagination. Here at last were the skulls and the megaliths, the leather masks, the amulets and neck rings of solid gold.

Deep in the jungles of South-east Nias lie the mysterious remains of . . . great terraces and altars, on which stand round tables with great monster heads, double rows of pillars crowned with figures of deer and rhinoceros-birds, mushroom-shaped stones on which graceful dancers once bent and swayed . . .

Crowds of heavily armed dancers were pictured stampeding across a hill-top parade ground watched from the verandah by cloaked dignitaries. Another photo showed a dressed slab of stone, about the size of a small car, cradled in timbers lashed with vines and being dragged on rollers by a hundred straining slaves while an impressive figure in a helmet and leather jerkin directed operations from on top of the stone. Schnitger, an Austrian given to flights of fancy that cost him the regard of other ethnographers, had captured the menace and the barbaric splendour as well as the academic interest.

At twilight a strange atmosphere pervades the place. Silent and ghostly the columns arise in the scarlet sunset glow, and animals stare with stony eyes into the western sky, where lies the land of the dead. Over the dusky mountains evening approaches and suddenly it is night, the silent blue night of Nias, night in an isle of dreams, filled with waving ferns and the crests of royal palms. A gentle whispering is heard; in the pale starlight the animals seem to be calling each other in muted tones.

Small wonder that Schnitger had left such an impression. Were social anthropologists in the habit of betraying such warmth for their subject, places like Nias could become popular. And that was the other half of the problem, the other source of my misgivings. Martine and Nathalie had not been the only foreigners on the Sibolga bus and nor, to judge from the night's passing traffic, were they the only ones on the boat.

Encouraging whiffs of Blue Sumatra alerted me to a world of pre-dawn pallor. They competed with those from the toilet and emanated from a kettle thoughtfully placed between the tap and the urinal. You could wash, pee and breakfast without shifting position. I returned to the deck and over a paper cup of sweet black coffee leant on the rail straining to catch the muted dawn chorus from Schnitger's megalithic menagerie. The breeze blew as hot and moist as the night before but a dark slit of land now divided grey sea from grey sky. As befitted the slumbering 'isle of dreams' not a single light was visible.

Several identical baggage items propped on the ship's foredeck looked in the half light as if they might actually be megaliths. Each was about ten feet tall and perfectly proportioned for a standing stone of arresting symmetry. Closer inspection revealed that their pictographs were all sports logos, mostly of surf-riders. Qantas and KLM baggage tags fluttered in the breeze. When we docked at Teluk Dalam a magnificent troupe of bronzed giants with streaming tresses and spectacularly hairy thighs issued from the cabins to hoist these megaliths with ridiculous ease and lash them to backpacks before trooping ashore. There small dark touts immediately swarmed about them, tugging at stray straps to win attention, slipping through the massively striding legs and leaping in the air to achieve eye contact. The invaders paid no heed. They consulted no books and they opened no dialogue. Like monstrous crustaceans obeying some familiar migratory instinct they simply tramped beneath their swaying carapaces to a row of parked motorbikes and bestrode the pillion seats. Lilliputian drivers leapt up in front and, slithering dangerously on the sandy tarmac, their bikes bore away the sea's improbable bounty. With surf boards tweaking the telephone wires and knees brushing the verdure they disappeared precariously down a lane of coconut palms, bandanas and dreadlocks flying in the slipstream.

The French girls and other assorted ethnologists were meanwhile deep in quayside negotiations with the town's three *becak* drivers. Eventually they too would head off to the palm-thatch *losmen* around and beyond Lagundri Bay. There I later found them happily beach-combing and barbecuing. Seduced by crevettes and lobster, they now talked less of tramping the 'dusky mountains' to experience Niah *culture* at first hand.

They were also indifferent to the high rolling right-handers on which distant riders were endlessly driving ashore in a pageant that could have been devised to rub in the Europeans' successful invasion of Nias' isolation. The surf at Lagundri is said to be the best in Indonesia although rumours were now passing among the intent watchers along the beach that in distant Simaleue (or was it Siberut?) a pioneer reconnaissance had stumbled upon 'a big one'. Over more beers opinions were laconically canvassed in accents that ranged from California to Auckland. Portable lamps zapped the mosquitoes and canned food crammed the cabins' shelves. For such single-minded nomads Indonesia appeared to exist as no more than another tiresome passport check and another change of currency. Simaleue, a primitive place even by Niah standards, was just another boat ride. In the waiting hours the surfers chomped biscuits and devoured dog-eared paperbacks while up the beach the ethnologists battled with their lobsters and their dictionaries. Like different species drawn by chance to the same waterhole, the two groups kept their distance, separated by a spit of sand and a wall of mutual incomprehension.

In the knowledge that the Niha had long since turned their backs on the sea, and because one tropical paradise is pretty much like another, I stayed in town. The books had been vague about both the origins of the Niha and the antiquity of their culture. More to the point, I still had no idea what remained of it. I needed a local informant with fair English and motorized transport, neither of which were much in evidence.

Teluk Dalam, six pot-holed streets and a harbour, seemed to have escaped the bureaucratic takeover of its real estate which has transformed most Indonesian towns into official cantonments. No one had heard of the government tourist department, let alone an archaeological department, and the most sought-after accommodation, perhaps the only accommodation, turned out to be a dark corridor above a lock-up for the municipality's two trucks. Here windowless cells of stark simplicity and all-over yellow tiling were screened by louvred glass partitioning which sacrificed both privacy and security for such light and air as might funnel down the corridor. Room rent was collected in a shop up the road; room service consisted of two boys in shorts and tee-shirts who wrenched themselves from a Nintendo to fetch iced beers from the town's only refrigerator. I slept through a steaming wet morning and woke to a steaming wet afternoon.

The rain did the place no favours. It confined the cockerels to barracks, where they crowed incessantly, and brought the ducks quacking into the garbage-filled ponds that were usually pot-holes. Along the quay small brown bodies inside transparent polythene sacks were manhandling bags of cement and 45-gallon drums with the ease of men used to megaliths. Regardless of the rain, the fuel was then siphoned into waiting motor bikes and the cement stashed in a corrugated shed. A domestic economy based on the sack, the gerry-can and the corrugated shed, though an inevitable attribute of far-flung places, somehow detracts from their exoticism. Sump oil stained the coral grit of the sidewalk; the gushing eaves failed to cleanse it. All twenty shops sold the same range of plastic hardware, fresh and fried fish, green mangoes, beef tomatoes, dry goods, umbrellas and cheap cottons. Strip lights lit their dark interiors. Under cover of a power-cut a bucket of surprisingly long-legged crabs made their escape into a puddle.

The main restaurant announced itself with a plate glass frontage and a cabinet displaying cans of Bintang beer, Carnation milk, 7-Up, and pot noodles, all neatly arranged with an eye for colour but little regard for digestive harmony. I ate fish and rice and put the word about that I was in search of a motorized mentor. Next evening, over more fish and rice, a fellow diner was introduced as the local schoolmaster. He wore a sweatshirt and jeans like everyone else, only a slight paunch and an endearingly weary smile suggesting he might be a senior member of the community. Elikasih Wau was his name and he came from Bawomataluo. I wrote them both down. Disentangling the syllables of the second, it suddenly struck me that it tallied with a place mentioned by Schnitger. 'High and inaccessible on a hill', this village had come as a revelation and boasted a chiefly residence that Schnitger rated 'one of the finest bits of architecture ever made by a primitive people'.

'Ah', said Elikasih, 'my uncle's house. You can see anytime, I will show you. Come tomorrow.'

High but no longer inaccessible, Bawomataluo could now be reached on a motorbike provided its cubic capacity was up to the climb. This challenge was grudgingly accepted by a moronic layabout who had been touting for my custom ever since I arrived. He wanted me to call him 'Johnnie' and on the strength of his assets – a pretty wife whom he treated with doltish indifference and, more to my purpose, a big new Yamaha on which he doted – I would happily have obliged. But he also lied, cheated, was universally disliked and had appalling halitosis plus a nasty way with the scatter of hairs on his upper lip. A distinctly Mongoloid cast of features, noticed by several observers as typical of the Niha, recalled Turkestan.

Sharing a saddle with this Genghis Khan I lost all credit in Teluk Dalam as we roared unnecessarily through each of the six streets, scattering livestock and splashing puddle water indiscriminately. The open road, when at last we struck it, meandered pleasantly between paddy fields and beach for a few miles before turning off up a steeply tilting incline. Tangled vegetation, which to anyone unacquainted with Sumatra might pass for jungle, closed in. In fact it was a fine example of mixed equatorial husbandry; every tree and shrub pertained to gumbooted woodsmen who could occasionally be glimpsed belaying the undergrowth with machetes, and every one of them was identifiable as the provider of some valued fruit, root, resin or timber. Raffles' Dr Jack, who had also been based at Teluk Dalam (which he thought would make an excellent site for a fort) had not exaggerated the fertility of the soil or the industry of the locals. As if to emphasise such bounteous convenience, just as the front tyre went flat a hut embowered in hibiscus turned out to be a one-man vulcanising depot. Which tree, I asked, had the vulcaniser tapped for his ball of adhesive? But Genghis fluffed the translation and the man returned with a banana.

The road, as if tiring of this tropical abundance, now burrowed into the hillside in a series of near vertical contortions. We skittered on the dust and dropped to an even lower gear; supercilious lizards swivelled their hooded gaze to watch us pass and a pedestrian with a baby on her back easily kept pace with us. There followed steeply terraced gardens cascading from houses that were still the basic one-room-and-open-verandah of anywhere in rural Indonesia. To the south the distant ocean appeared through wooded hills whose oppressive greenery made one appreciate the sparkle of coral sand and crashing rollers. The chances of man ever having made his mark on such pristine scenery seemed scant indeed.

Then quite suddenly we stopped at the bottom of a broad flight of steps. The steps were certainly of well-cut stone with a stone balustrade at the top. And the road, I now realised, was not the bottom but a mere landing on an infinitely longer staircase that went straight down the hill until lost to sight in the greenery. It needed weeding and some of the flagstones had been dislodged by floods. But it was still impressive and a wildly fanciful extravagance for a people whose houses were largely made of leaves and who kept dry by wearing plastic bags.

To give Genghis the slip, I barged through a throng of village gossips, dashed to the top of the steps and promptly buckled up with a sickening mix of excitement and embarrassment. It was like diving into a bar only to find oneself in a cathedral. Here, after so much riotous vegetation, was a realm of space and order that was almost classical in its formality. Geometry sprang to mind, then astronomy. Elikasih had told me that the real name of the Niha was *ono niha*, 'the children of the people', because they were all descendants of the first people who had come down from the sky at a place called Gomo. Consequently the *ono niha* much preferred the sky to the sea and at Bawomataluo sky both floated above and flooded up from below.

This effect resulted from the hill top being a wide, open and dead level expanse of paving, more parade ground than street. It was flanked by double pavements fronting identical terraces of housing which traversed the hill-top in straight lines; two hundred metres away, the ground met the sky on the other side at the top of another stone staircase. Inaccessible to wheeled vehicles because of the steps, this field of flagstones made a perfect farmyard and playground. Long-snouted pigs scattered squealing from a ruckle of footballers; hens scuffed among the hopscotch players. But with the houses all drawn up to face inwards, it also suggested a forum for more exacting rituals. And, in a street, where cars might have been, megaliths were parked.

The most prominent, because stalled in the middle, was not actually a megalith but a very short section of dry stone wall neatly fashioned to resemble a rather high gymnasium box-horse. I recognised it as such from photos and Elikasih, who emerged smiling graciously from one of the houses, pointed out the springboard, also of stone. He confirmed that, given plenty of notice and a sizeable fee, demonstration jumps could be arranged.

'Mostly for tourist groups and – how you say? – "president visits" is it? For generals, yes?'

Dodging a dog fight and an old hag selling necklaces of teeth, quite possibly her own, he led the way to what was obviously Schnitger's 'finest bit of architecture ever made by primitive man'. The ordinary houses were remarkable enough. All stood three or four feet off the ground on interlaced piers made of smoothly rounded timbers, and all presented to the street the same full width latticed verandah which leant slightly outwards as if intent on the goings-on below. The impression of a poop deck on some basic galleon was heightened by finely carved gunwales which projected below the verandahs like the runners on a sledge. But unlike Batak houses, they made no other concessions to marine architecture and, gable to gable, abutted one another so that each communicated with the next; the ridges of their roofs thus presented a continuous skyline while the verandahs became a long barred gallery. Within, like caged prisoners, family groups could be seen busy whittling icons.

In contrast the *omo sebua*, or 'big house', consisted mainly of a wedge-shaped roof, concave in profile and soaring to a pitch little short of the vertical. It towered above the two adjacent houses, themselves higher than the rest, like a rather menacing fang. All of sixty feet high, the roof finished with a row of ferocious spikes along its ridge pole, leaving the visitor with no doubts as to its owner's status. This was further emphasised by the revelation of its centrality. For opposite, another wide paved street flanked by houses formed the stem of what was now revealed as a T-plan village with the chief's house commanding the junction.

In the angle of the T stood the meeting house, somewhat like an open-sided medieval barn, while opposite, outside the chief's

house, a veritable forest of megaliths lined the pavement like waiting supplicants. Reclining stones, some boat-shaped, some possibly coffins, jostled with sprightly obelisks, crooked menhirs,
dolmens, benches, thrones, tables, grave slabs and what Schnitger
calls *niogaji*, the dancers' mushrooms. Some were distinguished
with low relief carvings of figures, patterns and symbolic objects,
especially lizards that could have been crocodiles. Elikasih said
there were well over two hundred megaliths in this one village but
some had clearly lost their significance and had been appropriated
for other uses. A dozy boar with vicious tusks was tethered to the
stump of a column and several blocks had become saddle-backed
with long use as battering boards for the villagers' laundry. Like all
the other houses, access to the chief's was by way of a ladder hidden among the substructure of supporting piers, some here a
metre thick and as smooth and rounded as marble pillars. We
emerged through the floor into a dark baronial hall of uncertain
height where brown-skinned retainers blended well with a floor
and panelling of smoked timber polished with use. I had never felt
so conspicuously white. The only other feature which stood out of
the gloom was a dado of skulls. It ran right round the apartment
somewhat above head height and was composed of several hundred curiously pointed crania.

'Pigs', said Elikasih, anticipating my question. 'All from one big
feast.' The feast had been part of the consecration ritual for the
house. Slaves too had been slaughtered for the occasion but their
skulls had since been removed. Judging by their excellent state of
preservation the pigs, and so the house, were not that old. Elikasih
confirmed this by pointing to one of the spirited carvings on the
wall which depicted a ship with both rigging and funnel plus some
very European-looking sailors engaged in line-fishing. I half
expected to see surfers riding the choppy waves. Later I noticed
that one of the megaliths outside actually had an inscription and a
date. It was 1990.

'You see, there is a line of big stones through the middle.' From
a high seat in the verandah we were gazing down across the paved
street where there was indeed a central pathway of larger, dressed
flagstones laid with great exactitude. 'Every man had to bring one

up from the bottom of the hill and present it to the chief.' The idea was that each stone thus represented a subject whose number the chief could easily count as he trampled them underfoot. So when was this?

'Long time ago. But not so long time ago. I think maybe two hundred years.' In fact it seems that the village was probably founded in the late 1860s when, according to Modigliani, the village of Orahili at the bottom of the hill was destroyed in a Dutch offensive that persuaded the villagers to move to higher ground. Other villages hereabouts and especially in central Nias are undoubtedly much older; but few boast such a splendid *omo sebua* or such uniform architecture and gracious planning.

Over the next few days I returned again and again to Bawomataluo. The name lost some of its magic as I mastered its pronunciation and I began to notice how even here every house had electricity. Ugly metal poles ran the length of the village and many of the roofs, including that of the *omo sebua*, were now clad in corrugated rather than thatch. The carvings – constipated figures with big heads and privities to match – were all for the tourists; gentle Elikasih himself turned out to be one of the main exporters. The heavy gold jewellery had all gone the way of the human skulls. Only the toddlers went naked. Their parents complained about the lack of television.

Needless to say, no one had the foggiest idea of when or whence, other than the sky, their forbears had come to the island. Schnitger argued strongly for a migration from Nagaland, east of Assam, where a similar culture had survived into the twentieth century. His conclusion that human sacrifice, head-hunting, pig feasts and megalithic erections were all ritual essentials in the 'feasts of merit' which solemnised certain chiefly undertakings – weddings and house-buildings – seems now to be generally accepted. But there is still no consensus about the origins of this enigmatic people. Around 850AD is the earliest for which there is any evidence of Nias and its people but in a place with so much 'prehistoric' material above ground no one has yet dug for signs of earlier occupation. Likewise the language, though Austronesian, is said to be closer to certain Polynesian and Madagascan tongues than it is to, say, Batak, let alone Malay.

Wandering about the village, like the 'children of the people', I too somehow lost interest in historical data. In this place of stone and bone and timber the chipping of chisels and the rasp of saws was more convincing that the most informative of stele. And far from being cause for regret, the village's lack of antiquity became a principal source of wonder, and its concessions to modernity a welcome reassurance. Because the people were not dramatically disadvantaged, nor their lifestyle hideously debased, one was privileged to witness a unique *culture* without being morally challenged by it. As is the way of these things, and not only in Indonesia, a place supposedly remote had turned out to be surprisingly accessible, and a society expected to be unspeakably primitive just agreeably different.

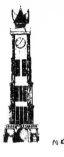

NL

5. Why is West Sumatra?

For administrative purposes Indonesia is divided into 27 provinces. Eight of them are in Sumatra but their arrangement is somewhat confusing. Two hundred years ago Marsden had found the island's breakdown 'perplexing and uncertain' and so it remains. Thus today, the province of North Sumatra (Sumatra Utara), which straddles the island to include Medan, the Batak country and even Nias, does not include the extreme north, which is Aceh. Similarly South Sumatra (Sumatra Selatan) does not include the extreme south, which is Lampung. There is no East Sumatra although the provinces of Riau and Jambi are sometimes referred to as such; and West Sumatra (Sumatra Bharat) turns out to be south and considerably *east* of North Sumatra.

This muddle partly stems from the island's perverse orientation. With its axis skewered by the equator at exactly 45 degrees, geographers have never been able to make up their minds whether it lies more east-west or more north-south. Thus the long Indian Ocean littoral is sometimes called the west coast, sometimes the south coast; likewise the east/north coast. In the 1950s, with a refreshing disregard for the niceties, the Indonesian government weighed into this debate and declared the axis north-south. And because the government also had very good reasons for not wanting to encourage regional loyalties, it opted for a system of provincial nomenclature based on this orientation. Hence North Sumatra, South Sumatra etc. Aceh, of course, objected. Its disputatious *ulama* took strong exception to the prospect of being outnumbered by the pig-eating, bible-bashing Batak brigadiers in North Sumatra and, by fomenting the usual 'troubles', eventually persuaded Jakarta to reconstitute it as 'virtually an Islamic state within the nation' (M.C. Ricklefs).

The precedent thus set of appeasing a regional, linguistic and sectarian entity could have had interesting consequences. Provincial units based on language as in India, or on ethnic groups as in the ex-Soviet Union, may seem logical and may gratify local sentiment; but they also preserve ancient loyalties and promote ancient antagonisms which can only exacerbate the centre-province tensions within a plural super-state. The centre becomes haunted by the spectre of secession and the provinces become paranoid about central regulation.

That the problem has to some extent been avoided in Indonesia is thanks primarily to what happened in Sumatra's most influential province, the one known as West Sumatra. Every Indonesian knows that West Sumatra is just an official euphemism for the land of the Minangkabau. Thoroughly Islamic, proud and progressive, with a unique social system and a distinctive language, the Minang (for short) – or sometimes *Orang Padang* (Padang people) – comprise 90 per cent of West Sumatra's population and thus might have been expected to make common cause with the Acehnese in demanding an autonomous Minang homeland. But they also had, and still have, a unique and decisive stake in Indonesian nationhood. Indeed so handsomely did they contribute to the leadership of the independence struggle, to its intellectual climate and to its social conscience, that it is hard to see how without them the Indonesian republic would ever have come about.

Typically none of this rates a mention in the museum devoted to Minangkabau *adat* in the provincial capital of Bukittinggi. It wouldn't be very responsible for such good Indonesians to trumpet their ethnicity. Here the emphasis is on a remoter past which, nevertheless, provides some clues to the ascendancy of this remarkable people. Most striking are two enormous family trees. One charts the descent of the Minangkabau kings from progenitors who include Asoka, the 4th century BC Buddhist emperor of north India, and 'Iskander Zulkarnain of Macedonia' – i.e. Alexander the Great.

The Minangkabau kings – in the 18th century there were usually three at any one time – were nothing if not illustrious. A king who was Marsden's contemporary, though reduced to an obscure and contested sovereignty, was still hailed as the brother, through a common ancestry, of both the Emperor of China and the Ottoman Sultan. Their imperial seals flanked his own on royal warrants issued from the thatched palace whose 'authority reacheth over the whole universe'. His royal honorifics ran to several more palm-leaf pages and included the viceregency of heaven, the sultanate of the golden river and the lordship of the air and clouds. His Majesty was also possessed of fabulous assets, like gold mines, and some awesome talismans including 'a buffalo whose horns are twelve feet asunder' and 'a blue *champak* flower not to be found in any other country than his (being yellow elsewhere)'.

Though mentioned merely *en passant*, it was the gold mines that lent substance to these pretensions. Mined and panned in the Minangkabau highlands, gold had accounted for Sumatra's ancient celebrity and possibly, as the Sanskrit *suvarna-dwipa*, even for its name. It was also the gold mines which, together with the region's pepper crop, brought first the Portuguese and then the Dutch who in 1663 established a bridgehead at Padang, one of the few sheltered anchorages on the west – or south – coast. They failed, however, to penetrate inland and it thus remained for the British, and in particular Thomas Stamford Raffles, to blaze a trail into the mysterious highlands.

Raffles, already impressed by the pedigree of the Minang kings as described by Marsden, would have been equally intrigued by the Bukittinggi museum's second family tree. This illustrates the supposed descent of the Minangkabau race from a three-pronged stock (Tibeto-Burman, Yunnanese and Indian) which unites to form the Mon-Khmer people who, dispersed to Sumatra, become the Minangkabau and who then beget the Malay people. Today's scholars may find all this as fanciful as the royal pedigree beside it; but in identifying the Minang with the Malays it coincides with Raffles' insistence that in this remote and unstudied people he had found the origins of what he liked to call 'the Malay nation'.

Marsden had already surmised some link between the highland Minang and the coastal Malays. The Minang language was much like Malay; both peoples were Islamic; and many Malay rulers traced their ancestry to Minang antecedents. He also noted that many of Sumatra's other peoples, including the Batak and the Acehnese, acknowledged a shadowy and remote Minang authority. Raffles collated all this information with what he knew of the Malays from several years residence in Penang and began to discern substance in 'the authority which reacheth over the whole universe'. More specifically he found in the Minang country stones inscribed with Indic characters from which he inferred an ancient association with the Hindu-Buddhist civilisations of Srivijaya and Melayu. Perhaps recalling 'the sultanate of the golden river', he then proposed that, in the course of exporting their gold down rivers like the Indragiri and Siak which drain west from the highlands to the north/east coast, it must have been the Minang who first settled the Srivijayan heartland around Palembang. If gold-rich Minang rulers had been Srivijaya's patrons in its 7th century Buddhist heyday, no wonder they claimed so many imperial connections. 'Here, then,' declared Raffles, 'for the first time, was I able to trace the source of that power, the origin of that nation [the Malay] so extensively scattered over the Eastern Archipelago.'

Emerging from the museum not a little envious of the conviction with which Raffles could pontificate on subjects now deemed far too ill-documented for historical purposes, I found myself in the zoo. As a founder of London's Royal Zoological Society and no mean menagerie-keeper himself, Raffles would have approved the juxtaposition. The museum stands on top of a hill (*bukittinggi*, high hill) whose terraced slopes, lined with the cages of the zoological park, completely surround it. From among the Sunday afternoon promenaders, mostly family groups in gay attire, there rose the piercing screams of a sex-starved macaque. Small children in crisp cottons excited its fancies by mimicking the screams, then trooped off to the playground to imitate its antics.

I too approved the juxtaposition. Of the commodities eagerly sought by any visitor to Indonesia, information and anonymity are the scarcest. Yet here were both. The museum had proved enlightening, if only because it was one of very few to have a system of labelling. And the zoo offered that reassurance which comes with rejoining the audience after having been part of the show. Restored to the ranks of *Homo sapiens*, I stalked through the crowd jammed between the cages like the invisible man. As objects of curiosity, victims of occasional abuse, recipients of edible titbits and the inspiration for endless jokes, animals beat foreigners hands down. I paused to empathize with a dozy curassow and muttered my gratitude to a grey-saddled tapir. Here too the exhibits were labelled, only a family of ginger orang-utans requiring no identification. For the island's other speciality, the small rare Sumatran rhino, there was a label and a cage but no inmate. Perhaps he had made a break for it, back into the misty mountains which ringed the horizon and blended with the clouds.

No doubt there are worse places of detention in Sumatra. On the other side of town the vertiginous cliffs of a moderately grand canyon are honeycombed with tunnels dug by Indonesian prisoners during the Japanese occupation. Their sufferings are less well documented than those of allied prisoners in the notorious camps of Palembang and Muntok. But no doubt both groups would willingly have swapped hard labour, malnutrition and beri-beri for the comparative ease of Bukittinggi zoo; so perhaps would some of the thousands of political prisoners currently languishing in Indonesian gaols.

'Hello Meester, Hello Meester.' Two small girls in pink taffeta, having exhausted the aviary, sidled up to squeeze the last drop of novelty from the afternoon. One shouldn't be ungrateful. At least in Indonesia you can still enjoy the company of other people's children without inviting accusations of paedophilia.

'How are you? How are you?'

'I'm fine, how . . . ' I stopped and, feeling suddenly rather weak, slumped on the grass. They hadn't asked 'How are you?' at all. What they had actually said, in unison, twice and quite distinctly, was 'Why are you? Why are you?'

One was retying a red ribbon in a pigtail, the other knelt on the grass and eyed me expectantly. Perhaps they had just got their interrogative pronouns muddled. But the innocence of the enquiry only made it worse. It was like being stung by a butterfly. Agonisingly self-aware at the best of times, the solitary traveller is prone to enough introspection without having to grapple with gratuitous metaphysical barbs. And this being Minangkabau country, there was the distinct possibility that it was not as innocent as it appeared. Some mischievous primary teacher could be instilling into his pupils a subtly adjusted greeting designed precisely to incapacitate intruders.

That evening, like most in Bukittinggi, I dined alone in one of the Roda Group's restaurants. *Nasi Padang*, their and West Sumara's spicy speciality, is the only regional cuisine which is giving American fast food outlets a run for their money. Floor and walls shone with ceramic dazzle and the tables were so clean that the dozen or so dishes of pick-and-mix curries which constitute Padang food could have been safely consumed without plates. The lighting seemed too bright even for mosquitoes; but in this crystalline oasis of gleaming modernity it was the service that deserved most stars. Of the six waiters in matching batik shirts and a variety of spectacles, all had degrees, three had PhDs and, except for one rather dreamy Javanese, all were Minang. The food was accompanied by a short analysis of the Sumatran economy; over coffee they drew up chairs to canvass my opinion about a difficult passage in *Jane Eyre*. Sumatran diner became Senior Common Room.

Inviting academic sympathy over the afternoon's existential poser was a bad mistake. They hooted with glee and thereafter invariably hailed me, and no doubt countless other foreigners, with shouts of 'Mister, mister, why are you, mister?' But on the Minang-Malay relationship the panel was divided. One, presumably a historian, thought Raffles was probably right. But even if he wasn't, his argument was plausible in its day and extremely convenient. For what brought Raffles into the hills was not antiquarian curiosity, geographical discovery, or even gold-fever; it was *realpolitik*.

'He wanted the Minang to rule Sumatra again.' As with Nias,

he also wanted, using Minang sovereignty, to establish in Sumatra a new field of endeavour for the East India Company and for Thomas Stamford Raffles. The famous visit was made in 1818 when both he and the Company had just been deprived of Java. It and the other Dutch possessions in the East had been occupied only to deny them to Napoleon. After Waterloo, the British were always going to return them to the Dutch, and nothing Raffles did or wrote dissuaded them. The transfer duly took place in 1817. 'Exiled' (his word) to the Sumatran wilderness, Raffles set up home in Bengkulu, 200 miles down the coast from Padang, to begin again his self-imposed task of creating an empire.

Time was short. The Dutch, brandishing exclusive treaties with some of the local rulers, were expected back any day. With the idea of forestalling them, he sailed for Padang on the Minang coast in July 1818. Thence with a baggage train of 200 coolies and an escort of 50 sepoys, the explorer, his wife and their geologist (for tracing gold-bearing strata) rode into the mountains or were carried aloft in litters. They followed river beds through the forest, slept in huts and bathed little. Pregnant as usual and eternally damp beneath full skirts and riding coat, Lady Raffles occasioned both anxiety and comment. The natives, she reported, 'seemed to be struck with amazement and the question was not *who* is that? but *what* is that?' Cleverly misused interrogatives were obviously an old Minang speciality.

Their route lay south of the busy main road that now links Padang with Bukittinggi and the Minang heartland. Raffles maximised its difficulties, exaggerated the isolation of the Minang country, and was quite wrong to claim that no European had ever visited it. (Thomas Dias, a Portuguese in Dutch employ, had written a detailed account of a much more formidable journey into the West Sumatran interior as long ago as 1684.) But he was only doing what all explorers did and, for political reasons, it was important to emphasize that prior to his visit the country was both unknown and unencumbered. The Minang chiefs confirmed this. Somewhat predictably they also wanted nothing to do with Dutchmen and pleaded for British protection. Raffles obliged by signing treaties and 'forming an establishment in two parts of the interior.' 'The measures I have taken will no doubt be considered strong' (they were; he was ordered to countermand them immediately) but a residual regard for Minang authority was still acknowledged throughout Sumatra and, revived with British encouragement, he believed that the country could again become the nucleus of a trading confederacy that would reunite the Minang and the Malay 'nation'.

To further his cause he also portrayed the country as a rich prize in itself and, for once, he did not exaggerate. Suddenly, instead of mountains and forests, 'the whole country . . . as far as the eye could distinctly trace, was one continued scene of cultivation, interspersed with innumerable towns and villages, shaded by the cocoa-nut and other fruit-trees. I may safely say this view equalled anything I ever saw in Java.' From Raffles no praise could be higher. 'The scenery is more majestic and grand, population equally dense, cultivation equally rich.' Irrigated rice terraces filled the open valleys and were stacked up the hillsides as in Java; but here they also had waterwheels for raising the flow and milling the grain. Some of these contraptions are still working today and along the roadside, where Raffles spied coffee as well as coconut, his 'fruit-trees' reveal a tropical diversity of durian, mango, banana, papaya and mangosteen interspersed with tapioca (cassava). Pepper vines cascade from trees which on closer inspection turn out to be budded with cloves or tipped with the pink new growth of cinnamon. They must be the most exotic hedgerows anywhere. Between them, switchback lanes traverse the choppy contours, plunging into dank shade to squeeze past a waterfall and then soaring to a sunswept pass as they edge round the nursery slopes of smouldering Merapi. All the lakes are craters, all the mountains volcanoes; the cloud haze that blurs their outlines could be smoke; the dust that enriches the fields is certainly volcanic.

For someone who knew of the Batak and Niha only by reputation, the houses too were a revelation. Many were 60ft long, exquisitely carved and painted, and invariably flanked by one or more lofty *lombongs* (rice barns). 'The ridge-poles of the houses, lombongs et cetera have a peculiar appearance, in being extremely concave, the ends or points of the crescent being very sharp.' In this they resemble Batak houses but where the Batak gable sails away extravagantly into space the Minang gable follows its tight crescent into a somewhat prim and startled peak. *Kerbau* being Malay and Minang for water buffalo, it is said that from this beast the people derive their name and the houses their profile. But Minang buffalo, even with horns twelve feet asunder, would need the upswept curve of a Highland cow to qualify. *Pinang kabhu*, 'an archaic expression meaning original home', seems a more probable derivation for the Minangkabau name.

'In the larger houses they [the roofs] give the appearance of two roofs, one crescent being, as it were, within the other.' The effect is similar to that of the Sydney Opera House but with concave peaks instead of the convex hoods. With several of these additions, each sheltering an extension to the groundplan built within the old gable, the roofline becomes prickly with pinnacles. Such a house, open within but with its floor pierced by masts braced to take the strain of the saddle-back roof, is the Bukittinggi museum. Other examples still dot the countryside, the finest being the palace near Pagarruyung, the ancient capital and Raffles' ultimate destination. Here, no doubt, he would be received in savage splendour and hence he would pen to Marsden a gloating account of royal favours conferred at the *fons et origo* of Malay nationhood.

Regrettably, though, in 1818 there was neither palace nor king. The present structure was built – perhaps 'rigged' better describes the construction process – only in the early 1980s. Raffles had arrived too late. A *Tuan Gadis*, or 'Virgin Queen', bravely deputised, but her court had dispersed and her capital was fast succumbing to agricultural encroachment. 'A few peasants now cultivated those spots which had formerly been the pleasure-grounds of the rich. Where the palace of the Sultan had stood, I observed a man planting cucumbers, and sugar-cane occupied the place of the seraglio.' Though further evidence of crop diversity, it was no compensation for the disappointment. 'Three times had the city been committed to the flames by a remorseless fanatic; twice had it again risen to something like splendour; from the last shock it had not yet recovered.' Nor would it. For West Sumatra was in the throes of a revolution that would prejudice its appeal to colonialists and transform it into a hotbed of what Raffles called fanaticism and what Indonesians recognize as authentic nationalism.

Twelve hours out of Sibolga on the long haul from the Nias ferry to Bukittinggi, the inevitable 'night bus' had pulled up before a badly lit hangar in the middle of nowhere. It was three in the morning, time for another meal stop. I reckoned we were nearly there and would now arrive about 4.30am, a bad hour for finding a bed. So why had we stopped?

'All buses stop.'

'Why? Where is this place?'

'This place Bonjol. It is Ecuador, no?'

In the clammy dark, abuzz with insects and the pumping of frogs, it could well have been Ecuador; it could well have been anywhere. But Bonjol, that was a name I had noted. It was near enough the halfway point on the Trans-Sumatra Highway and it was where one changed hemispheres. In the gents, a murky tin shack awash with soap and slime, the *mandi* (a square bath from which you bale water) was big enough for several Neptunes. When fellow passengers stripped off, I snuck off into the night. Perhaps they were just feeling in need of a wash but, if not, I must have looked like a likely candidate for first crossing frolics.

The equator – or 'ecuador' – is duly marked with a concrete pillar which says EQUATOR! On the other side of the road a blue globe, also concrete, is balanced on the pinnacle of another pillar, like a beach ball on the snout of a sea-lion. There isn't really a lot to say about the equator and this little ensemble seemed more than adequate. My own interest was purely scientific in that Bukittinggi being so nearly on the meridian, I would there indulge in a room with a conventional bath. The question – which way would the bath water revolve as it went down the plug-hole? – was the only equatorial mystery I could think of. Answer: the same way as in Aceh ($6°N$), my last bath, and the same way as in Jakarta ($6°S$), my next. The equator was a non-event.

Of more interest is Bonjol's other claim to fame as the birth-place and power base of a man known as Tuanku Imam [of] Bonjol. Like Teuku Umar of Aceh (the Tuanku/Teuku is an honorific reserved for religious leaders), his name is revered throughout Indonesia. Every city has a Jalan (street) Imam Bonjol and, equator or not, no self-respecting nationalist would want to pass through Bonjol without paying his respects.

From deserted Pagarruyung Raffles had turned back to the mountains and the coast. He never reached Bonjol nor even Agam, the Minangkabau district now centred on Bukittinggi. But Imam Bonjol was his exact contemporary and, as the 'remorseless fanatic', it was the Imam with his bearded cohorts who had just overthrown the royal family and laid waste their capital. Raffles called these miscreants 'Padri or Orang Putis' and assumed that the name stemmed from their dressing in white (*putih*) robes and turbans. To the Dutch 'padri' implied a suitably clerical fanaticism (Portuguese missionaries were *padres*) so they retained it. But a commoner spelling is *paderi* which is thought to derive from Pedir, a port in Aceh whence the Imam and two colleagues had returned to Sumatra in 1804 after performing the *haj* (pilgrimage to Mecca).

By chance their visit to Arabia had coincided with the occupation of the holy city by scimitar-wielding followers of Muhammad ibn Abd al-Wahab. Puritannical reformers who had already converted Riyadh into a forbidden city of white-hot Islamic orthodoxy, the Wahabis made a deep impression on the men from Minangkabau. Now dressed like the Riyadh zealots, the Imam and his friends regained their homeland in the Bukit Barisan determined to rid it, if necessary by force, of *adat* practices unsanctioned by the Qur'ān. These included gambling on cockfights, chewing *sirih* (betel), smoking and, terrible to tell, occasionally quaffing palm wine.

Such an ambitious programme met with resistance. Though nominally Muslim since the 16th century, the Minang were very attached to their particular brand of *adat* and would remain so. To this day they see no contradiction in, say, chewing the blood-red *sirih* while attending a circumcision party. (When, as is customary, one is taken to inspect the surgeon's handiwork, *sirih* stains make it look as if the boy has lost tongue as well as foreskin). In particular the king of the universe at Pagurruyung would have nothing to do with the reformers. But Pagurruyung's wealth depended on its gold mines and these were now nearly exhausted while to the north, in districts like Agam, new wealth was being created from new export crops. Here the Imams found willing followers whose zeal for the redemption of their fellow countrymen knew no bounds. Most of the Pagurruyung royalty were murdered in 1815 and by 1818, the year of Raffles' visit, the Paderi had carried their crusade to the coast and north even to some of the Batak clans.

A year later, with the restless Raffles now busy on a new imperial blueprint in which the place of West Sumatra was to be taken by an island called Singapore, the Dutch at last returned to Padang. Their help was quickly sought by remnants of the royal family and other upholders of the traditional mix of Islam and *adat*. In return for a treaty ceding to Holland the Minangkabau country, the Dutch took on the Paderi. The ensuing war lasted seventeen years (1821-38). It involved fewer troops than would the Aceh war but was equally vicious. Operations were facilitated by the construction of fortresses near Pagurruyung and in Agam. The latter, Fort de Kock, is still recognizable from some ramparts, an old cannon and an extensive view; a town grew up around it and was eventually renamed Bukittinggi in deference to nationalist sentiment.

Hostilities ended with the fall of Bonjol and the capture of its wily Imam. But the Imam lived on in exile to a remarkable 92 while in the hills of his homeland the Paderi blend of Islamic orthodoxy with colonial defiance became a Minang characteristic. As long ago as Marsden's day the Minang country had been regarded as 'the seat of religious authority in this part of the East' and second only to Mecca as a place of pilgrimage and Islamic scholarship. Now Qur'ānic schools raised literacy levels above those of anywhere in Indonesia and served as a conduit for new influences from the outside world, both Sufic and Modernist. In the 1920s the latter spawned the Muhammadiya reform movement which, concentrating on national rejuvenation through schooling and social welfare, was eagerly espoused by the Minang and soon became the largest mass organisation in the archipelago. At about the same time Malay, as *bahasa Indonesia*, was adopted as the nationalist *lingua franca*. With a first language so similar to Malay, Minang intellectuals were ideally placed to enter the nationalist debate and to formulate anti-colonial ideologies. But, critically, the authority conferred by their Islamic orthodoxy and their history of colonial resistance was further enhanced by aspects of Minang *adat* which, once in conflict with Islam, now tempered it and made Minang leadership of the Nationalist struggle acceptable throughout the archipelago.

If Parapat had been a disappointment, Bukittinggi soon restored my affection for hill stations, surely one of colonialism's better ideas. Though nudging the equator, its 900m elevation means a dramatic reduction in humidity and, though never cool, a more interesting variation in temperature. It helps, too, that it is built on *bukit bukit tinggi* 'high hills' (the duplication makes *bukit* plural). With its gradients shunned by the most noxious traffic, the city centre becomes the perfect place for *jalan jalan*, 'wandering about' (duplication is also used to imply lack of purpose). In fact it may be the only Indonesian city not built on the flat and not lethal to pedestrians. Horse-drawn phaetons, whose bells jingling among the conifers recall Kipling's Simla, ply roads which contour cheerfully round the hills, occasionally slithering down a terrace or abruptly terminating at the foot of a flight of steps. Big open skies and vistas of rolling verdure intrude at every intersection.

Here evening brings long shadows, none longer than that of the *Jam Gadang*, the big clock, whose chimes issue from the mini Minang house that crowns its tower in the centre of the main square. The short walk hence to the Roda restaurant became familiar; yet 'looking-looking', as English-speaking Indonesians say in a nice transference of idiom, it still held surprises. One evening I noticed that it passed no fewer than three *Gadih Ranti*, or 'Ladies' Banks'. Veils are not uncommon in Bukittinggi and, as in other Islamic countries, segregated banking facilities are deemed essential to eradicate the notorious hanky-panky of the safe-deposit queue. But three, all handsome new buildings, did seemed excessive; so I invited comment from the Roda round table.

They were unanimous. It was because the women had the money and because the women owned the property. Minangkabau society was still matrilineal. Surely everyone knew that.

Oddly, for very little escaped his attention, Raffles did not. He noticed the veils but he seems to have remained in complete ignorance of the one outstanding peculiarity of Minang society. For here, and nowhere else in Indonesia, property titles pass through the female line, descent is traced from mother to daughter, and society is divided into matrilineal clan groups. With a population of about four million, West Sumatra thus has the largest matrilineal society in the world.

'We are first feminist country,' said one of the PhDs. But what, I wondered, about Islam? Qur'ānic orthodoxy doesn't usually elevate the status of women above that of their menfolk. Indeed not; and many of the Paderi leaders had tried to stamp out this anomalous aspect of Minang *adat*. But they had failed. Now, with both Islamic and statutory law at variance with *adat*, and in the face of media propaganda supporting a global convention in favour of male primogeniture, the system was again under threat. But it had moulded Minang society and still did.

Since property belongs to the mother and will pass to the eldest daughter, men play a marginal role in family affairs. About the village they are, or were, somewhat redundant and were therefore free to take up religious duties, teaching or, more typically, trading. The consequent exodus of menfolk from the highlands, known as *merantau* or 'lowlandization' (*rantau* = lowlands), is deeply engrained in Minang culture and should have interested Raffles. For herein lay a ready explanation for the Minang diaspora not only to the Sumatran coastal towns but to the Malay peninsula, Java and as far away as Timor and the Moluccas.

Today it is said that there are more Minang in Jakarta than there are in Padang and Bukittinggi combined. A brief acquaintance with the capital's chattering classes had convinced me that all these Minang must be either newspapermen or academics; but apparently they are still equally prominent in trade, industry, and shipping. Also in catering and hence the position of *nasi Padang* as something like a national cuisine. Many Minang return home to the highlands for holidays or retirement; most remit part of their earnings to their distant families to be banked, no doubt, in one of Bukittinggi's *Gadih Ranti*.

Determinedly outward-looking, then, with pan-Indonesian interests, as well as being highly educated, admirably Islamic and traditionally anti-Dutch, the Minang, both male and female, possessed a set of nationalist credentials second to none. Of the quadrumvirate usually credited with engineering Indonesian independence – Sukarno, Mohammed Hatta, Sutan Sjahrir and Amir Sjarifuddin – the last three were all Minang. The national emblem, an eagle-like garuda (from Hindu mythology by way of Javanese tradition), and the national coat of arms were the work of another Minang nationalist and poet, Mohammed Yamin, while his fellow countryman and associate, the maverick Tan Malaka, became the leader of Indonesia's first communist party. But it was Hatta, a small bespectacled lawyer of formidable skills, who proved the ideal foil for the explosive Sukarno. As the only other signatory to the unilateral Proclamation of Independence which marked the birth of Indonesian nationhood in August 1945, he is revered as the co-founder of the Republic.

During the five tumultuous years that followed, Indonesia's case was presented to the world by its venerable foreign Minister, Haji Agus Salim, also Minang. The Republican government, then holed up in the Central Javan city of Jogjakarta, 'can almost with as much justice be called a Minangkabau government,' declared Dutch intelligence. Bukittinggi, not reclaimed by the Dutch until late 1948, served as a stop-over on the air-bridge between Bangkok and Jogja by which arms reached the beleaguered Republicans and, when Jogja was eventually overrun, it served briefly as the capital for the government-in-exile.

The Dutch responded with 'divide and rule' policies, disguised as federalism, whereby the Minang were promised autonomy. Elsewhere in the archipelago such concessions to regional and ethnic sentiment would gain support and, had they succeeded in West Sumatra, must surely have crippled the national consensus. Yet even Dutch advocacy of *adat* against Islamic intolerance failed to shatter Minang allegiance to the national ideal. Appropriately it was the tireless Hatta who in 1949 at last won Dutch recognition of the new state at a Round Table conference in The Hague.

6. Raffles country

A final test of Minangkabau loyalty to the Java-based Indone-sian Republic came thirteen years after independence when the young nation was wracked by what a foreign correspondent dismissed as 'the politest, most ambiguous civil war in modern history' (James Mossman). Indonesians, for whom being both polite and ambiguous is something of a national imperative, know this episode by a date, 1958, and a set of initials, PRRI. Initials and acronyms are much used for matters political. As well as saving newsprint, they spare the reader from having to confront whatever they stand for and, since every letter has a value, they reduce official jargon to the quantifiable units required for divina-tion and numerology. Thus PRRI, which actually stands for *Pemerintah Revolusioner Republik Indonesia* or The Revolutionary Government of the Republic of Indonesia, becomes a sort of alge-bra open to all sorts of sorcerous interpretations. Only when some-one, usually a foreigner, with a dismal regard for good taste and no appreciation of mystical ambiguities, actually calls it a revolution and probes its significance does the subject become taboo.

As if all this were not sufficiently discouraging, the political cir-cumstances which prompted PRRI typify that impenetrable com-plexity which so diminishes Indonesia's news value. Grossly over-simplified, what had happened since international recogni-tion of Indonesian independence in late 1949 was that universal suffrage and a multi-party system had merely highlighted regional, sectarian and ideological divisions.

Elections in 1955 turned disquiet into alarm when returns indicated a clear polarity between Java on the one hand and the outer islands on the other. In Java pro-Sukarno nationalist and socialist parties predominated; further afield it was the Islamic and Christian parties who made gains; the only party that appeared to be advancing on all fronts was the PKI, the Communist Party of Indonesia.

The PKI had two natural enemies, the Islamic parties and the army. But the former were hopelessly divided between those in government who accepted the secular constitution and those out of government who still hoped to Islamize it. More effectual opposition therefore had to come from the army; but here too division soon appeared. Formed from local militias originally raised during the Second World War by the Japanese, the army had always had a strongly regional character and a propensity for exploiting local business opportunities. With these franchises now being exposed by Communist activists, regional commanders in Sumatra and Sulawesi took the law into their own hands and began suppressing the PKI. Thus in Medan Colonel Simbolon, the Christian Batak commander of North Sumatra who had a profitable sideline in rubber smuggling, simply abrogated the civil government.

In 1956 Mohammed Hatta, the brains behind Sukarno and the one man who commanded respect from all camps, resigned as Vice President. A year later, with the situation deteriorating fast, Sukarno virtually suspended the constitution when he introduced a form of personal rule under the euphemism of 'Guided Democracy'. Looking more Javanized than ever, the central government stepped up its radical rhetoric and began expelling Dutch nationals. Conservative-minded politicians felt threatened and began to slip away from Jakarta. In January 1958 leaders of the largest Islamic party, including two ex-premiers, met some of Sumatra's disaffected commanders at Padang and issued a joint ultimatum demanding that Hatta be restored, that Sukarno revert to his role as figure-head and that new elections be held. Jakarta responded by labelling the Padang protest a rebellion and in February the 'rebels' hit back by setting up their Revolutionary Government (the PRRI) with headquarters in Bukittinggi.

The republic now had two governments. Significantly the PRRI, though committed to greater autonomy for the provinces, said nothing of secession and made little attempt to foster Minangkabau separatism. Though based in West Sumatra, its leaders included Batak like Simbolon and even disaffected Javanese socialists. By undertaking to protect foreign investments, especially in Sumatra's oilfields, it wooed international support. And to enhance its pan-Indonesian credentials, it forged links with another army revolt (*Permesta*, Eternal Struggle) based in distant Manado (North Sulawesi). There the rebels actually enjoyed some American backing, although the little good it did them was outweighed by the propaganda coup afforded to Jakarta when a US pilot was shot down on a bombing raid over Ambon.

In Sumatra promises of arms and aid from the US and Malaysia came to even less. The only bombing here was that of Padang and Bukittinggi by the Indonesian airforce as, with remarkable speed, an invasion force was organised from Jakarta. The rebels appealed to Hatta. He sympathized and, by urging compromise, incurred Sukarno's further displeasure; but he declined to head the PRRI. Meanwhile under the command of Colonel Ahmad Yani, of whom more would be heard, the task force effected a landing at Padang. Resistance, at first brisk, quickly crumbled. Yani's troops swept up into the highlands and the PRRI, unsupported by the civilian population, faded into the hills and jungles there to continue the struggle as guerillas.

A reconciliation of sorts was signed in the auspicious setting of Bonjol but not until 1961 did the ringleaders surrender. They were treated with leniency. Meanwhile, a few PRRI guerrillas fought on in the Sumatran forest. They were still there in the 1970s, occasionally waylaying officials and raiding settlements and, so far as anyone knew, they were still there in the 1990s. It was the only explanation on offer when, in the dead of night about a hundred miles out of Bukittinggi, a small explosion and a shower of glass halted my Bengkulu-bound bus in the middle of nowhere.

For the long haul through central Sumatra a train would have been a better idea. Several squiggles of track feature on the map and with envious gaze I had actually followed a neat layout of level-crossings, sidings, signal boxes and stations alongside Lake Singarak near Bukittinggi. The line, said to be used for hauling coal down to the coast, snaked back and forth across the road and the stations were gay with hibiscus and bougainvillea. But I never actually saw a train. If there were any, they must be patient trains; buffalo and goats would first need to be untethered from the rails, washing lines removed from the signals, and whole villages removed from the tracks. Like other railways in Sumatra, this one seemed not to go anywhere and soon disappeared into a gloomy gorge. Railways would have to wait for Java. It was back to the bus station.

So much time is necessarily spent on this unromantic form of travel that any journey through Sumatra is liable to degenerate into a series of bus incidents. Ten years ago, before the completion of the Trans-Sumatra Highway, there was some justification. In the rainy season – here a relative term denoting the period from November till at least April, sometimes October – whole busloads went missing. Rafts in the process of ferrying them across rivers might be swept away in a spate; landslides sometimes claimed both the road and its traffic; and potholes of legendary dimensions could swallow a forty-seater. You allowed a month for the 1,500km from Aceh to the Java ferry and rarely made it.

Now a stage that could take a week takes barely a day. Rivers are bridged and the road surface is mostly tarmac. Accidents, of course, are more frequent, but no more so than might be expected from any high speed chase along a thin ribbon of asphalt through impenetrable rain-forest and across notoriously unstable mountainsides. Complaining about a driver who is merely trying to cut the journey time in the interests of all concerned is churlish; so is criticizing the rugged suspension and minimal upholstery when quite half the passengers may be without seats at all.

Some buses, like the air-conditioned Aceh-Medan *bis malam*, compare favourably with anything operated by Greyhound. Everyone gets a blanket, a pink satin pillow with white lace edging, and a cardboard box containing a piece of cake, a banana and a bottle of water. Between the lavatory at the back and the film show up front, frequent loudspeakers ensure lively listening even for the hard of hearing.

Sadly the service operated out of Bukittinggi by a company called Bengkulu Indah provided none of these amenities except the music. The bus, not a new one, had recently been painted in the company's unusual livery of matt black with highlights in Prussian blue. The effect, in keeping with the bodywork and in anticipation of the ride ahead, was of a bad bruise. We took to the road at midday, two hours behind schedule. But arrival in Bengkulu was still confidently predicted for 5am next day. This remained attainable until the second puncture. By then it was dusk and sensitive Sumatran stomachs were at last adjusting to the motion of the bus.

Through two meal-stops and several fruit-calls the binge-vomit syndrome usually associated with *bulimia nervosa* had found classic expression. Hens lined the roadside ready for the *plastiques* full of undigested rice and vegetables that rained on the verge barely five miles from the last *warung*; five miles later palm fruit and banana crisps were being taken on board to relieve the pangs. *Plastiques* being now in short supply, the fruit was returned, still recognizable, to the bags in which it had come and then jettisoned like the rice.

The second puncture slowed progress because the first had accounted for the only spare wheel. By now we had left the hills and were in the midst of forest so rampant that in places the canopy had already closed over the road in an arch of Gothic tracery and was now lowering chains of foliage to ensnare high-sided vehicles. Lesser growth ventured from the hard shoulder, preceded by tendrils of creeper which explored the bitumen. I watched as a monkey, all prehensile tail, went soberly about its dinner at the extremity of a branch; a fat vermilion moon lay back, full-bellied, on the tree tops.

Elsewhere, weird rock formations – white stalagmites against the green of the jungle or colossal curvilinear cones of thrusting masonry – had recalled Angkor and provided a reminder of Sumatra's lost Indic cities. But here nothing challenged the soft heave of nature. Behind the curtains of vegetation the darkness gently chattered; giant leaves inexplicably flapped or rasped as if activated by the flickers of the distant lightning; as the twilight faded and the air softened for rain, the forest drew breath before beginning again its nightly foray into the road space.

Ill at ease, passengers milled about as the crew jacked up the bus. Luckily the back axle had double wheels, one of which was removed to replace the punctured front wheel. That meant we were a six-wheeler running on five which evidently affected the steering. Top speed was down to 40mph and the ride was getting rougher. It was also raining.

A third puncture meant depriving the other side of the back axle. I thought that, by evening things up, it might restore the driver's control. In fact, it merely induced that side-to-side swing to which caravans are prone. Swaying perilously we now crawled forward at little more than a trot. The rain drummed on the roof. The fourth puncture, to which there could be no answer, seemed only a matter of time.

Sure enough, shortly after midnight a sharp explosion announced the inevitable. In the darkness I vaguely registered that it was a big bang even for a blow-out. Then a child started to cry – it was more a whimper than a howl – as rain plus glass gusted amongst us.

A stone, I thought. But there had been no other traffic for hours and the window that had shattered was not the windscreen but one of the large side panels. Much of it had landed in the lap of a veiled mother who had been surreptitiously suckling her baby. From mother and child the husband now quietly and meticulously began removing each splinter of glass as if he were picking out lice. The lights were on, the bus halted. When the driver scrunched down the aisle to assess the damage, I asked who would stone a bus.

'Stone? No, bullet. PRRI.' And he made as if taking aim with a rifle. At that speed we must have been an easy target. Small wonder he liked to keep the foot down.

As part of being so exceedingly polite and ambiguous, Indonesians cultivate what often seems like an indifferent sang-froid.

Mere gestures of impatience, like hands on hips and uplifted eyes, let alone exhibitions of temper, betray evil breeding and a dismal lack of social skills. The voice is rarely raised; aggression must be contained, dismay subdued. Foreigners habitually mistake this for the innate passivity which made Indonesia 'a nation of coolies'. They forget that this was also the nation which gave to the English language a word, *amok*, synonymous with uncontrollable rage. Feelings like resentment and anger, though habitually repressed, are not forgotten.

As if it were an everyday chore of travel, like topping up the radiator, the driver ordered his assistant to the roof rack for a sheet of polythene to replace the window. Passengers dusted glass from their hair, the husband went on picking splinters from his wife and their baby went back to sleep. Not a word was said in anger. Anywhere else the panic and pandemonium of an ambush would have stampeded the passengers and doubled the injuries. Here it brought only a slight urgency to the repair and a palpable sense of relief when the bus resumed its crawl.

'Perhaps we will be late,' said the man beside me. He smiled as he wiped a cut on his scrawny neck and picked glass from his *peci*. He came from Java; without his hat, he reminded me of a turtle.

The night wore on. At Lubuklinggau a three-hour halt was needed to replace the missing wheels and to file a report on the ambush. It was 5am by the time we left the Trans-Sumatra Highway for a spur road through the Bukit Barisan. Dawn found us high in the hills, exploring steep declivities on an execrable road that repeatedly tossed my Javanese neighbour into my lap. Each time he smiled more broadly.

By now a strong sense of shared experience bonded us Bengkulu Indah passengers together. I had names for many and obligations to most for minor kindnesses and information. In return they knew my age, nationality, preference in cigarettes, family members, itinerary, professional status, probable length of stay in Indonesia and earnings for the last tax year. To be reduced to such statistical data does one no harm. We live too much in our own estimation. As the man who liked oranges, had four children, spoke painful *bahasa Indonesia*, shared his biscuits, and came from somewhere called Scotlandia where it snows, I briefly enjoyed that cherished delusion of being accepted into local society.

Poised for the final descent into Bengkulu, we stopped for the last meal at a place called Curup. 'Wisma Rafflesia' said a sign on a clap-board frontage. It was appropriate, for thirty miles south-west, on the first of his forays from Bengkulu, the restless Thomas Stamford Raffles had made the incidental discovery for which in Indonesia he is now best known. I can't recall a Raffles Hotel south of Singapore, but Rafflesia hotels, *losmen* and *wisma* (both guest houses) abound. They commemorate not the man but the fungus which, if fungi may be said to blossom, Raffles rightly guessed to have the largest flower in the world.

Fortunately on this excursion he and Lady Raffles ('the perfect heroine' as she rafted white-water rapids lashed to the mast) were accompanied by a botanist, Dr Joseph Arnold. *Rafflesia Arnoldi*, their joint discovery, extruded from the bark of a vine, the parasite of a parasite, and had neither leaves, stem nor root. But in the course of a couple of years its spore budded prodigiously to the size of a child's head and then, for a week, unfolded its orange-brown covering to release an appalling odour of rotting flesh with a bloom to match. Shading from lurid purple to livid red and dotted with white 'pustular spots', Raffles measured its circumference at 'rather more than a yard'. The nectarium was 'nine inches wide [and was] estimated to contain a gallon and a half of water, and the weight of the whole flower fifteen pounds'.

Like the equally repulsive dragons (really giant lizards) of Komodo in the eastern archipelago, the *Rafflesia* has become a major attraction. Its more accessible habitats are national reserves and news of an impending efflorescence is faxed round the tourist offices as if it were a once-in-a-lifetime event. How Raffles had so quickly stumbled upon this rarity remains a mystery; and, seeing all that impenetrable forest, I wondered what other mysteries yet remained to be discovered. A hundred years ago reports were still current of a Sumatran anthropoid apparently related to the orang-utan ('forest man'). Called the *orang kubu* it was much sought by trophy hunters until anthropologists cleared up the matter by identifying a primitive tribe of hunter-gatherers in the South

Sumatran forest as the only Kubu.

Between Curup and Bengkulu the local population are Rejang, a handsome people, late converts to Islam, who claim descent from a Javanese called Jang. But the Javanese homesteads which line the roads here and all over southern Sumatra are the result of more recent migrations. The word in *bahasa Indonesia* is *transmigrasi*, a controversial solution to the overpopulation of Java, Madura and Bali whereby settlement of less-populated parts of the archipelago is encouraged – some would say enforced – by transportation. The policy was inaugurated by the Dutch but Indonesia, like the ex-Soviet Union, remains one of the few countries which still transports its own citizens. It is also, like the Soviet Union, one of the few countries where you can be exiled within the national frontiers.

A marathon like the 20-hour ride from Bukittinggi to Bengkulu merited some reward. I ordered a late breakfast and, while puzzling how best to despatch two very soft-boiled eggs without spoon, egg cup, or bread, was urgently summoned by reception.

'It is Tabot. Quickly. See Tabot'. We raced across an ornamental bridge over a pond full of small crocodiles, through the aviary where toucans cocked their heads in disgust at such unseemly haste, and out into the street. For a hotel it bore a strong resemblance to a zoo. Reception, though, was charming and, through festive crowds which now lined the pavement, the two twin-setted girls drew me firmly to the front and pointed down the street.

Wild music and extravagant dancers announced the cavalcade of tinsel towers. There were forts and castles, ships and mosques and palaces, some topped with mythical monsters including a bird, less toucan than vulture, which flapped its wings and kept getting entangled with the telephone wires. An elephant with a monstrous howdah was followed by a thirty-storey *gunongan* which shamed its Aceh equivalent and was obviously modelled on Borobudur. Each tower had a number (there were 63) and was drawn, carried or, if motorized, simply accompanied by a gang of dark-skinned lascars with bandanas round their heads and knives in their waist-bands. Some manned drums and gongs while among them cavorted a strange miscellany of tigers, horses, sultans, monkeys and Elizabethan pirates. There was also a whale, a Disney Pluto, and a mermaid with a very fetching salute who wore sunglasses and a peaked naval hat from which flowed her Godiva tresses.

It was my day. By the happiest of coincidences I had stumbled into Bengkulu on the 9th after Muharram. In a civic calendar not packed with festivities I had unwittingly struck the one day in the year when this normally somnolent town stages Sumatra's only real carnival.

'Tabot means history,' said one of the receptionists. 'Tabot means tower,' said the other. And where, they both asked, was my camera? Without this universally accepted badge of tourist accreditation, one becomes a suspicious character, especially at such a photogenic event as Tabot. The girls drifted off; I joined the procession. Not the least of the occasion's mysteries was how one was supposed to know of it. In Bukittinggi no one had heard of it; on the bus no one had mentioned it. The hotel was empty and even reception seemed to have been taken by surprise.

Though, from the date, it is assumed that Tabot commemorates the martyrdom of Husayn, grandson of the Prophet and the inspiration of Shiite Muslims, the celebrations were not noticeably Islamic. In Iran and elsewhere Muharram occasions frenzied mourning and self-flagellation. But Bengkulu has practically no Shiah (nearly all Indonesian Muslims are Sunni) and marks the occasion with an eclectic symbolism and riotous frivolity which must seem blasphemous to Muslims of any persuasion.

After a perambulation which knocked out most of the town's telephones and fused power supplies, the procession split. Half headed for an area of waste ground where the towers were measured and then dismantled. Boys as agile as monkeys scaled the tottering superstructures to tear from the bamboo skeletons their covering layer of streamers, tinsel, fretted board and garish paper which were then thrown to the mob of trophy hunters below. In watching this I lost track of the other half of the procession. It had gone to the beach, I was told. The towers would be floated out to sea.

Images of fragile fairground structures gaily bobbing to a water-logged oblivion stirred memories of India. In Hyderabad the Muharram penitents process among similar *tazia*, and in Benares they commit such paper and plywood images to the mighty Ganges. The palaces, surely, were maharajas' palaces, the monkeys hanumans, the birds garudas. The date might come from the Islamic calendar but the inspiration, the colours, the craftsmanship and the ambience – all were Hindu, and not the esoteric Brahminism of classical Java or Srivijaya but the vibrant popular Hinduism of post-Moghul India.

Post-Moghul India, of course, was principally British India. After pioneers of the London East India Company such as James Lancaster had tried and failed to prevent Holland's monopoly of the archipelago's spice trade in the early 1600s, the English had concentrated on India. But they retained one toe-hold in what is now Indonesia and that was Bengkulu (or 'Bencoolen'). They moved here in 1685, after being ejected from Banten in Java, and they remained here for 140 troubled and largely pointless years, Raffles being the last-but-one Governor.

Throughout most of this time the settlement was attached to the Presidency of Madras whence came the sepoys, or Indian troops who formed its garrison. Few of these were Madrasis. Fighting troops were recruited from India's so-called martial peoples – Rajputs, Rohillas, Gurkhas and Pathans – while ancilliaries, such as tailors, washermen and cooks, were largely Bengalis. Posted to somewhere as remote as Bengkulu, nearly all took local wives (as indeed did the British) and it was their mixed progeny, looking not unlike Nepali Gurkhas with their bandanas and kukris, who in the garbled symbolism of Tabot still displayed something of their forebears' culture. Or so I fancied.

The British withdrew from Bengkulu as a result of that swap whereby the Dutch got a free hand in Sumatra in return for relinquishing claims on the Malay peninsula (to Malacca and

Singapore). This was in 1824 so, strictly speaking, Bengkulu was not part of British India but of Company India; and Company nostalgia being, unlike colonial nostalgia, an unthinkable indulgence, Bengkulu's British past has not been exhaustively studied. More is the pity, for the records contain rewarding insights. From a random trawl in the course of writing about the Company, I had conceived a warm affection for its usually luckless Bengkulu agents. Next day, encouraged by Tabot and refreshed by sleep, I sallied forth to seek out their haunts in the still just bearable heat of a sparkling seaside morning.

The four-square fort, its sloping ramparts and castellated parapets dazzling in their new whitewash, stood back from the beach and was remarkably intact. A cannon, too hot to touch, basked on one of the bastions and slender palms peeked over the wall-walk like dishevelled sentries with reveille still ringing in their ears. It lacked only its watchtower, destroyed by an earthquake; but since this, like the fort itself, had been faithfully reproduced at yesterday's Tabot, I could well visualize its confident profile with a capacious Company flag, red on white like that of St George, hanging lifeless from the flag-pole.

The fort, completed circa 1717, was named Marlborough after the 1st Duke, the victor of Blenheim and other battles in the War of Spanish Succession. And 'Long may this fort retain that glorious Name and may it sometimes be said that Govr. Collet built it,' wrote Governor Collet. Superseding Fort York (two miles to the north, never impressive, and now only of archaeological interest), the new creation is still 'Benteng Marlioboro' while Joseph Collet enjoys the distinction, unique for a Bengkulu agent, of having had his letters edited and published.

Like the settlement's founders and like practically everyone else who ever served in this forgotten outpost, Collet came to Bengkulu reluctantly. As a bankrupt he had to borrow even the wherewithal for a Governor's outfit and as a born-again Baptist he was further handicapped by a hypersensitive conscience which demanded he repay his creditors in full. And well he might, for there were excellent opportunities to speculate in local trade and no obvious means of spending the proceeds. But for a Bengkulu agent, making money was a secondary consideration. The real challenge was to stay alive.

If mortality in India was high, here it was higher. 'Some unusual malignity infects our air and strikes at all,' wrote Collet in 1713. Half his staff, including the minister and the doctor, were either dead or dying, probably from smallpox which swept up and down the coast with monsoonal regularity. The garrison became reduced to a few fevered pensioners; the fit were too fearful to care for the sick and the sick too feeble to bury the dead.

Between such epidemics, those who ventured inland got malaria while those who stayed in town went mad with boredom; Benkulen fever ('which invariably results from mounting a native woman') was a popular alternative to suicide. So was alcohol poisoning. In one month Collet and his 19 assistants got through 900 bottles of claret, 300 of beer, and more than 200 gallons of other assorted spirits and beverages. 'It is a wonder to us that any of you live six months and that there are not more quarrellings and duellings amongst you,' sneered the Company's directors in London.

Their only interest, and Fort Marlborough's *raison d'être*, was pepper, most of which was purchased from local growers like the Rejang. But, as Marsden noticed during his own spell in Bengkulu (1771-9), pepper was an exacting crop. The vine which produces the strings of berries has to have something to climb up and that means erecting suitable poles or growing suitable trees. It takes time and effort and, since Sumatran cuisine has no use for the resultant condiment, it was worthwhile only if prices were high and guaranteed to stay so. From London the directors lambasted the incompetence of their agents in failing to stimulate output and from Bengkulu the agents begged, bribed and browbeat the growers. But all to remarkably little effect. Production stuck at a few hundred tons a year and seems not once in 140 years to have yielded a return commensurate with the overheads of the Fort Marlborough establishment.

At an intersection near the fort a domed mausoleum of Moghul pedigree commemorates Thomas Parr, one of Collet's successors. In the course of a boring December evening he was stabbed to death by intruders and then decapitated. No one quite knew why. Here animosities might fester for months until suddenly something snapped and all hell broke loose. It was the nature of *amok*; and Bengkulu was the sort of place where the natives ran *amok* all too readily. In 1719 just after Collet's departure, the entire establishment had to take to the boats as the new fort was besieged and then fired by the disgruntled populace. Thirty died in the attack; the rest faced the galling indignity of Dutch protection.

Truly, then, the lot of a Company man was not a happy one. Reviled by his employers, cordially detested by his suppliers, wasted by fever and drained by the heat, he embraced death consoled only by the thought that hell could hold no surprises. More than half did die, most within their first two years. The upkeep of their graves was probably more than their contemporaries could manage, let alone posterity, but a few stones survive in the overgrown confusion of the cemetery; some are also built into the fort. They bear the simplest of heavily abbreviated epitaphs, as if all the fine words had long since been exhausted and the engraver's chisel was required elsewhere. Some are little more than dates and initials, algebraic formulae as cryptic as 'P.R.R.I. 1958'.

Within the walls of the fort the erstwhile guardhouse and armoury seemed to have the makings of a museum. Cannon balls were displayed in various arrangements and a few period prints and drawings had been assembled. But the main exhibits, mostly photographs, recalled a more recent inmate who found exile in Bengkulu almost congenial. Indeed, unthinkable to the Company man, he was actually removed to Bengkulu for convalescence. This was in 1938, the convalescent being a young and beaming Sukarno who had contracted mild malaria at his previous place of detention in Flores. Exiled by the Dutch as a trouble-maker and already the acknowledged leader of Indonesia's nationalist groups, he was receiving rather better treatment than colleagues like Hatta, who had been held in the dreaded labour camp of Boven Digul in Irian Jaya.

Sukarno, accompanied by his wife and adopted daughter, spent only a few days in the fort before moving into a chintzy bungalow in one of the town's new garden suburbs. He got a teaching job in the local Muhammadiya school, joined the badminton club, and seduced and eventually married Fatmawati, the belle of Bengkulu. It was a pretty relaxed kind of exile. Family photos and a well-stocked library give the bungalow the air of a deserted holiday home rather than a place of detention. Thanks to the subsequent eclipse of his reputation, it has been fortuitously preserved from heritage status. On the book shelves, among many works on music, A.J. Cronin's *The Citadel* looked well-thumbed. I searched for a copy of the history of Bengkulu which he is said to have written but failed to find it. Of an evening he directed the local dramatic society, pedalling forth on his bike, which I tried for size. The stirrup brakes were jammed; otherwise it was in good order.

For the ebullient Sukarno, as for Raffles, the numbing malaise of Bengkulu must have been more taxing than exile itself. Cut off from the rest of Sumatra by the cloud-shrouded Bukit Barisan, with no harbour worth the name, no industry, an indifferent beach and a vile climate, the town dozes in a haze of aimlessness. One evening, in a Chinese restaurant where no fewer than 15 calendars formed the only decoration, the television news carried a belated report on Tabot. Already it was hard to credit the place with such scenes of animation. Perhaps, like an outbreak of *amok*, Tabot cleared the air, excusing the townsfolk from all endeavour for the rest of the year. The news was followed by an episode of 'Twin Peaks'. The lugubrious proprietor paid no attention to either, preferring to stare out of the window at the deserted street. Why, I wondered, did he need so many calendars? 'Because they look pretty.' He cleared his throat before and after speaking, then resumed his contemplation of Bengkulu's non-existent nightlife.

I felt especially sorry for Raffles. For Sukarno, the soon-to-be Father, President and personification of the Indonesian Republic, a stint in the wilderness was no bad thing. Contacts formed here and in Flores would enhance his standing as a truly pan-Indonesian leader; and colonial detention was an essential for one of the century's most charismatic anti-imperialists. But it was different for Raffles. He had already won his prize – Java – and then seen it snatched from him. He returned to the East and to the backwater that was Bengkulu no longer plain Tom Raffles but Sir Stamford

Raffles, 'the man who would not let the East rest'. Yet the tide had turned against him and rightly he now likened his situation to that of Napoleon exiled on St Helena.

He often thought of Napoleon. The most un-British of empire-builders, Raffles too was a dangerous dreamer with all the pushy assertiveness of a short and self-made man. Of colleagues he made adversaries, of friends disciples. But his sympathies were sincere and his enthusiasms infectious. In exploring every aspect of Java's culture he had consciously followed Napoleon's example in Egypt. And after Java he had actually called on the emperor in his island exile. He continued to sense some affinity with the great man and, whether from raw ambition or righteous zeal, was convinced that he too had some dispensation to force the pace of history.

Arriving in Bengkulu he found 'a dead land', 'the most wretched place' he ever beheld. To its air of hopelessness and decay an earthquake plus a tidal wave had recently added whole-sale devastation. The roads were overgrown, the houses deserted. 'Ravenous dogs and polecats' welcomed him to the abandoned Government house where Lady Raffles, their just-born daughter, the nursemaid and the rest of the gubernatorial menage were to set up home. A fine Adam-style country house, it was soon repaired, the cornices restored, the cracks filled and the policies reclaimed. From England Raffles had brought the livestock for a home farm and the seeds for a gracious garden. Here, in defiance of the fevered ghosts and the packed graveyard, an ever-growing troop of children and pets filled the sweltering air with nursery rhymes and laughter.

And all the while, flagrantly flouting the Bengkulu malaise, Raffles himself laboured prodigiously. Slavery was abolished, the procurement of pepper (and now coffee, cloves and nutmeg) was reorganized, Sumatra's natural history was catalogued, its political history rewritten, new treaties signed, new lands explored, new empires planned. A British base was to be established in the Sunda Strait, a south Sumatran protectorate was to be set up with the Minangkabau, Bali was to be denied to the Dutch, Nias to be occupied. And when each of these was in turn denied him by orders from above, he turned to the Malacca Straits. From

Bengkulu, on the last of his colonial forays, he sailed in 1819 to the island called Singhapura to stage its dubious handover; and from his desk in the Bengkulu residency, like a law-giver of old, he then developed the principles of its free trade status, sketched its groundplan, and pondered a constitution for what would become its university. Tirelessly too he argued, lobbied and fought for the retention of 'this, my political child'.

Five minutes walk from Fort Marlborough, down dusty streets past dilapidated godowns, the shell of the Governor's residence still stands. The roof is gone and the ravenous dogs are back, plus goats. They scratch amid the mounds of refuse from which writhe the roots and branches of would-be trees. Weeds sprout from the wall-head where a corniced balustrade once surrounded the roof-top; sinuous creepers entwine the pilasters to glide from the empty window sockets like escaping anacondas. Whether nature is supporting the architecture or crushing it I couldn't decide.

That this forlorn ruin in a run-down quarter of an insignificant town in the back-woods of Sumatra could have hosted a classic idyll of enlightened government and domestic bliss beggared belief. But for Raffles it was so.

'He was beloved by all those under his immediate control [wrote Sophia, Lady Raffles]. The natives and chiefs appreciated the interest he took in their improvement and placed implicit reliance upon his opinion and counsel . . . Uninterrupted health had prevailed in his family, his children were his pride and joy . . . . and it was a curious scene to see the children, the bear, the tiger cubs, a blue mountain bird and a favourite cat all playing together . . . The evening was spent in reading and music and conversation. After the party had dispersed he was fond of walking out with the Editor [Lady Raffles edited his letters], and enjoying the delicious coolness of the night land-wind and a moon whose beauty only those who have been in tropical climes can judge of . . . '

I stared again at the skeleton of a house and noticed what looked like a vulture's nest on the balcony over the porticoed entrance. It was easier to imagine the place as the charnel house it soon became. Or as what Raffles himself would call 'the complete hospital' with drapes drawn, visitors shunned and the singing silenced.

In September 1820 he was still indulging in Napoleonic rhetoric about 'laying the foundations of the future civilisation of Sumatra'; he would import 30,000 English colonists and himself become 'the great Moghul of the island'. The unexpected demise of Lady Raffles' brother passed with little comment. But six months later death took up permanent residence. First to go was young Leopold Raffles, two years old and the apple of his father's eye. Harry Auber, another brother-in-law, was carried off in the same month and both Sir Stamford and Sophia were dangerously ill. They were slowly recovering by Christmas but in January 1822 both Charlotte Raffles, five years old, and Marsden Raffles, two-and-a-half, were also 'taken from us'. That left just baby Ella who, lest she too succumb, was despatched to England on the first available ship.

'Now that I am in other respects childless' Raffles tried to concentrate on his 'political child'. But for weeks he too lay in a semi-coma and still the vengeful spirit of the place was unsatisfied. Later in the year died the last of their three doctors and Mr Winter the chaplain. Dr Jack, the botanist who had reported so fully on Nias, followed his predecessor, Arnold of the *Rafflesia* discovery, to an early grave in 1823. And though that year brought a new child, Flora, by December she too was dead. Greedily the soft sandy soil swallowed its fourth cradle-sized coffin.

Like so many Company men before him, Bengkulu's near-demented Governor now frantically scanned the horizon for a sail. Early in 1824 the *Fame* hove in sight. Though running from a nightmare, Raffles took infinite care to pack aboard her what was certainly the greatest collection of Sumatran flora, fauna, fossils, rocks, maps, notes and statistics ever amassed. Denied possession of the island, he could yet appropriate it for science. To one who had rendered to its 'unusual malignity' four of five dearly loved children, a dozen good friends and the ambitions of a lifetime, it was compensation of a sort.

But what he always called the Eastern Archipelago, the world which people said Raffles would not let rest, would not now let Raffles rest. A few hours after sailing, while still within sight of the look-out on Fort Marlborough's watchtower, the *Fame* caught fire, exploded and sank. All hands were saved but they trailed back ashore with nought but the night clothes on their backs. When the Raffles finally reached England six months later they were travelling lighter than when they first set out. And Sir Stamford was a dying man. No further honours came his way, only the usual censures and penalties meted out by the Honourable Company to their few employees who survived the horrors of Bengkulu. Like them he died, according to his secretary, 'not generally known' in his homeland.

7. Dire straits

Sumatra is separated from Java by the 20-mile-wide Sunda Strait plus, according to Raffles, about 1,000 years of civilization. As a linguist and scholar as well as its Lieutenant-Governor (1812-16), Raffles had enthused over Java as 'this other India', a place so rich in history and so culturally sophisticated as to merit the adjective 'classical'. Indeed, there was evidence of that rarest of phenomena 'a strong sense of nationality . . . [which] supports a hope of future independence which they [the Javanese] are not backwards to express'. Raffles saw a nation in the making and his sweeping reforms, though not as liberal in practice as they appeared in theory and though designed to discredit Dutch rule as much as to improve the lot of the Javanese, could still be called enlightened. According to one of his severer critics he 'opened windows and doors so that the wind could blow through the old house' (B.H.M. Vlekke).

But Sumatra was a different matter. Crossing the Sunda Strait had been like passing back through time from Enlightenment France to Saxon England. Instead of civilization he found forest and instead of a sense of nationality, rank tribalism. Here Raffles the antiquarian deferred to Raffles the natural scientist; and here the benign liberator reverted to an authoritarianism which he likened to that of a feudal baron.

Although he undoubtedly exaggerated, the contrast would have been heightened by that between Batavia, already a major international metropolis, and Bengkulu, an irredeemably provincial backwater. Batavia is now called Jakarta; otherwise nothing in this respect has changed. In spite of its fragmentary configuration, Indonesia suffers more than almost anywhere from the centripetal pull of the capital and the peripheral push of the provinces. Wealth, resources and manpower slide inexorably into the metropolitan vortex only to be spewed forth on to its hinterland, like lava flows from a volcano, as suburban slurry, ribbons of industry, and concrete corridors of infrastructure. These reach deep into West Java's countryside and, because Jakarta is only three hours from the Sunda Strait and its busy ferries, they are also making their mark on south-eastern Sumatra. Raffles' differential of a thousand years of civilization is being concertina-ed into the modest span of a couple of five-year plans.

After climbing back into the Bukit Barisan, the road from Bengkulu, so new I couldn't find it on the map, had raced beside the upper reaches of the Musi, here a cheerful torrent proscribing sandy curves through lush meadows and then scouring wooded ravines to suck the soil from under unsuspecting forest colossi. After Lahat, having rejoined the Trans-Sumatra Highway for the last time, we encountered traffic worthy of a highway. Oil-rich Palembang, the capital of South Sumatra and supposed site of ancient Srivijaya, lies on the lower Musi only a hundred miles to the east. Thence came bulk carriers, trailerized containers, timber lorries, tankers and a stream of hurtling buses that completely overwhelmed the trickle of transport from upcountry.

Feeling very superior in an air-conditioned minibus, I was myself enjoying something of the capital's pulling power in that this lightning service – 24 hours from Bengkulu to the heart of Jakarta and all of it in what the Bengkulunese regarded as unheard of luxury – was a new venture designed to test the market. The shock absorbers absorbed even Sumatran shocks and the seating allowed for what was almost a sprawl. As we wove through the juggernauts, I glimpsed from behind the smoked glass windows suburban streets with satellite parabola, as big as *Rafflesiae*, uniformly beamed to receive the call of the metropolis. The Padang restaurants along the roadside were now facing stiff competition from Kentucky Fried Chicken and Burger King; and the great pot noodle war, waged relentlessly in TVRI's advertising breaks, at last burst from the forest in gigantic hoardings. Sumatra chose 'Super-Mie', said an unctuous starlet masquerading as a house-wife. 'Indo-Mie' outsells all, rejoined a fresh-faced brat. I heard too the whistle, actually more a gong, of my first train and saw a long trail of goods wagons disappearing into a rubber plantation.

As had unfailingly been the case in the long haul through Sumatra, we hit the highlight of the journey in the dead of night. Not that Bakauheni was dead. From here to Merak ferries criss-cross the Sunda Strait round the clock. Acres of arc-lit marshalling yard were jammed with freight as into the cavernous holds of throbbing vessels rolled the produce of Sumatra. The reek of exhaust sat like a slick in the sweltering humidity. To the grating of ramps, the clank of rusty chains and a cacophany of bell, buzzer and hooter, we slewed into the Strait, full speed for Java.

Keen to savour sea air and to see this historic waterway, if only by night, I absconded from the minibus and scaled a companion-way up the side of the vessel. At the rail stood an immaculate school party from Padang, off to Java for the first time. The boys were in blazers and the girls in *jilbab*, the Indonesian version of the Islamic veil. Usually a pastel shade and not unattractive, it hides neck and hair but leaves the face exposed. Flawless complexions benefit, appearing full of delicious nun-like innocence.

Introductions brought to mind an observation in Marsden's *History of Sumatra*. 'The hands of the natives are always cool to the touch.' Also silky smooth, they nestled in the palm as if seeking a confidante. Marsden put the coolness down to languid blood circulation. Could this also, I wondered, explain that superhuman restraint – Marsden would have called it torpor – and, since blood so languid must be liable eventually to form a brain clot, did it also explain the dreaded abandon of *amok*? Although it was Raffles' *History of Java* that became a classic, Marsden's *Sumatra* contains the better insights. I dished out segments of mangosteen and watched impeccable teeth suck from the stone the white translucent flesh. 'The pride of the Malay countries,' wrote Marsden of the mangosteen, 'its qualities are as innocent as they are grateful'.

While beacons probed the night with their pencils of light, we scanned the approximate horizon for a glimpse of Krakatau's inferno, then debated our chances of survival in the oily waters below. Others had eyed these features with greater apprehension. Not surprisingly, since Padang had suffered severely, the students displayed much vulcanological knowledge but were less well informed about local castaways. Either way, what transpired in the Sunda Strait has had a considerable bearing on both native and foreign perceptions of Indonesia.

Like a long curving breakwater, the arc known as the Sunda Islands (i.e. Sumatra, Java, Bali, Lombok, Sumbawa, Flores etc.) shield from the empty Indian Ocean the busy maritime world of the Asian archipelagos. And just as the land-locked Mediterranean and Black Seas had once formed a self-sufficient trading world and a cradle of civilization, so it was with this other favoured lagoon of the Java and China Seas. But while the Mediterranean has only the Straits of Gibraltar, the Java Sea has several points of access. For shipping from India and the Arabian Sea, the Malacca Strait was, and still is, the main route of entry. That way, in the 16th century, came the Portuguese pioneers who from their citadel at the town of Malacca soon controlled the Strait.

To bypass this obstacle the Dutch and the English headed east for the Sunda Strait which anyway proved to be a shorter route for ships coming direct from the Cape of Good Hope. Through Sunda's narrows sailed Lancaster and his English successors and through them came Jan Pieterzoon Coen, their great rival and the founder of the Dutch empire in the East. They were followed in the 18th century by a generation of Pacific navigators: Anson and Carteret, Byron and Bougainville, Wallis, Tasman and Cook. Not to be outdone, the 19th century brought the tea-clippers, those racy frigate birds of the high seas, Thames-bound from the Pearl River with more canvas than a touring circus. Truly a history of the sea could be written here; and few would call themselves sailors who have no yarns to tell of the Sunda Strait.

The best such yarn was that of a Captain Watson, probably from Belfast like his barque, who timed to perfection his passage

of the Strait. On the night of 25 August 1883 he entered the fun-
nelling waters from the south and next afternoon was beating up
the Strait just ten miles from the island marked on his chart as
'Krakatoa'. It was shrouded in cloud or, more probably, smoke.
Volcanic activity had been evident for the past three months with
several minor earthquakes, continuous emissions and a modest
eruption on 27 May. By chance, this had actually been pho-
tographed by a tourist on a passing vessel. His picture shows a
thick column of smoke raging from the far side of the already
denuded island and showering all in its shadow with what looks
like torrential rain.

Just such a scene now confronted Watson. Only it wasn't rain
and it was growing worse. To 'a strange sound as of a mighty
crackling fire or the discharge of heavy artillery' smoke and solid
matter 'or whatever it was' was being propelled 'with amazing
velocity towards the north-east'. He took in sail and kept close to
the Java shore.

'At five the roaring noise continued and increased; wind moderate from the south-south-west; darkness spread over the sky,
and a hail of pumice stone fell on us, many pieces being of considerable size and quite warm. Had to cover up the skylights to
save the glass while feet and head had to be protected with boots
and southwesters. About six o'clock the fall of larger stones
ceased but there continued a steady fall of the smaller kind,
most blinding to the eyes and covering the decks to three or four
inches very speedily, while an intense blackness covered the sky
and land and sea.'

All night the sea churned and 'chains of fire' ran up and down
between the island and the sky. The wind, though from the opposite direction, blew hot and sulphurous. Scorching cinders still fell
from above while from the sea-bed the ship's lead came up hot to
the touch. Lesser fireballs coursed through the rigging; the iron-
work gave off shocks; and all the while the island ground its sub-
terranean teeth and rent the air with agonized roars. 'Our situation
a truly awful one,' noted Watson in his log.

The 27th, a Sunday, dawned late and reluctantly. Ash no longer fell but the sky was overcast and the sea suspiciously calm. Now thirty miles to the east of Krakatau, Watson saw signs of the night's devastation around the Java port of Anjer. Trees had been uprooted and a work camp flooded. It was as nothing to the visitation that lay in store. The big bang, heard from Rangoon to Bangkok and Perth, was logged at 10.02am. Like others in the vicinity, Watson seems to have been little awed by the noise of the greatest-ever recorded explosion; he mentions no blast and, being in deep water, his ship barely felt the *tsunami*, the mighty rush of water, that followed. But he saw its effects. Sangaing Island athwart the Strait was thrice inundated by walls of water which also ran fatefully on to the Java and Sumatra shores. There, having swept the coasts, they drove inland, compressed by the hills into hundred foot bores heavy with tree trunks, roofing timbers, rocks and bodies.

Watson barely glimpsed the horror, for by 10.30am night had fallen again. It was so black that his men had to grope their way about the ship. 'The darkness might almost be felt.' Indeed it was felt. Instead of ash they were deluged by 'a downpour of mud, sand and I know not what'. On the deck and the spars the aggregate compounded with the pumice and volcanic ash into a deep cement. And it was the same on the sea. For weeks floes of solid volcanic matter would clutter the Strait and compact along its shores.

Not till the late afternoon did a wan light return. Watson, who had wisely kept under way throughout the crisis, was then past Merak and at last emerging from the jaws of the Strait into the Java Sea and safety. His ship was so encrusted it looked like the survivor of a polar winter; yet, had Charon been its commander, it could have sailed no closer to hell.

It has been estimated that the great eruption was equivalent in its energy release to at least a thousand Hiroshimas and that it ejected about four-and-a-half cubic miles of matter, most of it as pulverized dust. This formed the cloud that turned day to night even in Batavia. Reaching into the upper atmosphere, it circled the earth many times, confused meteorologists and rewarded the romantic with a couple of years of sensational sunsets.

The big bang caused mainly confusion. Several navies went on alert, others thought it was either a salute or a distress signal. In Borneo the murderers of a Dutchman fled their village thinking revenge was nigh; and in Aceh the beleaguered Dutch forces rushed to arms thinking the Acehnese were mounting yet another offensive.

The great killer was the *tsunami*, the 'tidal' wave. For some reason it travelled mainly west, its effects being noticed as far away as the Cape of Good Hope, the English Channel and even Cape Horn. In Sri Lanka it claimed its most distant victims but, when it receded, rewarded survivors with a bumper crop of stranded seafood. Sumatra's ports, from Bengkulu to Aceh, were all inundated, but the major loss of life was here along the coast of Lampung (Sumatra) and, across the Strait, along the even more densely populated coast of Java. Places like Merak and Anjer were totally devastated, scarcely a tree left standing or a creature breathing. It was the same at Bakauheni and at Teluk Betung, the old port on the Lampung side. There a Dutch gunboat and a crew of 28 was swept up and eventually found, with all hands dead, stuck in a hill, 30ft above sea level and more than a mile inland.

Krakatau's total death toll is usually put at about 35,000. Yet it was not by any means Indonesia's (and so the world's) greatest eruption. In prehistoric times Toba probably held the record. More recently Tambora, a thousand miles to the east on the island of Sumbawa, blasted some 25 cubic miles of matter into the air, more than five times the output of Krakatau. This was in 1815 when Raffles was in Java. From the accounts he collated it appears that Tambora left ash several feet deep in eastern Java, plunged Makassar in Sulawesi into a 24-hour night and, always a dreaded possibility, triggered other volcanoes into action including Bali's Gunung Agung and Java's Merapi. The latter, poised over the island's densely populated heartland, has long been a force to be reckoned with in Javanese history. An eruption in c1000AD may have put paid to the first kingdom of Mataram and another in 1672 presaged the demise of the second.

★

When I asked my young companions on the rail of the ferry why no sparks from Krakatau now lit the night, they shrugged.

'He is sleeping,' ventured a serious face, moon-like in its *jilbab*; she was leaning against me, half asleep herself. 'Volcanoes sleep a long time'.

'No, now it is *anak Krakatau*, son of Krakatau, a new island but small.' The know-all of the group, no giant himself, wore gig-lamp spectacles just like Mohammed Hatta. 'It has been rising for a long time. You can visit by boat. But better you visit Bromo or Merapi, I think.'

Offshore and with no great physical presence, Krakatau scarcely counts among the 70-odd still active volcanoes which, like beacon cones, line the breakwater formed by the Sunda Islands from Sumatra to the Moluccas. They average about 10 eruptions a year, mostly benign in that the ash enriches the fields and the lava once provided an easily worked laterite for building purposes. On the whole they are well regarded. Javanese and Sumatran *adat* personifies most and acknowledges all as righteous referees in the affairs of men. When they occasionally run *amok* it is always with good cause; the social order has been disturbed, a dynasty has outrun its allotted span, a new order is in the offing. Tambora's rage was an expression of disgust over Raffles' recent assault on the noble city of Jogjakarta; Krakatau spoke up against Dutch treatment of the Acehnese.

So had there, I asked, been a notable eruption in the first weeks of 1942? The class looked blank. Only our bespectacled know-all grasped the drift of the question.

'1942. Hollander colonialists defeated by Japan. No eruption. But you know Joyoboyo?'

If the volcanoes had remained silent perhaps it was because at first Japanese rule looked like a real improvement after 350 years of Dutch bullying. Sukarno's exile in Bengkulu abruptly came to an end and, in an uneasy alliance with the new invaders, he and Hatta were back at the Nationalist helm. Everyone donned the pillbox *peci*. The newspapers switched to *bahasa Indonesia*, the new national anthem of *Indonesia Raya* was being openly sung and, thanks to the ease with which the blue in the Dutch flag could be snipped off to leave just its red and white bands, the streets were ablaze with the nationalist *merah-putih.* The Japanese might be an unknown quantity and would soon reveal a contempt for the welfare of their fellow Asians which made Dutch rule seem almost paternal. But Indonesians would bear it all with admirable fortitude. They knew that Japan's days were numbered. Joyoboyo had predicted it.

Information on Joyoboyo has proved hard to come by. He seems to have been a king of Kediri in eastern Java during the 12th century whose utterances only gained popular currency some 600 years later. One such, sufficiently cherished for Sukano to evoke it with powerful effect, predicted a 'great ordeal that would exterminate Java and all that is upon it', a reference, obviously, to Dutch oppression. But eventually, said Joyoboyo, there would come to the assistance of the down-trodden Javanese a force of liberators from the island of 'Tembini'. They would be 'yellow of colour, small of height' and might resemble chickens; and they would occupy Java for the duration of a maize plant. And then they would go home and Java would be restored to her ancient state and to the custody of her own sons, possibly even to the *ratu adil*, a long-awaited messiah and 'just king' with whom his most ardent followers liked to identify Sukarno.

Only a people as mystically obsessed as the Javanese could have derived much comfort from all this when thousands of them were dying of starvation and forced labour. Howsoever, 1942's maize crop was in due course harvested; then it was requisitioned; still the occupation went on. So had the Kediri seer got it wrong?

Not at all, explained Padang's most precocious pupil. The maize plant might have died but, as every farmer knew, the corn of its cob lived on; it remained capable of germination for up to three years.

'So three years, and add the five months till the first crop. 1942, 1943, 1944, 1945, yes?' He counted them on his fingers and then slapped the ship's rail in triumph, thereby imperilling the extremely long claw-like nail on his little finger. 'Persons of superior rank; ' says Marsden, 'encourage the growth of their hand-nails, particularly those of the fore and little fingers, to an extraordinary degree.' So the prodigy was of noble birth, a mandarin in the making.

We were now in mid-strait with a twinkling light to port which I took to be Sangaing Island where Watson saw the effects of the *tsunami*. The island has another claim to fame and, though it meant nothing to my companions, to pass the time and retain their company, I launched into an account of the battle of the Java Sea and of its aftermath, the battle of the Sunda Strait. For a whole generation these engagements, plus the long years of detention and death that followed, irrevocably soured whatever charm and romance attached to Java and Sumatra. On the survivors they left scars that have yet to heal and in the history books they left associations of which few visitors can be unaware. It could do no harm to remind my companions that man was seldom as innocent and grateful as a mangosteen; and that it didn't take a volcano to transform a paradise into an inferno.

The speed of the Japanese victory in South-east Asia is still hard to credit. Barely three months sufficed. Pearl Harbour was hit on 7 December 1941; by the end of January (1942) Hong Kong, Indo-China and Malaya had fallen and Sumatra and the Philippines were being invaded; two weeks later Singapore had surrendered, the eastern archipelago had been overrun and Burma was under attack; Java fell three weeks later, on 8 March.

In Indonesia the only set piece battle came towards the end when on 26 February, with Java already isolated, an Allied naval force hastily collected at Surabaya in the north-east of the island and ventured forth into the Java Sea. It was to offer what amounted to a last-ditch defence against the converging Japanese invasion forces and then to escape through the Sunda Strait to the comparative safety of the Indian Ocean. The five cruisers and nine destroyers included vessels of the Dutch, American, British and Australian navies, the last two battle-hardened from the Mediterranean. But command went to the Dutch who, it was soon being said, had not fought a naval battle since the 18th century. It remains debatable whether, with no aerial reconnaissance, against

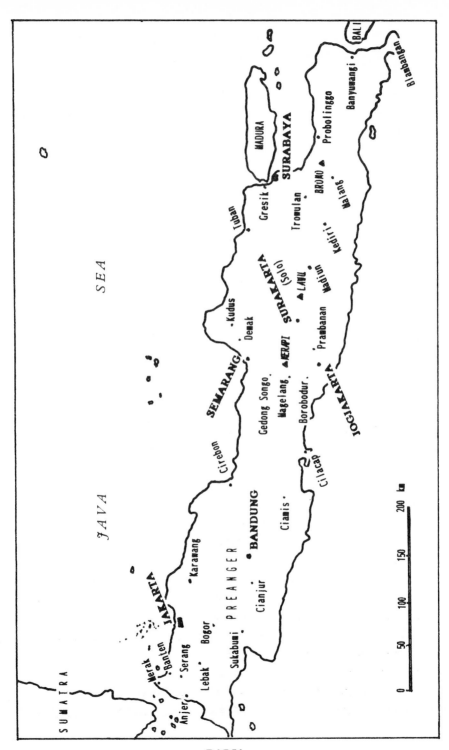

JAVA

a vastly superior enemy with air and submarine support, more tactical awareness would have made much difference.

The enemy, finally sighted on the afternoon of the 27th, quickly took advantage of the situation. By midnight the allies had lost their two Dutch cruisers plus two British and one Dutch destroyer. Another cruiser, the British *Exeter*, had been disabled and forced to retire to Surabaya with escorting destroyers. Of the 14 ships only two cruisers, the American *Houston* and the Australian *Perth*, continued west for the Sunda Strait. They called at Tanjung Priok, the port of Jakarta, for fuel and ammunition and, securing little of either, steamed on for the Strait and safety.

(This was the bit I remembered best. Sleepy eyes and solemn faces hung on my every word. I wished I could tell it as Ray Parkin had in that classic of its kind, *Out of the Smoke*. But I didn't have the book and the English had to be simple.)

They nearly made it. At 11pm on 28 February the light on the cape just north of Merak that marks Java's extremity and the entrance to the strait was already in sight. (I pointed to a likely beam; the class faced about.) But also in sight was what proved to be a Japanese destroyer. Other flashes suggested it was one of five, then of nine plus a cruiser, then of ten, possibly twenty, with five cruisers and untold support craft.

Encircled, the *Houston* and the *Perth* gave better than they got; but they had no chance. When the *Houston* was hit, the *Perth* tried to make a run for it. She was nose into the Strait at 28 knots when the torpedo struck. Another followed; the cruiser slowed and settled; and as shells rained aboard like pumice, the survivors abandoned ship. She was still steaming into the Strait, racked by explosions which showered the sea with oil, when she finally nose-dived to the bottom. The *Houston* followed minutes later. For the hundred or so survivors, clinging to overcrowded life-rafts, bits of wreckage or nothing at all, many of them wounded and all suffocating with oil-clogged lungs, a second battle began.

Of those who stayed afloat, some made it to the Java coast near Merak (now full ahead). But most were swept into the Strait by the current and washed ashore either on the lighthouse rock known as Toppers Island or the much larger Sangaing Island.

(The ferry seemed to have passed between the two.)

On Sangaing they found other castaways. From Singapore, hours before its fall, thousands of non-combatants – engineers, nurses, administrators, planters, journalists – had been packed aboard all available shipping. With the Malacca Strait already in Japanese hands, this flotilla had also headed for the Sunda Strait, the only hole in the encircling Japanese net. It was halted by an enemy task force about a hundred miles from the Strait near the island of Bangka off the coast of Sumatra. From the forty-odd ships that were sunk, survivors came ashore on Bangka where all were rounded up. A few, though, made it to Sumatra and some further. Sangaing's castaways included a party of six, two of them children, with a small skiff in which they were heading for Timor and Australia. Encouraged by this example, the marooned men of the *Perth* and the *Houston* began to forage, to improvize, and to hope.

I had to precis the rest of the story. A faint silvering of the night sky presaged dawn and, amid the lights of Merak, wharves and cranes were now visible. To a point south of here near Anjer, most of those from Toppers and Sangaing were ferried ashore on rafts. They hoped that friendly 'natives' would feed and clothe them (few had more than oil-encrusted shorts) and then send them on their way to wherever the next evacuation was being organized. Again they were just too late. The Japanese had landed on Java three days earlier and were now about to take its surrender. The 'natives' were not friendly; capture came as a relief. Only one group of Australians, who had improvized mast and sails for a lifeboat, put back to sea.

In a ten-day odyssey which took them through the Strait and out into the Indian Ocean, they seriously considered making a bid for Darwin. But the winds were against them, the boat sailed badly and they had neither food nor water nor chart. Parched, emaciated, barely able to stand, they reached Cilacap, half way along Java's south coast. To their surprise they were received with kindness by their Japanese captors who respected their courage. Once recovered, they ceased to enjoy such favours. It was *en route* to a labour camp on the notorious Burma-Siam railway that they were briefly held in Bandung where the *Perth's* Chief Petty Officer, bearded and as oblivious of his surroundings as the Ancient Mariner, first told his story.

His audience – with more time on their hands than my young friends who now bolted back to their bus ready for landing – included Laurens van der Post, a fellow prisoner who later encouraged publication of the story and wrote a foreword to it. For the ensuing three-and-a-half years in Japanese prisoner of war camps, no one was better qualified than van der Post. To the advantage of a Dutch name in camps where Dutchmen predominated, he brought the survival skills of a South African bushman and the assurance of a British officer. He was also a natural leader; he spoke fluent Japanese; and he enjoyed a profound sense of destiny like Raffles (whom he thought 'the most imaginative leader that Sumatra and Java had ever known'). After the war he was destined for a part in taking the Japanese surrender and brokering Indonesian independence, or rather 'a principal role in what was to be a repeat performance in contemporary dress of the piece of high history enacted round Raffles'. But in 1942 his standing among both his fellow prisoners and his captors rested on another distinction; he was one of the very few who had been captured in action in Java.

It had taken the Japanese just four days to pocket the jewel of the Dutch East Indies. One invasion force, barely delayed by the battle of the Java Sea, landed on the north coast between Semarang and Surabaya; the other, having disposed of the *Perth* and the *Houston*, swept into Merak as unopposed as Krakatau's *tsunami*. From the port's road and railhead, still the busiest in Indonesia even at five in the morning, the Japanese controlled West Java and menaced Batavia. Resistance seemed hopeless. The Dutch forces felt betrayed by the British surrender of Singapore and were anyway quite inadequate for the defence of the large and scattered communities of Dutch civilians, let alone the Indonesian population. A hard-fought war across the most densely populated island in the world was unthinkable.

But in a wider context the Allies desperately needed to slow the Japanese sweep through the Pacific and to tie down in Indonesia as many enemy battalions as possible. For this purpose British and Australian forces had been rushed to Java and fought valiantly. When the Dutch, without consultation, quietly surrendered just four days after the landings, it was they who felt betrayed. Van der Post's contempt for the fat Bols-swilling *myneers* and their cotton-frocked *mevrouws* loses nothing for being the one blind spot in his almost infuriating eye for the good in others, not excluding his captors.

Sensing betrayal, the Allies' South-east Asia Command had been hurriedly evacuated, but not before inviting selected officers to recruit their own troops and fade into the hills, there to prolong resistance as guerillas. Van der Post was to operate from the mountains near Merak. He was not at large for long. Most of his recruits were rounded up before they reached the mountains. He himself 'walked into a Japanese trap one morning on a mountain in the far west of Java called Djaja-sempoer'. Presumably it counted as 'captured in action' because his surrender was involuntary.

From the ferry, my Bengkulu minibus skirted Merak to join the Jakarta expressway. It was still barely light when I bailed out at the Serang slip-road. To the south a sky of schist glinting with the mica of day betrayed a horizon of dark shaggy mountains. Any one of them could have been Djaja-sempoer; and it was to Serang's cinema that most of the *Perth/Houston* survivors had been taken after they came ashore at Anjer. But I didn't bother to look for either. I was back on the spice trail. Though Serang is the main town, the district is still commonly Banten and it was at Banten that both Dutch and English East India Companies first set up shop.

I paused only to find a room and breakfast. While waiting on the *losmen*'s verandah, a salvo of shrieks from the parakeets announced the dawn chorus. It was followed by a volley of song from deep in a mango tree, and then, through strident trills and anxious twitters, quickly degenerated into the quack, the crow and the honk of domestic birds and the cough, belch and expectoration of their owners. Java's coffee, after another sleepless night, made up for everything; and for eggs no bigger than parakeets' I found that a jar of Vicks served well as an egg cup.

Indonesian hens come in all sizes from turkey to pigeon. They have in common only a fleshless physique – there is more meat on a Sumatran spider – and a capacity for producing under-size eggs. To the Company men of three centuries ago Banten was always 'Bantam' and as such still claims a mention in the English dictionary as the place where small fowl originated. But, though I scanned the yards and roadsides from the back of a *bemo* all the way from Serang to Banten Bay, I failed positively to identify a single bantam that might not have been a half-grown pullet or a stunted rooster.

It seems, then, that with diminutive chickens as with pepper Banten served as a conduit for the produce of elsewhere. The pepper came mostly from neighbouring parts of Sumatra and the chickens, probably, from upcountry Java. They came to Banten because in the 16th-17th centuries its sultanate controlled both sides of the Sunda Strait and possessed in Banten Bay a vast and sheltered anchorage of strategic as well as commercial value. To it came not only the Dutch and the English but also Thais, Burmese, Bengalis, Gujeratis and an annual armada of junks from the ports of China. It was the busiest entrepôt in the whole archipelago and the hub of another of those trading spheres into which so much of Indonesian history resolves itself. But unlike that of the Malacca Strait, control of which passed bewilderingly from Srivijaya to Melayu to Aceh etc., this one, based on the Sunda Strait, was disputed by only two contenders, Banten and Batavia/Jakarta. And it was Banten that lost out.

The city in 1600 was about the size of Amsterdam but more cosmopolitan, according to its Dutch visitors. They, and then Lancaster's fleet for the English Company, both picked Banten for their first trading posts. Known as 'factories', these establishments required a permanent staff and an armed guard for they housed the chests of bullion and the bales of cloth (mostly fine batiks and muslins bought in India) with which payment was made for pepper. Relations with the Sultan's court were generally good. European trade brought all sorts of novelties, including muskets, cannons and much tableware to supplement that coming from China. But for the common Javanese, 'notorious pickers and thieves' according to Lancaster, the establishment of these exotic European emporia represented an irresistible temptation. Palisades had to be erected around the 'factories', the guards doubled and trebled, and brickwork preferred to timber. From the security precautions taken by those first Dutch merchants grew the overweening might of the Netherlands East Indies. Van der Post would wryly call it 'the world's third largest empire' which, 350 years in the making, in 1942 crumbled to nothing in just four days.

Climbing a stubby minaret which appeared to be modelled on a Regency pepper pot – and given the vogue for pepper and European tableware, very plausibly was – I surveyed the site. A Brahminy kite, its ermine head and gilded wings aglow in the early sun, mewed plaintively as it scavenged over a wasteland of scrub. But for a flapping tarpaulin and a nest of bamboo scaffolding, evidence of archaeological activity, I would probably have missed the masonry – steps, pillar stumps and walls, a pavilion arch and a slab of bastion – which nestled in the undergrowth among several acres of pits and tumuli. So this was the Surosawan, the royal palace whence the Sultan issued, dripping with finery, to give public audience. The masses, including Dutch and English merchants, would have assembled in the *alun-alun*, an open square now more like a village green where a few stallholders were setting up shop immediately below me. The stalls offered food and drink plus skull-caps and *peci* to suit all heads. Enquiries confirmed that they were expecting not tourists but pilgrims.

As a power base, Banten's innings was short. The Dutch removed their headquarters to Batavia in 1618, returning to Banten only to drive out their English rivals in 1684 (the English moved to Bengkulu) and to assume the sovereignty of the sultanate. They marked their triumph by building the gloomy Fort Speelwyck on whose grassy parade ground I watched Banten United practising penalties. It lies well to the north of the Surosawan and suggests that even in the 1680s the Java Sea, and with it the port-city's *raison d'être*, was on the retreat. The canals that served as the royal processional routes would have been drying up, the Sultan's baths draining and the palace gardens parched. Now, even from the fort, the sea is little more than a distant promise across miles of reclaimed waste, fish ponds and mud flats.

As a declining port, a troublesome fief and a run-down palace, Banten lingered on in the records until 1815 when the Sultan abdicated with Raffles' encouragement. Thereafter its decay must have accelerated dramatically. To have sunk to the enigmatic middens and earth-works of an archaeological curiosity in less than two centuries was no mean achievement for a place that rivalled Amsterdam. In the on-site 'Museum Arkeologi' artefacts ranged erratically from prehistoric scrapers to 19th century beer bottles. Its 'Cultural Resources Management' ('developed as a multi-disciplinary approach to optimally improve cultural resources') scouted the idea of eventually 'restoring Old Banten'. Some hope.

What makes the devastation so impressive is the survival, in excellent condition, of a structure that predates all the ruined pavilions and was probably the first ever erected by the sultans of Banten. This is the *Mesjid Agung*, the great mosque, a set of build-ings grouped round a raised *pendopo* (roofed platform) with tim-ber pillars and a lot of tiled roof including a five-tier pagoda tower. Any tiered tower is liable to be credited to that Hindu-Buddhist obsession with *gunongan*, the mountain shape of Indic cosmology. And this is indeed a decidedly un-Islamic mosque. But it recalls others, dating from the first coming of Islam, in the coastal ports of central Java and particularly one in Demak whence came Ban-ten's founders in c1525. Sharif Hidayatulla, his son Hasanuddin and grandson Jusuf, also founded the dynasty and the kingdom. Both are now defunct but in sowing the seeds of Islam in West Java the Demak men achieved a more lasting celebrity as saints and miracle-workers.

Their followers were thronging the makeshift market on the *alun-alun* as I left. For the first time, instead of the charming *jilbab*, I noticed black veils and a huddle of shrouded figures in the all-embracing *chador* of Arabia. To compensate for its lost glory Banten explored the solace of Islam with un-Javanese single-mindedness. During the independence struggle it became 'the Aceh of Java' and here too fanatics fought and killed for a *Dar-ul-Islam*, an Islamic homeland. They included descendants of the royal family and they advocated the restoration of a godly sultanate. Recalling that idea of restoring the vanished city I wondered about their representation on the Museum's 'Cultural Resources Management'.

8. *Living dangerously,*
dying horribly

'So you think it's OK for the these Indonesians to be torching East Timor, do you? And kicking the Irian tribes off their land and, and, and clear-felling Kalimantan? It's OK by you mate, that it?'

The Australian anthropologist, two years into a research fellow-ship on Timorese language structures, knew what he was talking about. Against my three days in West Timor back in 1986, he practically lived there.

'Well no. Of course it's not OK. But, I mean it's their country. It's up to them how they want to run it. When we start telling them who should live where and how many trees they can fell, they smell neo-colonialism and . . .'

'But it's not their country. Timor's not theirs. Irian's not theirs. Not according to the UN. These places it's the Indonesians who're the colonialists, not us.'

We were breakfasting at a long communal dining table with a white tablecloth. Deckle-edged plates piled with white sliced bread were strategically located among double dishes of scallop shell design containing margarine on one side and chocolate dis-guised as iron filings on the other. A picture of the Last Supper hung on the wall.

Checking in, I hadn't realized that 'PGI' as in Jakarta's PGI Guest House, stood for the Indonesian Communion of Churches. I was missing my eggs, I was sorry to be cooped up inside during the most delicious hour of the day, and I was quite unqualified to mount a convincing defence of Indonesian policy. So changing tack, I enquired whom he held responsible; who were these dreadful Indonesian colonialists?

'Well the Indonesian military, Jakarta, Java, Javanese imperialism.'

'And Bali?'

'Yeah, OK, Bali, Sumatra, whatever.'

'Including the Minang, the Batak, the Acehnese?'

'Sure. Batak especially.'

'But what about the Acehnese? They aren't much happier than the Irianese. And they too have taken the trouble to fight for their autonomy.'

'So?'

'So it's not that simple. Indonesia's a lot of different peoples, some more used to the idea of integration than others.'

It was an irrelevant argument and we both knew it. But sensing a point worth making even if it wasn't the right one, I pressed on regardless.

'It's like India. You reckon the place is doing pretty well if there's enough food to go round and no more than a couple of states under martial law and the occasional train being waylaid by Maoist guerillas. The tidy little consensus on which other nations pride themselves is too tall an order for a sprawling multi-ethnic super-state.'

Old India hands used to say that no one who knew about India ever talked about Indians. Sikhs, Marathas, Bengalis, yes; but not Indians. By a happy coincidence the same sentiments had surfaced in the book I was reading by an old Indonesia hand. 'The man whose acquaintance with the Dutch East Indies is confined to Java can no more have a correct idea of the Malay, the Ambonese, the Batak, the Alfuro, the Timorese, the Dayak, the Bugi or the Makassar than if he had never left Europe.' In fact the man acquainted only with Java would think twice even about using the term 'Javanese'. The Tengger people of East Java, Hinduistic hillmen, did not qualify and, more to the point, 'the western residencies of Bantam, Batavia, Preanger, Krawang and part of Cheribon . . . are not regarded as part of Java.' In other words the whole of

West Java province plus metropolitan Jakarta, about a third of the entire island, is not Java at all; it is Sunda and 'its costume, tribal character and language are so totally unlike those further east that the Sundanese or *orang gunung*, 'the man from the mountains', differs more profoundly from the real Javanese than an Englishman from a Dutchman.'

Max Havelaar or The Coffee Auctions of the Dutch Trading Company, from which I quote, was written under the pen name of 'Multatuli' by Edward Douwes Dekker in 1859. D. H. Lawrence, in an introduction to the English edition, declared it a satire on the Dutch bourgeoisie; others have called it 'the one Dutch classic' and 'the most powerful indictment of colonialism ever published'. It provoked a furore which eventually had important consequences for the character of Dutch rule when the 'cultivation policy' of the 19th century was abandoned for the marginally more enlightened 'ethical policy' of the 20th. But I was reading it because, though a novel, the Indonesian sections of the book are pure autobiography. Havelaar is Dekker; both served as Assistant Resident of Lebak; and Lebak is the sub-division of West Java, or rather Sunda, immediately south-east of Serang.

It would have weakened Dekker's diatribe to make too much of Sunda's distinctive character. He was gunning for the whole colonial system and the controllers, residents and regents (native agents) through whom it operated. The peculiarities of the downtrodden victims of the system were not relevant. Yet Sunda was, and is still, a place apart. Outside the pages of the tourist brochures differences of costume no longer arrest the attention; but Sundanese remains a distinct language, there is at least one tribal novelty, and thanks to its history and its economic importance Sundanese society has stresses all its own.

In keeping with the Indonesian custom of evoking historical pedigree when naming universities, that in Bandung, the West Java capital, is called Pajajaran University. (Palembang's is Srivijaya University, Surabaya's Airlangga, Denpasar's Udayana etc.) The kingdom of Pajajaran seems to have been based near Bandung and to have held sway over most of Sunda in pre-Islamic times. It may have succeeded an earlier Hindu-Buddhist kingdom known as Tarumanegara and, judging by inscriptions, was also Hindu-Buddhist. Other than this little is known of it until the 16th century when Pajajaran's authority over Sunda's north coast ports was called into question.

Maritime trade, as so often, was at stake. Further east the recently Islamized ports of Demak and Kudus were attracting the lucrative supply and exchange business of their Malay and Indian co-religionists engaged in the spice trade. To meet this competition the Portuguese from their base at Malacca sought allies and facilities in Java. They found both in Hindu-Buddhist Pajajaran. Of its two ports, Banten and Sunda Kelapa, the latter was made available to the Portuguese. But in 1525 Banten fell to the zealots from Demak and two years later, before the Portuguese had taken up this option, Sunda Kelapa was also conquered.

One may judge of how comfortable with their new religion were the conquering converts of Demak and Banten not only from their pagoda-style mosque in Banten but from the fact that they now renamed Sunda Kelapa 'Jayakarta'. It means 'City of Victory', an appropriate title and definitely an improvement on Sunda Kelapa, the 'Sunda Coconut Palm'; but the language is the Sanskrit of ancient kingdoms like Pajajaran, not the Arabic of Islam. 'Jayakarta' was quickly abbreviated to 'Jakarta' which for some unknown reason the Dutch spelled 'Jacatra'. When they in turn renamed the place Batavia, the Javanese, not to be outdone, corrupted this into 'Betawi', a name which still enjoys popular currency although Batavia itself has since reverted to Jakarta and will hopefully, after such prolonged uncertainty, remain so.

Pajajaran went the way of its ports when it was itself overrun by Muslim forces in 1578. Thereafter the Sundanese were all nominally Muslim and most, as at Banten, profoundly so. But somehow in the mountains south of Dekker's Lebak there survived a pocket of determined non-believers called the Badui. Possibly their inhospitable terrain accounted for their initial survival; but only a conspiracy of toleration can explain their still being there today, five centuries later. Technically not a tribe since they are ethnically identical with their Sundanese neighbours and speak an archaic form of the same language, the Badui yet cultivate an extreme form of tribalism in that they forbid not just marriage with outsiders but any contact with the outside world at all. To preserve this isolation Badui society is divided into two groups, the inner (or White) Badui and the outer (or Black) Badui with the latter operating a *cordon sanitaire* for the former. Thus the Black serve as go-betweens with the outside world, trading any surplus and turning away casual visitors.

Under such circumstances it is not surprising that Badui beliefs have been little studied. They are said to abominate money, transport, police, cosmetics, schools and just about anything else that their ancestors of five centuries ago managed to dispense with. Their clothes and domestic arrangements are of the simplest. And any outside authority like that of the Jakarta government they decline to acknowledge. Yet their own authority is very considerable indeed.

For what preserves the Badui is the widespread belief that as the descendants of some ancient Hindu priesthood, they retain esoteric and mystical contacts with the supernatural world which can be of untold value to those admitted to their counsels. They are, in short, the most sought-after of *dukun* ('magicians'); and the ancient Indic world which they represent has become the source of that spiritual communion so central to both Javanese and Sundanese life. Sukarno chose for his house in nearby Bogor a site adjacent to a Pajajaran inscription so as to appropriate its magical properties. West Java's crack military division is auspiciously named after Siliwangi, the last Pajajaran king; and Suharto, the president and icon of free-market Indonesia, still consults a Badui seer on matters of state. Perhaps even in the naming of 'Jayakarta' there lay method rather than ignorance in that a Sanskrit name conferred both magical and political legitimacy. This was certainly the thinking when in the 1960s Indonesia celebrated its acquisition of the west half of New Guinea by renaming the land Irian Jaya ('Irian Victory'); likewise its capital of Hollandia, after a brief appearance as 'Sukarnopura', became 'Jayapura', both the 'jaya' and the 'pura' being impeccable Sanskrit.

The Badui apart, Sunda's early submission to Islam isolated it from the sophisticated culture and the elaborate etiquette of central Java's ossified Hindu kingdoms. When, during the last century of Dutch rule, Javanese moved into Sunda in large numbers, the *orang gunung* quickly learnt to resent their treatment as backward hillsmen and under regional, religious and ideological banners, turned on both Javanese and Dutch.

The seeds of an incipient separatism eventually bore fruit during that crucial phase of the Independence Struggle between the 1945 declaration and its 1950 recognition. In 1947 the young Republic actually had to redirect its troops from the Dutch enemy to deal with a revolution in Banten. Against the rebels, who had achieved an improbable synthesis of monarchism, Marxism-Leninism and Islamic revivalism, was sent that great trouble-shooter Abdul Haris Nasution at the head of his Siliwangi Division.

A year later separatism resurfaced in a very different guise when a Sundanese state, known as Pasundan, was actually constituted. This was part of The Netherlands' last-ditch attempt to preserve something of their authority by fragmenting the country into a fully independent Indonesian republic in Central Java and several federal units, like Pasundan, in the outlying provinces. The ploy not only failed but fatally discredited the whole idea of a federal structure in the eyes of nationalists.

'But now I think things are changing,' said Amir, the editor of one of Indonesia's national dailies. 'This federalism, it is not dead. Local, cultural, religious and linguistic grievances are reviving in the freer political climate of the 1990s. And these grievances, mostly against Javanization, will have to be addressed.'

Amir lives in Editor Street between intersections with Sub-Editor Street and Columnist Street. The whole bungaloid colony, which ten years ago was on Jakarta's rural fringe but is now considered desirably central, was developed as an enclave for newspapermen. Academics, lawyers, bankers also have their enclaves; and the country's different ethnic and linguistic groups lay claim to whole suburbs. Like other exponentially growing cities, Jakarta is a metropolis of villages and townships.

When last we met, Amir's paper was banned. It had reported on a demonstration disapproved of by the authorities. The paper was contesting the ban. Meanwhile the spartan bungalow in Editor Street hosted impromptu gatherings of radical activists. Slung about with batik shoulder bags they made straight for the bathroom to slosh away the dust of undivulged journeys and then talked late into the night.

Five years later the paper was still contesting the ban; but Amir had moved on. The house had doubled in size; its scrawny yard had become a shady lawn and the driveway was jammed with hatchbacks and a station wagon. His wife was in Paris; nanny and the children were out; so was the cook. A surly servant in a *peci* served up the rice and prawns.

'He is from Lampung.'

'How can you tell?'

'Not easy. But you can tell sometimes. Name, for instance. Someone with a name ending in "o" and maybe beginning with "s" is Javanese. Sujono, Suharto. Just one word. But if it ends in "a" probably he is Sundanese. Muslim names, Habib, Abdullah, Tariq, Taufiq and so on mostly have father's name too and are typically Minang, also Malay and Paisir [coastal Java]. Batak names often end in "ing" or "on". Christian names have Johannes etc. Bagus, Made, etc. are Balinese. But it is not easy. Chinese often adopt Javanese names. People with Javanese names may adopt Christianity. Yani, for instance. You know Ahmed Yani, the general, he was a Christian but with Muslim name.'

'Must be a problem for the Javanese. I mean how many names can you have beginning with "s" and ending with "o"?'

'Oh, so many. You see name is chosen with the help of a *dukun* and it usually includes a Sanskrit root word. So "Suharto". The "su" means "more" and the "harto" means "wealth". So "more wealth", a good name, ya? He is married to Mrs Suharto who is officially "Madame Tien". Very powerful, so many business interests. We used to call her "Madame Tien per cent". Now she is "Madame Tien times Tien per cent".'

'And Sukarno?'

'Sukarno – "su", "more", "karno", "ears". More hearing, hearing more.'

'Big Ears?'

'Ya, Big Ears. Very good. And Nasution for Noddy. But Big Mouth would have been better.'

High-pitched giggles, so out of keeping with his editorial *gravitas,* broke the ice and recalled old times. I grabbed the moment to question whether his switch to a mainstream paper and a much improved salary had prejudiced his radical sympathies.

'It is a new paper. *Kompass* is owned by Catholics and the other one by Protestants. So this one is more Muslim. Already we have 130,000 circulation. Perhaps I have changed. I think, though, the climate has changed. You will agree that it is much easier now.'

He borrowed my *Indonesian Observer* and pointed out a report on the death of a union activist; a woman, she had been murdered by assassins hired by her employers. 'In most cases [it read] workers who demand higher wages are dealt with by security units (i.e. police) acting on behalf of the Company proprietors. They are subject to all kinds of intimidation and are fortunate if they are not accused of being Communists, the dreaded word, which could see them spend the rest of their life in prison.'

'Now this sort of report could not have been published five years ago, you will agree. And this woman, now she is a national hero.'

'But what about the Communists? Still the dreaded word?'

'Ya, still the dreaded word. It will take a long time. Thirty years is not enough. Maybe forty. But by then Communism may not exist. I think we made the right decision in 1965 and now history seems to tell us so. Only China is Communist. That's why the Chinese here so often adopt Javanese, even Muslim names. Many have become Christian and Buddhist, anything rather than be accused of Communism.'

The drive out to Lubang Buaya proved interminable. Car showrooms alternated with random blocks whose only obvious function was as climbing frames for the neon signs and as pedestals for the billboards and the satellite parabola. In an attempt to persuade the traffic that the elevated through-way was well worth the toll,

our choked boulevard repeatedly tangled with the Bogor Expressway in a knot of underpasses. The taxi driver was unimpressed. As
red light succeeded red light, scalding water dripped on to my feet
from somewhere behind the glove pocket. He said it was the air-
conditioning. But the air was conditioned only by the fiery
draughts from round the door and the bonfire of cloves that spluttered and sparked at the end of his *kretek*. It was like being dry-
roasted.

'Lubang Buaya, Cro-co-dile Hole ya? Crocodile Hole.'

He was just checking. I confirmed the destination and he
exhaled despairingly. There was no accounting for tourist tastes.
Here we were, fifteen kilometres out of town and within easy striking distance of Madame Tien's Mini Indonesia Theme Park,
surely the city's most popular attraction, and all I wanted to see
was the Crocodile Hole.

It turned out to be rather more than that. Skirting Halim air
base through what seemed to be the officers' lines we arrived at the
entrance to a handsome park. A ceremonial way swept through the
massive gates and on past gracious lawns to a parade ground
whence steps mounted to the Hole, actually a deep well just wide
enough to take a general. Beyond, on a concrete podium, stood
seven life-size statues of the officers whose mutilated bodies had
been dragged from the well by frogmen. All were in uniform, six
generals and a lieutenant, but instead of standing to attention they
were informally portrayed as if advancing on to the stage to perform at a forces concert.

I recognized only Yani, centre stage and eternally youthful, plus
the Lieutenant who had been on Nasution's staff. But here, for
once, the labelling was faultless; and, lest the illiterate flounder or
the imagination fail, blood-curdling screams and deafening gun-
shots came from an adjacent glass rotunda through whose panes,
darkened to simulate night, one could gawp at a blood-spattered
recreation of the massacre with full audio accompaniment. More
audio-visual awaited in the great hall of fame across the car park.
Up dim ramps, ferociously air-conditioned to detain the on-
looker, a dozen or more glass-fronted tableaux conducted one
through the set-pieces of recent Indonesian history. It was like the

Stations of the Cross as realized by a designer of aquaria.

Each scene included figures in uniform and depicted an occasion when the army had been called on to mobilize for the defence of the people. One, for instance, had Yani suppressing the 1958 PRRI and another showed Nasution's Siliwangi Division freeing the people of Banten from their eclectic revolutionaries in 1947. The climax was, of course, Lubang Buaya itself. Curiously for a national monument, the enemy was seldom the Dutch colonialists, seldom even misguided separatists but, nine times out of ten, the insidious PKI, the Communist Party of Indonesia.

Outside, families picnicked in the shade and coach parties filed back to the car park via the ice-cream kiosks. No doubt my young friends from the Sunda ferry had trooped through while I was in Banten. They would not have been allowed to miss Lubang Buaya. For Indonesians from Sabang to Merauke and from the Bay of Bengal to the Arafura Sea this gruesome spot is a 'must' as the most cogent and the most authoritative statement of today's political orthodoxy.

Its message is simple. As a young nation with a horrendous colonial handicap of social and economic retardment, Indonesia was peculiarly vulnerable to the divisive and ungodly heresies of Marxist-Leninist propaganda. Like Indo-China it was a domino waiting to fall, and it nearly did fall. Only ABRI, the Armed Forces of the Indonesian Republic, stood against this menace and at considerable cost repeatedly intervened to save the nation. Communist insurgency climaxed with the attempted coup of 1965 when Yani and the rest of the army's top brass were massacred on this very spot. But ABRI, promptly mobilized by General Suharto, proved equal to the challenge; the PKI was finally outlawed and economic progress ensued. To Suharto and ABRI the nation owes its growing prosperity, its apparent tranquillity and its very gradual progress towards freedom of expression. The highways and the in-bus karaoke, the school trips and the new hopsitals, the refurbished mosques, the pot noodles and the three television channels, all are thanks to the New Order and the man now paternalized as 'Pak Harto'.

'Pak' is short for 'Bapak' or grandfather, a respectful but familial title which Suharto prefers to that of General. It suits a man of few, mostly anodyne words, whose inscrutable dignity instils more awe than affection. It also contrasts effectively with the populist 'Bung' ('mate') used by Sukarno. 'Bung Karno' was a man of the people and his devastating appeal owed everything to an uncanny ability to identify with them. In fact he *was* the people. They were his *alter ego*, he once explained to a mass gathering in Merdeka Square, the city's Central Park; and in addressing them he felt himself to be engaged in 'a two-way conversation between Sukarno-the-man and Sukarno-the-people.'

His oratory has stood the test of time better than his rhetoric. Listening to an old BBC recording, and without understanding a word, it was still possible to be mesmerized by the sheer virtuosity of his performance. Staccato phrases burst from rambling asides; pitch and tone veered erratically; long pauses ended with a throw-away joke. The crowd was hypnotized, inhaling his words, holding its breath during the pauses, sighing, laughing, and cheering at the punch lines. In translation the speeches reveal a heady mix of exhortation, allusion, ideology and bewildering jargon. Some of his conceptualizing remains embedded in the national mythology. 'Pancasila', for instance, a Sanskrit word denoting the five principles of Indonesian nationhood, was enunciated at the time of independence and remains central to the constitution. So does the principle of *'gotong royong'* or 'mutual co-operation' to which the Pancasila is reducible. But demons like 'Nekolim' (Neo-Colonial Imperialism) and 'Oldefos' (Old Established Forces) no longer stalk the land. Gone too from the political vocabulary are their acronymic adversaries, 'Nefos' (New Emerging Forces), brave 'Manipol-USDEK' (the 1959 Political Manifesto that enshrined Guided Democracy) and big-hearted 'NASAKOM' (an invincible slogan for the parity of Nationalism, Religion and Communism).

From the same stable of incantatory jargon came 'Tavip' or the 'Year of Living Dangerously'. On every 17 August, the anniversary of the declaration of independence, Sukarno would commune with his people in Merdeka Square and declare a revolutionary theme for the year. 'Tavip', two auspicious syllables culled from an odd mix of *bahasa Indonesia* and Italian, denoted *'Tahun Vivere*

Pericoloso'. It later became the title of a novel and of the Peter Weir film starring Mel Gibson. But, like Krakatoa which a Hollywood title perversely located 'East of Java' rather than of Sumatra, the 'Year of Living Dangerously' was really 1964 and referred to the 'Konfrontasi' with Malaysia; the 'Konfrontasi' with Communism came a year later in 'Takari', the singularly mis-named 'Year of Self-Reliance and of Standing on One's Own Feet.'

'Standing on One's Own Feet' meant implementing an eight-year development plan which owed more to numerology than conventional economics. Thus its chief merit lay in its being divided into 17 parts, printed in eight volumes, and containing 1,945 clauses, a conjunction of digits which, faithfully reproducing the date of independence (17/8/1945), guaranteed success. Yet, strange to tell, hyper-inflation persisted and so did the food shortages. Bung Karno was no economist and, infinitely worse in the eyes of his adoring public, he was reliably rumoured to be dying of kidney trouble. Only his sexual prowess and his genius for relentless politicization remained unimpaired.

On the night of 30 September 1965, true to form, he addressed a meeting and then, collecting Dewi (a Japanese escort girl who was the third of his five wives) from the Hotel Indonesia's nightclub, he retired to her house and bed. Whether he was blissfully unaware of what ensued or whether his evening had been contrived to make him appear so, is one of the many unanswered questions. Another, no less relevant, is whether his successor, Suharto, knew what was happening. Thirty years on, the trail has not so much gone cold as been locked in the freezer. Few in a position to answer such questions are still alive and few of them will speak out.

But now, with Suharto in his seventies, Indonesia faces only the second presidential succession in its history. The first, as well as those six generals, cost more than a quarter of a million lives. It would be helpful to have a better understanding of how it was managed and why it went so wrong.

For a man supposedly recording his version of events for the first time, General Nasution showed little reticence and an excellent recall. I was interviewing him at his home in Menteng, the colonial heart of Jakarta and the scene of much activity on that last night of September 1965. The interview, part of a BBC programme, dragged on. Already we were on to the second spool of tape and Nasution was still sketching in the background.

To summarize, then, it appeared that in the early 1960s Sukarno had fallen out with the UN and increasingly relied on a Jakarta–Peking axis which meant promoting domestic support for the 'KOM' in 'NASAKOM'. With five million members, the PKI was already the largest Communist party outside Russia and China and, having just celebrated its 45th anniversary, it was also one of the oldest. At last it looked as if its hour had come. But as in 1958 (PRRI), Nasution and the army were alarmed; and now all the more so since Sukarno appeared ready to endorse Communist demands for a 'fifth force'. Consisting of paramilitary cadres for whom the Chinese were eager to supply arms, this force would be a direct threat to the army's authority and duly provoked rumours of a pre-emptive military coup.

'Our situation was very complex, huh? They say Yani and I were planning a military coup for Armed Forces Day on 5 October. I know very well it is not true. I was against bringing so many troops to Jakarta and I told Sukarno not to bring them.'

Nasution's English, though good, was thick with the accents of one who had first learnt Dutch. It was also heavy with the measured tones of a last will and testament. Gout-ridden,well into his seventies, and long since side-lined, the general spoke like one who had nothing to lose. As we paused for coffee and biscuits he grumbled about the garden. Age had reduced his impressive Batak physique to a stoop and two walking sticks; his features had shrunk, like those of a wizened Chinese, to minor interruptions in a pattern of wrinkles.

'So, 30 September I went to bed, but four o'clock in the morning – God help me uh? – that I was awake because there was a mosquito in the room; and I was busy hunting the mosquito; and many trucks we heard coming then. Then my wife heard the front door being forced open. I said to her: "I will go out, talk to them;

they are soldiers, uh? I understand soldiers." But my wife said: "Don't do it. Maybe they murder you." You see, she had had a dream. I opened the bedroom door. Already first man is there. I saw him hit the trigger, ya? The trigger. I fell down immediately, automatically. They have the order maybe to take me alive or dead. My wife was closing the door with her body. They were shooting through the door, all around her. But only some hairs have been cut by the bullets.'

He chuckled, though whether at the incompetence of his assassins or the courage of his wife I could not tell. His daughter, who beamed at us from a school photo on the table, was not so lucky. She died later from wounds received in the attack; and his ADC was shot outside the house. In the dark his assailants grabbed a Lieutenant whom they mistook for Nasution while he himself escaped over the garden wall into what was then the Iraqi Consulate. There he hid in a water butt till morning. The mosquitos were excruciating and he had sprained his ankle.

'Yani also. He went to bed and then four o'clock, tock, tock, tock on the bedroom door. He came out and standing in the door is the presidential guard. They say: "The President needs you immediately in the palace. Very serious situation." Yani: "OK, but I must change my pyjama for uniform." "Not necessary. You go with us." And he is turning to go inside when against his back automatic fire. He fell there and dead already.'

Of the five other generals on the hit list, two more were killed resisting capture; the other three were taken, with the corpses of their comrades, to Halim airbase. There they were tortured and killed, all the bodies being then hidden in the Crocodile Hole. Jakarta woke to 1 October with troops in unfamiliar places and an unscheduled programme on the radio announcing the glad tidings of a military coup forestalled. The announcement came from something called 'The 30th September Movement' and was followed by the suspension of all existing ranks and the creation of a Revolutionary Council.

In referring to this 'movement' Nasution consistently used the acronym 'GESTAPU'. It derives from *GErakan [Movement] September TigAPUlu [Thirty]* and, with its connotations of Nazi

Germany's military police, is very much part of the new ortho-doxy. It may also serve as a good example of Javanese allusion. A movement susceptible to such pejorative associations must be evil incarnate and could only be doomed to failure.

So it proved. Although the plotters had secured the person of Sukarno, they had let Nasution escape and, in one of many scarcely credible oversights, had made no attempt to neutralize the capital's Strategic Army Reserve or to eliminate its commander. This was General Suharto. Proceeding without let or hindrance to his office next to the captured radio station, Suharto found the army communications network intact and quietly proceeded to mobilize against the GESTAPU men at Halim. Nasution joined him and it was all over within twelve hours. Sukarno was detached from the plotters and packed off to his country palace at Bogor. Although still technically President, his time was up. Fatally side-lined by events, he was now under close military scrutiny. The ring-leaders were dispersed and later either captured or killed. And the bodies of the murdered generals were tracked down to Lubang Buaya and hauled from the well. Designed to forestall an imaginary military take-over, GESTAPU had merely precipitated the real thing.

My questions for Nasution included why Suharto had not been on the hit list and why he, Nasution, had not assumed control instead of the more junior Suharto. The first he ducked; I would have to ask whoever drew up the list. He could have claimed, as does Suharto himself, that the latter's name was indeed on the list but that he evaded capture. Yet there is no corroboration of this and it begs the question of how Suharto managed to reach his office unmolested in the morning. Alternatively he could have claimed, as many do, that Suharto was too junior to merit inclu-sion on the list. But were this the case, why did he not defer to Nasution as soon as it was known that the latter had survived?

'Yani was Army Chief of Staff. He had taken over from me, uh? I was passed over. When Yani died, Suharto automatically took his place. That was the army protocol.'

'I thought you were Chief of Staff.'

'I was the Armed Forces Chief of Staff but this was army affair.

I gave Suharto my support but this was his responsibility you see, and he was contacting all these army groups.'

I was none the wiser. Shattered by the night's events and deeply worried by his daughter's worsening condition, perhaps Nasution was simply too unprepared and too distracted to take over command. Suharto, on the other hand, acted with the decision and despatch of one who knew exactly what was happening and had laid his plans accordingly. It would, though, be irresponsible as well as seditious even to hint at such precognition. Better to credit him with brilliant improvisation plus a few fortuitous interventions that those favoured of the gods may expect in critical times.

One such came next day when, in a scarcely credible bit of self incrimination, the PKI's newspaper hailed the already disgraced plotters as saviours of the nation. It was known that some Jakarta cadres had been involved in the affair and that the party boss had been among the ring leaders at Halim. But so had a lot of disgruntled officers of no known party affiliation. Now, with the PKI alone acknowledging support for GESTAPU, it could be portrayed as a straight Communist *putsch*. Presented with a chance to discredit and outlaw its ancient foe, the army under Suharto's acting command did not hesitate.

Out at Lubang Buaya it began with an elaborate piece of carefully orchestrated theatre. Like rabbits from the hat, the bodies of the murdered generals were conjured from the murky depths of the well for the edification of the world's press. A medical panel testified to their sufferings; photographs were taken and quickly circulated throughout the country; there were speeches and scenes of mass mourning; then seven ceremonial corteges set off for the deceased's homelands. Yani, as the most senior figure, became a national martyr. After him was renamed the principal street in towns throughout the nation and in villages that had never before had a street name. Getting the message, Jakarta's political parties began demanding the suppression of the PKI; their young hotheads stormed and burnt the party's offices. The army, reluctantly of course, bowed to popular pressure and the PKI was banned.

But Communism's traditional strength lay not in the cities but in the rice bowls of Central and Eastern Java. Thither army units were promptly despatched. They rumbled out of Jakarta in long convoys, cheered on by crowds baying for Marxist blood.

'In some areas,' said Amir, 'the people anticipated them. PKI members and sympathisers were attacked and killed mostly by Muslim groups. Other places it was the army that went hunting. Many who died were not Communists at all. People just took the opportunity to settle old scores. Peasants with inadequate land killed peasants with no land. Brothers killed brothers. Some places the people just ran *amok*, other places lists were drawn up and death squads formed.'

The image that crops up in so much testimony is of rivers clogged with bodies. Only the lucky had been shot; most had been butchered like the Lubang Buaya victims; the farmer's *parang* (axe) and the ceremonial *kris* (dagger) shared the honours. Some talk of a natural calamity like Krakatau; others of a cultural paroxysm, an ideological cleansing, a simple holocaust. No one knows how many died; no one dared find out. The usual figure of 200,000-500,000 was deduced later from regional samples conducted along the lines of a product survey. 'On a scale of one to a thousand how would you rate GESTAPU suppression in your village?' The madness spread to Medan and Sumatra and to Makassar and Sulawesi. In Bali, still retaining its 1930s tag as an earthly paradise, the death toll may have reached 100,000; to the usual skirmishes in the rice fields were added ritualized massacres and the Balinese speciality of mass suicides.

The killing peaked during the first months of 1966 and rumbled on until mid-year. Sukarno could possibly have recovered some of his authority with the armed forces had he offered to sanction their actions. But though his faults were many, inhumanity was not among them. For thirty years he had striven to create national unity and now it was in tatters. His pleas for clemency, order, restraint went unheeded. They merely fuelled speculation about his ambiguous role in the GESTAPU plot and his erstwhile accommodation of the PKI. He lingered on merely as a figurehead president, and died in comparative obscurity in 1970. All real power was now with the army.

Out of it grew Suharto's 'New Order'; and because the elimination of the PKI represented a rare defeat for Asian Communism while the New Order meant a pro-Western realignment of Southeast Asia's largest political economy, liberal Western consciences were not unduly troubled. In fact there is good evidence that Suharto enjoyed speedy US encouragement and that a timely consignment of small arms from the CIA boosted military firepower during its suppression of the PKI. Unsurprisingly, therefore, the greatest calamity in Indonesia's history and one of the largest peace-time massacres on record received only modest news coverage, most of it retrospective. Subsequent massacres, especially in East Timor, have received more sensational publicity. The difference is not merely one of scale but of priorities. If many Indonesians seem indifferent to the human rights abuses currently logged against their rulers, it could be something to do with still raw memories of the killing field next door and of the precarious nature of any national consensus in such an untidy, experimental and volatile construction as the Indonesian Republic.

9. *Every little breeze*

Leaving Jakarta in style was a way of making up for the austerities of the ecumenical guest house. After a surreptitious counting of rupiah in the station forecourt, I threw caution to the winds, swept past the queues for *Ekonomi* and *Bisnis* and booked *Eksekutif* class on the Bandung Express.

Then I repaired to the bar of the Hotel Indonesia, hallowed ground for Sukarnoists. Dewi, the good-time-girl from Ginza who became one of the President's wives, might have perched on this very bar stool. Even if she hadn't, she was still hot news. For, never slow to proscribe an undesirable publication, the government had that morning banned the import and sale of a book of black and white photography which featured the young Dewi adopting a variety of kimono-less poses. These, though familiar enough to Japanese *eksekutifs*, were thought to be novel to Indonesians and possibly shocking to those used to a Madame President, like 'Mrs Tien Per Cent', of less obvious athleticism and more generous dimensions.

I wondered where Dewi was now. Last reports had her in trouble with the Colorado police over some social fracas in Aspen. I wondered too about the mysterious 'Miss Manx', the latter-day Mata Hari. Amir, my newspaper friend, had added greatly to her mystery by claiming that she was also a Balinese princess, by name K'tut Tantri, and probably also 'Surabaya Sue', a 1940s radio announcer for the Republic with a slight Glaswegian accent.

He also said that she had resurfaced here in the Hotel Indonesia in the 1980s. She stayed some weeks, ran up a substantial bill, and then invited the state to pay it. As a heroine of the independence struggle and a close colleague of Sukarno and the other founding fathers, Indonesia owed it to her. In fact, according to the barman, she had only returned under the public-spirited impression that her life-story would make an edifying film in which she might even be persuaded to star. If so, she had badly misread the spirit of the New Order. 'But someone, maybe government, paid her account.' Where was she now? He didn't know. 'Maybe Australia, maybe America, maybe dead.' And was she really the same person as 'Surabaya Sue'? 'Maybe same. You ask in Surabaya, I think is best.' I made a note to do just that.

Though substantially redeveloped, the hotel still vaunts its tacky Sixties glitz. A poster in a clip-frame showed a fine expanse of beach and palm trees. 'Indonesia was created when God smiled,' said the caption. 'Hotel Indonesia was created when God got given Lego,' retorted a local wag. It was the first high-rise structure in Jakarta and symbolized Sukarno's international ambitions for his young nation. Dalton calls it 'the grandest structure put up by the Indonesians since Borobudur 1,000 years earlier.' Like the Javanese princes of old, Sukarno saw himself as an embodiment of the people, and his court and capital as an embodiment of the state. After experimenting with representative democracy in the 1950s, his personal rule, euphemistically known as 'Guided Democracy', had rested on the idea 'that the welfare of the country proceeds from the excellence of its capital, the excellence of its capital proceeds from the brilliance of its élite, and the brilliance of its élite proceeds from the spirituality of its ruler' (Clifford Geertz). The Hotel Indonesia, like Borobudur, was designed to demonstrate the legitimacy and mirror the perfection of a Javanese autocrat.

It has since been hopelessly upstaged by the new order of stainless steel tubes, cubes of mirror-cladding and galleries of glass that have turned the rest of Jalan Thamrin into the feisty futurama beloved of Pak Harto's regime. Further afield, Sukarno's monuments yet litter the roundabouts with social-realism; but the clenched fists and taut sinews of proletarian struggle as conceived by the Marxist school of metal-workers are now corroding in the exhaust from a million Japanese saloons. Only MONAS, short for the *Monumen Nasional,* still commands attention. Said to be higher than the Eiffel Tower and to symbolize not Sukarno's spirituality but his sexuality, this erection soars from the centre of Merdeka Square in a single white column topped by a confectioner's whorl of gold which is supposed to resemble a flame.

In Dutch days, as Koningsplein (King's Park), the square served as a parade ground. Now as Medan Merdeka (Freedom Park or Square) it has become the national *alun-alun,* the traditional forecourt and ceremonial amphitheatre of a Javanese court. As such it is fronted by palaces and other unremarkable buildings of state which peek through the trees from its kilometre-long fringes. Apart from MONAS, the only substantial building allowed within this hallowed space, as opposed to around it, is Gambir Station.

Java must be proud of its trains, I thought. The platforms were elevated above the station and, as the Bandung Express exited the square at tree-top level, we were treated to a long tall farewell from the enigmatic MONAS. Thereafter it was down to street-level as the train negotiated the city's sprawling southern suburbs. Here the tracks seemed to have been laid as an afterthought. We were continually trundling down narrow alleys, obliging cyclists to flatten themselves against walls or dart into someone's garden. Chickens scattered from under the wheels; mangy dogs limped aside to sit within inches of annihilation while they attended to flea-bites. The sharp corners necessitated a frequent blaring of the horn which resonated down the rails like the long-suffering moos of a dairy herd on its way to the milking parlour. My fellow *eksekutifs* adjusted their pillows, ordered beer and prawn crackers from the car attendants, and settled back to watch Indiana Jones on the in-train video. I remained glued to the window.

It could have been the air-conditioned *eksekutif* luxury, or perhaps it was just the intimacy, engendered by the unusually low suspension, of being eyeball to eyeball with the pedestrians outside. Whatever, as we crawled through other people's backyards and brushed past clapboard shanties, the prickling of a normally comatose conscience made itself felt. The district we were negotiating housed, after its fashion, what economists call 'the informal sector'. People washed windscreens, sold matches, begged, portered, peddled *becak*, pushed barrows, and battered laundry. They all had work and so they all contributed to the Indonesian economy. But the work was either underpaid or unpaid. 'A safe estimate is that at least 60 per cent of our workforce is presently unemployed or underemployed,' said a leader in the *Jakarta Post*. But the Minister for Manpower was to be congratulated. Never before had a government spokesman conceded more than 3 per cent unemployed.

Ecologists, normally among the country's fiercest critics, could also take heart. In this part of town recycling had been finessed to include not just bottles and paper but cans, plastics, timber, tin foil, clothing, recoverable foodstuffs, fasteners and nails, electrical parts, cigarette butts and certain kinds of leaves. Whole rubbish tips were being meticulously searched and sorted, creating yet more informal sector jobs. And whole lanes had been requisitioned for the flattening of tin cans and the straightening of bent nails.

While the carriage halted hard by a lean-to kennel that apparently housed a family, I watched an old man with a home-made bow saw and a broken bit of plank. His intention was to convert the wood into a useful rectangle of board by removing the jagged bit. But either the saw was very blunt or the wood very hard. For he was stripped to just a soiled sarong and, as he strained to little effect, his backbone arched prominently in cruel mimicry of the bow of his saw. And when he straightened, a narrow consumptive chest revealed ribs as proud and blunt as the saw's teeth. Here was a sick old man with the physique of a home-made saw expending his last energies on reclaiming a fairly useless bit of wood. From the international agencies that so readily condemn countries like Indonesia for cutting down their rainforests and squandering other precious resources, such heroic endeavours were, I felt, deserving of recognition.

Further on, where the industrial sector took over from the informal, the rainforest's rape victims were queueing for attention. Too big for a truck, each section of trunk was arriving on several sets of wheels, hauled by what was more a locomotive than a lorry. It went in at the back of a tin-roofed hangar and came out the sides as mountains of sawdust and out the front as wardrobes and bed-heads. They were lined up along the road for several miles. Then came the brick kilns. Beneath what must be some of the largest expanses of tiled roof in the world, finished bricks and tiles were stacked over several acres. Hard by, deep pits had been dug into the biscuity alluvium to provide the raw material. All vegetation to a considerable distance was coated with dust and so were the tur-banned figures who were unbuilding the latest firing. A hooter sounded and they downed bricks to troop off to their terracotta hutments. Between the monochrome worlds of sawdust and brick dust it was hard to distinguish what was so reprehensible about the former and so laudable about the latter.

Freeing itself at last from the metropolis's grimy tentacles, the train picked up speed over a dead level expanse of *sawah* (paddy fields). We were heading east across the grain of Java's hydro-graphy. From the distant mountains rivers swollen with the rain and silt of the Preanger highlands swirled round the piers of end-less bridges. Banana trees, up to their armpits in the flood, waved their fronds in panic; slender papaya trunks bent with the flow, their umbrellas of foliage tilting precariously. Bogor is said to have the world record with an average of 322 thunderstorms a year but Bandung, somewhat further east, must run it a close second. The daily deluge keeps the rivers full and the coastal plans flooded, making Krawang one of the most productive rice growing regions in the island.

Waking to this watery panorama after a catnap, I thought I was in an aeroplane. There was cloud above and cloud below. It took a chevron of ducks to set me right. They were passing just beneath us, but with wings folded; and every so often they up-ended in uni-son. Then came a conical straw hat whose wearer waded a straight line across the cumulus. Other lines connected with it in distant right angles to chequer the whole expanse like the grid on a map. Within some of these rectangles the wisps of freshly planted rice seedlings sprouted green from the cloud cover.

When next I woke the train seemed to have got a second wind. Charles Bronson, Indonesia's favourite actor, had replaced Harrison Ford; fried rice was being served on paper plates; and, as teak plantations drifted past the window, the carriage took on a slight tilt. We were not only cornering but climbing. Conversation resumed among my fellow *eksekutifs*. The car attendant insisted that I at least have a beer and the ticket collector proudly indicated that Indonesian Railways were so confident of running on time that the hour of arrival, as well as of departure, was printed on the ticket. We were, of course, bang on schedule.

Every foot of altitude not only reanimated the carriage but appeared to breathe new life into the engine. As we cornered sharply on bridges of lacy Meccano I could see the diesel heroically hauling the blue and orange livery of *Ekonomi* into the next tunnel. We were hugging a hillside, brushing precipitous rock faces to sail across bottomless gorges with a hollow rattle and then whoosh back into the forest. Linesmen clustered round a tin kettle; we sounded a short boom of greeting. The tiny terraced fields were gay with women in tightly buttoned blouses of hibiscus red and flaming orange. Instead of the conical straw hats they wore scarves of many hues; and the stations were abloom with flowers. On their neatly tiled platforms there paced in white linen uniform the inevitable 'Train Operator'. His stiff gendarme's hat was made of crimson velvet with its peak covered in gold braid.

Although found only in Java and, like most things Javanese, not boisterously promoted, Indonesian railways were proving a secret well worth discovering. Unencumbered by the railway cultures of China or India, Java's trains go quietly and politely about their *bisnis* of trundling people round the island in moderate comfort. Sumatran bus companies could learn something.

Altitude being the most significant statistic about any equatorial destination, I had established that Bandung was 2,500ft above sea level. Knocking off 10 degrees of humidity and 5 of temperature for every thousand feet, that made it pedestrian possible. I walked to a likely *losmen* and then strode into town.

West Java's capital proved neither old nor typically Indonesian. Dutch planners laid it out in the 1920s as one of the East's first 'new towns'. Now second only to Jakarta and Surabaya in population, it aspires to still greater modernity and patronage as the chosen seed-bed for Suharto's high tech revolution. Here is ITB (the Bandung Institute of Technology), the country's élite place of higher education; and it is no coincidence that here too are based both of the prestige projects with which Indonesia is celebrating its first 50 years of independence. Forty years ago it was also in Bandung that Sukarno launched the country's international credentials in one of the great political jamborees of the twentieth century. There was a lot to see. I wondered only at how few visitors there were to see it. Not exotic enough presumably. God had been paying the bills when Bandung was created.

Hemmed in by hills and richly endowed as to soil and climate, Bandung's privileged status arose from financial necessity. Through this valley in 1810 Marshall Willem Daendels drove his *Grote Postweg*, the Grand Trunk Road of Java. As the new broom sent by Napoleon's puppet Dutch republic to dust the cobwebs of neglect from its tarnished Eastern prize, 'The Thundering Marshall' assailed Java with a flurry of reforms. Some anticipated those of Raffles; nearly all alienated the Javanese and so disposed them to acquiesce in the imminent British invasion. For the *Grote Postweg* Raffles had reason to be especially grateful. The lives lost in its construction still rankled; and it was thanks to what even Douwes Dekker would acknowledge as 'a magnificent piece of work' that the British so quickly over-ran the island. It was also thanks to the *postweg* that the Preanger came to figure so prominently in the colonial economy.

'Preanger' and 'Priangan' are corruptions of *Parahyangan*, which means 'the Home of the Gods'. It refers to the mountains and upland valleys of West Java, or Sunda, which extend from Bandung west to Bogor and beyond to Douwes Dekker's Lebak district. Dekker's *Max Havelaar*, with its long and discouraging subtitle about coffee auctions, provides the clue to its importance. Long before Medan hosted Indonesia's greatest plantation boom, the Preanger had undergone a similar transformation. It was to serve its immensely profitable coffee plantations that Daendels chose this challenging alignment for his *postweg* and for the same reason Raffles exempted the Preanger from his land reforms. Coffee was just too important. It was the first crop in Java to be produced under the forced cultivation system (whereby land rent was paid in produce bought exclusively by the government at its own valuation); and it was the last crop to be released from this iniquitous system. During the 18th century, along with sugar, coffee had gradually replaced spices as the East Indies' most valuable export and throughout the 19th century it maintained this position. Dutch empire depended on coffee for longer than any other crop; most of it was grown in Java and most of that in the Preanger.

Running dead straight from east to west, a section of the old *postweg* became the main street of the 1920s new town. Fashionable shops and cafes catered for the cosmopolitan clientele of planters and exiles which upland coffee invariably attracts. And allied to the famed charms of Sundanese womanhood, these features won Bandung that tired sobriquet of 'Paris of the East'. Now the new town is the old town, the *postweg* has here become Jalan Asia–Afrika, and even pie-eyed Dutchmen would disclaim any similarities with Paris.

Pre-War P&O seemed more the decorative order of the day. Moored to the *postweg* and connected to it with a drive-in ramp, the decks of the Savoy Homann Hotel rose in diminishing tiers to a brownstone funnel of striking profile but uncertain purpose. Since Bandung is as far from the sea as anywhere in Java, perhaps it was designed to console its guests with the illusion of being homeward bound. Over the railings of its wrap-around balconies baggy-suited Bogarts and lean tippeted ladies in cloche hats should have been waving their protracted farewells. 'Every little breeze seems to whisper Louise' wafted through reception. But it came from the Muzak system; in the ballroom, its ceiling so encrusted with a cut glass firmament of pale blue, sea-green and beige that it looked as if it might melt, the smartly dressed marketing men of Garuda Indonesia, the national airline, were holding a sales conference.

I padded on down corridors of apple-green carpeting bordered with a bold linear design. A dado accompanied me; fan-shaped wall-lights, angular with chrome and glass, glowed wanly. On to an open verandah fronting an ornamental fish pond, well-cushioned wicker sofas strayed from a shady recess where white-aproned barmen juggled cocktails before a display of polished glasses and exotic liqueurs. Buffed brass and mahogany panelling preserved the nautical feel; but the long bar, unquestionably Bandung's finest, confounded the decorator's linear art to loop informally, its foot-rest coiling like a snake among the potted palms.

To the breeze that whispered Louise a long painted fingernail waved above a bent head of peroxide hair and bare freckled shoulders. Otherwise the bar was deserted. But in former times a whole divisional mess could here drink together. I imagined the skeletal Colonel van der Post toying with pipe and tomato juice in bemused solitude while, in another of the bar's ample bays, raucous subalterns plied the General's ADC, a Captain Dirk Niven van der Bogaerde, with dry martinis and duty-free Players. It was October '45. The war was over and the prison camp gates were open. But Java was in turmoil.

Nationalist youths and irregulars, many of whom had no time for the constitutional niceties that preoccupied Sukarno's self-declared government, were blowing up roads, bridges and any other installations that might assist an eventual reimposition of Dutch rule. Into this category, too, came both the Chinese community, handy scapegoats whenever Indonesian nationalism faces a set-back, and the British officers and their mostly Indian troops who were supposed to be evacuating the POWs and policing the post-war settlement. The British, awarded the doubtful honour of reclaiming the whole archipelago after the Japanese surrender, held what was still called Batavia and were endeavouring to occupy Surabaya. Bandung could also be reached but only in a heavily armed convoy that was invariably ambushed as it crawled up into the Preanger. In just such an attack the dapper young ADC had got his first taste of action.

Whether thankful, like van der Post, for having survived the prison camps or merely, like van der Bogaerde, for having survived the convoy, the British felt entitled to make the most of Bandung's creature comforts. I have no evidence that these two British officers with their every Dutch names every actually met, let alone drank at the same bar. But both were about Bandung at the same time. Dirk Niven van der Bogaerde (or to give him the stage name which he now used in the army, plain Dirk Bogarde) certainly patronized the Savoy Hotel. And it seems highly probable that his Bandung billet was the same as that in which van der Post's Java war both began and ended.

Naturally I wanted to find this historic site. Described as an old colonial villa, it was also where Wavell had briefly set up his high command in 1942 before the catastrophic battles of the Java Sea and Sunda Strait necessitated evacuation. To it van der Post was summoned to receive his orders for that short-lived guerilla resistance in the Serang district and to it, forty long and ghastly months later, he had returned to take the official surrender of his Japanese captors. A month later the first British convoy arrived from Batavia and General Hawthorn took up residence. Bogarde, his ADC, moved into a sort of pavilion in the grounds which was big enough to accommodate his growing entourage of Gurkha batman, 'ravishing' Eurasian mistress and pet panther. There was also a swimming pool; and it was on a hill. Surely this was enough to be getting on with.

The Savoy's manager looked doubtful. Bandung had grown beyond all recognition in the last 50 years. He suggested the Tourist Office and then scuttled back to reception. To the barman a British presence in the city was, frankly, implausible; even the war was news; and Bogarde, surely, was a brand of gin. Just for a minute, though, I thought I detected a flutter of interest from the only other drinker. She remained slumped over the bar, peroxide mane, mauled rather than brushed, spilling on to the mahogany. But between the bare shoulder-blades it seemed that a wasted muscle faintly twitched. And the raised finger had missed a beat. Could it be that one of those Dutch names had rung a bell? Or was she just passing through some alcoholic pain barrier?

As well as memoirs, both Bogarde and van der Post wrote autobiographical novels based on their Indonesian experience. With matinée eyebrows cranked to the near vertical, Bogarde quizzes the inanities of service life. The 'indolent, easy-going Indonesians' feature only as vindictive 'extremists'. Likewise the Dutch, all ex-POWs and mostly women and children, are stereotyped. His Eurasian interpreter, 'long legs, long hair, long neck – a sort of Modigliani creature', elegantly epitomizes exotic Java, but their affair is dogged by the chasm of race and the transience of a military posting. Bogarde is best on the social stresses of the officers' mess. He takes on the divisional newspaper, directs a variety show and gets his first broadcasting assignment as an English newsreader on Radio Batavia. No doubt his impeccable delivery was calculated to refute the insidious propaganda coming from the lady announcer with the Glaswegian accent on Radio Surabaya. For Bogarde, Bandung and Batavia represented a bizarre chapter in a life of bizarre chapters.

It was different for van der Post. Most of his forty months in prison camps had been spent in and around Bandung. The Preanger was the world over the wall for which all prisoners hankered. Day after day he had woken to the distant profile of Tangkuban Prahu, Bandung's tutelary volcano. The name means the 'Upturned Ship' and for the Dutch internees, remembering the good times aboard the Savoy Hotel but now reduced to begging favours from their erstwhile servants, it had seemed an appropriate comment on the state of society. But for van der Post, an incorrigible romantic, 'there was no scene of greater beauty on earth' than the flat-topped volcano. It epitomized Java's soft and lush contours where 'everything still had upon it a kind of sheen, like that on a new-born calf'. The island itself was as somewhere just created. Through its thin skin the seismic and tectonic forces that formed it could still be felt. Even the rumblings of nationalism and the rage of *amok* came from the umbilical cord which still tied the people to their seething native soil.

The irony of being a prisoner in such a paradise was exceeded only by that of a starvation diet amid such plenty. While the Javanese farmers harvested their five crops of rice every two years, prison rations were pared to three ounces of rice a day – about half a small cupful. At first van der Post and other inspirational figures like the Australian doctor, Weary Dunlop, had organized the camps into model communities with a full curriculum of classes and chores to fill every waking moment. But as the months wore on and the rations dwindled, the fit were siphoned off to labour and die on projects like the Burma–Siam railway while those who remained gave up their Spanish lessons and their elementary biology to wrestle with beri-beri, dysentery and black dog.

In a land without north or south or seasons, where the sun rose through the zenith without variation and where the trees stayed in leaf all year, time itself seemed to stand still. Marooned in their stockade of disease and despair, men came to hate the 'Upturned Boat' and to curse this merciless island. Perhaps they also cursed van der Post. To him every new trial seems to have been but another chance to affirm the 'triumph of the spirit'. He could not hate the Japanese for they 'never saw us as human beings but as provocative symbols of a detested past'. Indeed they had been so humiliated by the Western powers that he now professed to be amazed at their moderation. But the Dutch he could despise. They seemed to have learnt nothing from the war. It should have been a catharsis from which man could emerge with shared human values and goodwill to all. But the Dutch could not even bring themselves to acknowledge the injustice of their rule and the inevitability of Indonesian independence.

To this wholesale condemnation he made one exception; and it was of her that I was reminded in the bar of the Savoy Hotel. In *The Seed and the Sower* Laurens van der Post, thinly disguised as 'Lawrence', tells of how he was sustained through his captivity by an encounter with a Dutch girl on the eve of the Japanese invasion. They met by chance in a deserted hotel – possibly the Savoy – and shared their last night of freedom. No prurient details of the occasion are given. Van der Post is the perfect officer and gentleman and his companion a paragon of feminine grace and virtue. She takes his hand, he begs forgiveness 'for what men have taken so blindly and wilfully from women all the one thousand and one years now vanishing so swiftly behind them.' Their love-making is simply 'a pact of faith with life' at a moment when reason and events were conspiring to proclaim 'the end of life as we have known it'. Then comes a vivid description of Java's seething natural history and of its elemental instability. Thunder and lightning, earthquake and volcano, beating wings, upthrusting plants, tiny voices and the whole vocabulary of creation are summoned as testimony. Both were 'so stirred by their nearness to each other and to all other living, singing, flashing, shining creatures that they made love close to tears'.

The whole incident may, of course, have been invented. Perhaps the girl never existed. Perhaps van der Post never went near the Savoy Hotel. And perhaps the raddled mannequin now slumped across the bar was not a relic of Dutch rule but a package tourist who had opted out of the day's programme. After the war van der Post made no attempt to track down his companion. The symbolism of their act of life-affirmaton amid the riot of Javanese creation could no more be repeated than could the special circumstances of war which made it such a vital gesture of defiance. For less worthy reasons I made no attempt to interrogate my drinking companion. She was too far gone; and it was all too long ago. I never even saw her face. But as I left, the raised and painted finger nail still waggled in time to the music. Every little breeze, even the birds in the trees, seemed to whisper Louise.

Following his release van der Post acted as an adviser on Indonesian affairs to Mountbatten and to the British Minister in Jakarta. He got to know and admire Sukarno, Hatta and the other independence leaders. And he argued passionately and successfully against the British becoming involved in the restoration of Dutch rule. Though with a bloodied nose in Surabaya, the British forces, including Captain Bogarde, had all withdrawn by the end of 1946. But he failed to reconcile the Dutch to the inevitable loss of their colonial empire and he failed to convince the Indonesians that outright independence might be premature.

To argue this point with Sukarno he claims to have enlisted the help of Jawaharlal Nehru, then poised to become independent India's first premier. In a letter to Sukarno, Nehru is supposed to have confessed that even with 'a non-political and incorruptible civil service, a non-political and incorruptible judiciary, and a non-political and incorruptible army' he was worried whether the British were not leaving India too soon. Sukarno, with none of these priceless assets, 'had therefore better pipe down'.

Sukarno, of course, did no such thing. Indonesia lacked these essential building blocks of nationhood like it lacked territorial cohesion, ethnic integrity, economic stability and ideological unanimity. The odds against its succeeding as a nation could not have been stacked higher. Yet the declaration of independence read out by Sukarno and Hatta on 17 August 1945 made it the first of the colonial territories to claim full independence and its international recognition on 1 January 1950 made it among the first to achieve full sovereignty. Five years later this most premature of nations presumed to speak out for all colonized peoples when it emerged as the champion of the Third World. Far from piping down, Sukarno had talked his way on to the world stage.

From the Savoy Hotel to Gedung Merdeka (Freedom Building) is only a hundred yards along the broad pavements of Jalan Asia–Afrika. In a pedestrian-friendly city this is the 'Bandung Walk' *par excellence*. To the delight of the world's press, every morning in late April 1955 the galaxy of independence leaders who had gathered for the Afro-Asian Conference sauntered down Jalan Asia–Afrika like summer school students on their way to class. The walk was symbolic. Instead of arriving at the conference hall in bullet-proof limousines flanked by police and sharp-shooters, the peoples' representatives in the brave new post-colonial world strolled to work like everyone else, open shirted and apparently unprotected.

Three generations of the Nehru family walked side by side, Krishna Menon glowering behind them. In his pandit's coat, Jawaharlal looked like a magician, the sari-ed Indira like his assistant. Behind them might come U Nu of Burma and Sihanouk of Cambodia flanked, perhaps, by the tall hieratic figures of Egypt's Nasser and Cyprus's Makarios. One forgets what a novelty it must all have been. In the drab 1950s the world still expected its leaders to appear in formal attire; Churchill and Attlee were seen in frock coats, Eisenhower and Stalin in uniform; and beneath the peaked caps and the Homburgs the features were invariably grave, craggy and white. But in Bandung the sun shone and there was scarcely a pasty Caucasian face to be seen. Safari suits and Maoist fatigues mixed with Arab gelabiyeh, Indian saris and African prints. Peering at the photographs on display within the Gedung Merdeka, I sensed something of the glorious novelty of the occasion. Just when rock 'n' roll was slashing through the moquette conventions of the dance hall, Bandung revolutionized diplomatic attitudes and introduced a whole new cast of performers on the international stage.

Another photo showed a trio of lanky black dudes in rakishly angled trilbys with flapping double-breasted suits and two-tone 'co-respondent' shoes. They could have been the Savoy's dance combo but were in fact Liberia's delegation. Uneasy in such populist company, the then Prince Feisal of Saudi Arabia came alone, scowling. Ho Chi Minh was represented by Pham Van Dong and Mao Ze-dong by Zhou En-lai. Raul Manglapus of the Philippines appeared to be offering the latter condolences. The People's Republic of China was making its first diplomatic overtures to its non-Communist neighbours and its delegation should have been the largest. But somewhere over the South China Sea eleven of its members had disappeared when a bomb went off in their plane. Was it the CIA or the KMT? In the eyes of the West, nearly all these men had a price on their heads. But in Sukarno's Indonesia they felt safe enough. The informality of Bandung would long be cherished.

In all, twenty-nine nations were represented at the conference. Its impressario was Ali Sastroamidjojo, one of Indonesia's many polysyllabic premiers during this period of swiftly changing coalitions. But Sukarno was its star. 'Brothers and Sisters,' he declaimed, 'how dynamic are the times'. At last the world was awakening from the sleep of centuries. With the irresistible force of a hurricane nations were casting off the shackles of colonialism. 'The voiceless ones, the unregarded, the people who had had decisions made for them,' should now themselves demand a say in world affairs. In their shared hatred of colonialism lay the seeds of unity. And in their numbers and the justice of their cause lay a strength greater than economic leverage or industrial might. 'Yes we, we the people of Asia and Africa, far more than half the population of the world, we can mobilize what I call the moral violence of nations in the cause of peace.' His youthful good looks and expansive manner mirrored the excitement of the occasion. Beneath the flag of anti-colonialism was born the Non-Aligned Movement, a third force for a Third World, to broker peace between the two global super-powers and prosperity for the underdog.

It was heady stuff and, forty years on, surely well worth commemorating. But the curator of Gedung Merdeka knew of no such plans. Some of the photos in his exhibition were curling with age and the dust lay deep on the stenographer's portables. The Movement had fared badly. India and China, its two biggest players, had been at war within six years. And now, though non-alignment had never meant ideological neutrality, it was hard to see what it did mean when alignment itself was meaningless. Besides, Bandung had a more important anniversary on its mind. If 1995 was forty years since the Asia-Africa Conference, it was fifty since Indonesian independence.

'Ninety-five is Take Off of Technology Year,' explained Amir, my editor friend from Jakarta. 'We celebrate with two projects, both in Bandung. One is C250, the other is *Al-Qur'ān Mushaf Istiqlal*. Best you see C250. I can arrange. Habibie, yes? I know him. Perhaps he will take you in his helicopter.' Minister Habibie, the outstanding technocrat of Suharto's New Order, had championed the development of Indonesia's aeronautics industry. The country's first home-designed and home-built jet was his pet project and it would be making its maiden flight in 1995. But what about *Al-Qur'ān Mushaf Istiqlal*?

'No helicopter flight,' said Amir. 'But you could ask for Dr Nukman.'

I had asked for Dr Nukman. I asked in town and I asked high on the slopes of Tangkuban-prahu whence 'extremists' had once lobbed shells across the railway tracks at Bogarde and the British

but where now Bandung's silicon revolutionaries sit silently at
their Japanese work-stations plotting the technology take-off.
Beneath dripping pines I pounded through the cloud-wrapped
campus of ITB. In the 1920s the young Sukarno, in what was then
the first technical college in the Indies, had here welded the secular
nationalism of E.F.E. Douwes Dekker, a nephew of *Max Havelaar*'s author, to the Communist dialectics of Tan Malaka, the
most mercurial of the Minangkabau intellectuals. But radical stu-
dent movements, like radical diplomacy, had since gone underground. The alumni darted devotedly from classroom to lecture
hall. No one had heard of Dr Nukman.

Eventually mention of *Al-Qur'ān Mushaf Istiqlal* brought directions to a nearby mosque. It was brand new. In fact it was still
being built. Injunctions for the removal of shoes seemed premature as a mark of respect; perhaps it was because the concrete floor
was still drying. None of the scaffolders had heard of Nukman but,
after an interminable wait in a bare waiting room, a veiled matron
gave me directions of extraordinary complexity. Even the taxi-
driver could make nothing of them. He surmised, however, that
we were on the trail of a graphics project and, with frequent
enquiries at repro shops and photo-fax bureaux, triumphantly
deposited me in the unpaved forecourt of a clapboard shop
covered in Fuji stickers.

Within, a man in a *peci* dished out visiting cards, four in all, each
from a different print gallery, studio or design partnership and one
from a bank. He was not Dr Nukman. Dr Nukman was in Jakarta.
But this was indeed the home of *Al-Qur'ān Mushaf Istiqlal*. He was
Mahmud Buchari, co-ordinator of print and design, and he would
be delighted, nay proud and honoured, to show me their work.

As yet I was not quite sure what *Al-Qur'ān Mushaf Istiqlal* actually meant or why this apparently obscure production was to share
centre stage with the C250 jet trainer. Obviously it was a new
edition of *Al-Qur'ān* (the Koran). But not just new, said Buchari,
'it is the first ever illuminated edition based on Indonesian
designs.' His enthusiasm was a joy to behold. Ushered into a
window-less and fiercely air-conditioned sanctum, I was issued
with light table and magnifying glass as sheets of calligraphy and

transparencies of the most delicate art-work were reverentially displayed for inspection.

Work had started in November 1991. Seventeen artists and five calligraphers had laboured over their drawing boards ever since. The paper came from Germany and the paints from Windsor and Newton; but the artistry was purely Indonesian. There were 900 pages, 45 of them illustrated plus the 'very exclusive' designs of the first and last pages. Finance had been organized by the Ministry for Religious Affairs, mostly from private sources, and the designs had all been approved by the government. They were 'very canonic'. 'Not to draw humans or animals, yes?' So the designers had concentrated on floral patterns.

As we pored over the intricate brushwork, I was delighted to spot a small red and indisputably vulva-like *Rafflesia*. Buchari identified jasmine, orchids, hibiscus and several trees. He traced their tendrils through lacy friezes in which he also discovered patterns derived from Javanese batik and abstract designs which originated in Minang woodwork or the stone carving of Borobudur. The 4,000 de luxe editions were already in production; for the Istiqlal Festival, which would coincide with the independence celebrations in August 1995, all one million copies of the standard edition should be ready. It was probably the most ambitious publishing project ever attempted in Indonesia.

To the sobriety of the crisp Nakshi-style calligraphy the ravishing colours added a suitably Indonesian gloss, as if softening the desert austerities of Arabia with the decorous gaiety of the Pacific. I hoped that in this secular state no bigoted Christian would be moved to query its suitability as a national achievement.

'Of course not,' said Buchari. 'This is Indonesian achievement. Next we do Bible, not illuminated but fully illustrated with humans and animals, yes?'

'Yes; and birds in the trees, please.'

'Of course, of course.'

NK

10. All is palace

I continued east by train. The line meandered down from the Preanger through lumpy and dishevelled hills which jostled round a sleek volcano, elbowing aside the steep flights of *sawah* that tried to scale it. Where West Java becomes Central Java, the island narrows to a thickish waist and on the map the railway appeared to brush the southern coastline. But I couldn't see the sea; and it was here that the futility of an end-to-end journey down the archipelago struck home.

Travelling through Sumatra by bus, often at night, seldom luxuriously and for the most part amid dense forest had reinforced the illusion that little of consummate interest was being missed. Day time travel in the relative comfort of Indonesian Railways suggested otherwise. Cilacap, the only sizeable port on Java's south coast, was where the last surviving Sinbads from HMAS *Perth* had staggered ashore after their epic voyage from the Sunda Strait. It was also probably where in 1580 the *Golden Hind* made its only Javanese landfall and where Francis Drake, hearing music 'of a very strange kinde yet . . . pleasant and delightfull', registered the first European appreciation of gamelan. But Cilacap required a break of journey and a branch line excursion. The momentum of an end-to-end progress precluded both.

And still the sea was out of sight. To the Javanese the 'Southern Ocean' is quite unlike the Java Sea along the island's north coast. The latter laps a low shoreline of dunes and marsh interspersed with sandy beaches and sheltered estuaries. Inter-island steamers and tall-masted *pinisi* shuttle across its horizon while every breeze fills a swarm of smaller sails bent, with net and line, on plundering its shallow waters. It's Indonesia's main highway and one of its richest assets. But the 'Southern Ocean' is altogether more hostile and mysterious. It pounds, they say, against high cliffs where small boats flounder; the sand is black and the horizon empty. Strange creatures emerge from its unfathomed depths in which Ratu Loro Kidul, the siren goddess of the southern seas, rules over a kingdom of drowned mariners. Very occasionally she too comes ashore, dressed in the palest green, to claim connubial union with Java's senior Sultan. Today could have been her day. I would never know.

Frustration was compounded by Central Java being one of the most densely populated and historically significant regions of South-east Asia. Indeed Mataram, its heartland which we and possibly the lovely Ratu Kidul were rapidly approaching, is over-populated and culturally well-endowed even by Central Javanese standards. This is Indonesia's equivalent of the Lower Nile, the focus and fulcrum of the whole archipelago. Yet here I was, rattling through it in *bisnis* class, with no more to record than lumpy hills and whatever else presented itself to view.

We clattered through a village where all life was frozen to a standstill, watching the train. It was like a photograph framed in the window. Suddenly I badly needed to be out there, to be taking a glass of sweet black *kopi* in the shade of that mango tree as the children drifted back to school in their plum red uniforms. I wanted to check out the antiquities of Ciamis, climb to the smouldering crater of Galunggang and explore the Pagandaran Reserve. Most of all I wanted to squelch barefoot among the rice-fields and feel the soft Javanese mud-powder slither between the toes. I wanted to get out there and hug those lumpy hills; I wanted to loll in the back of a *becak* puffing on a *kretek*; I wanted to melt into that thick syrupy air heavy with the gongs of a distant game-lan and the cloying attar of mango.

Flying once from Bali to Jakarta, I had passed this way and watched out the window a landscape of sheer fantasy. It was late afternoon, the sun low, and the only cloud a few wisps of smoke curling casually from the parched volcanoes. What impressed me most was the majestic symmetry of these conical smokestacks. They stood in line, some higher, some more sharply pointed, but all equally spaced and all distinct one-off mountains. In a land where the invasive vegetation normally smothers all contours, their discoloured slopes were bare and of geometrical precision. Steeper than any pyramid, they lent to the scenery an ordered and architectural quality which the terraces of *sawah*, built as if to buttress and underpin their foundations, faithfully complemented. It was landscaped landscape, designed to order by imaginative giants with a penchant for pyrotechnics. There was nowhere else in the world remotely like it. Perhaps it was Eden. But it was also too strange, too grand and too fantastic ever to become familiar or comforting. Only the Javanese, steeped in their distinctive, ancient and impossibly complex culture, could feel at one with it. The visitor might revel in its riot of sensory externals but the logic or symbolism of its ordered grandeur defied penetration. Though a ripple of gamelan readily seduces the senses, the mind may remain confused, suspicious. 'A very strange kinde' of music for 'a very strange kinde' of landscape, yet 'pleasant and delightfull'.

Revisiting Borobudur, the image of those volcanoes soaring from their encircling terraces of *sawah* stayed with me. It was a handy starting point. Like everyone else I had left the train at Jogjakarta to explore Mataram's 1,200 years of art and antiquity in 72 hours flat. A hundred thousand tourists manage this feat every year and, provided one starts at the beginning, it is perfectly feasible. The important thing is to forget about the history but to hold tight to the chronology. For in spite of its antiquity Java, and especially Mataram, is blessed with a dearth of historical detail. The materials for a continuous narrative of the past – chronicles, inscriptions, coins etc – are simply inadequate while the few retrospective accounts which do survive are almost certainly unreliable if not downright misleading. We know more about the Pharaohs than we do about Java's dynasties. Instead there is a dazzling and clearly ancient culture, related to the often better documented cultures of mainland Asia but distinct, pervasive and remarkably consistent. The trick, therefore, is to concentrate on the processes of cultural change, on ideas, influences, symbols and styles, and to forget about politics, wars and religions.

It is easier said than done. Borobudur is commonly acclaimed as the largest Buddhist monument in the world. A gaggle of yellow-robed monks with shaven heads picnicked on pot noodles and cartons of lemon tea in the shade of the visitor centre. From Japan and Thailand, Sri Lanka, Tibet and all over Indonesia followers of the Middle Way converge on this enigmatic mound of masonry. Yet archaeologists now think that when construction began in about 780AD the inspiration came not from Buddhism but from Hinduism or possibly from some indigenous cult concerned with mountain spirits. A stepped plinth or pyramid, smaller but not dissimilar to today's monument, was evidently intended; but it had reached only the third tier when the design was changed and enlarged to conform with new notions of what such a structure might represent. Other changes quickly followed with a reworking of the plan roughly every decade for the fifty years it took to complete. Either its patrons were extraordinarily flexible in their ideas about the supernatural or, more probably, they did not acknowledge the rigid distinctions between belief systems that we take for granted.

Buddhist or not, I was fussing more over whether it was actually a monument. When in 1812 Raffles didn't discover it (although he was certainly the first to collate and publish a full description of it) the dome of the crowning stupa had collapsed, the bell-shaped stupas which surround it were mostly reduced to rubble and the topmost terraces were rippled with subsidence. Lower down, the supporting galleries were choked with debris while trees thrust their roots through the stonework to explore the earth beneath. For just as Java's landscape has an architectural quality, so its architecture has a landscape quality; and nowhere more so than Borobudur.

It is, in fact, not a building but a hill, albeit a hill cut into steps and clad in stone. Even the groundplan, which at first glance appears to be rectangular, is in fact indented to follow the rounded circumference of the hill's base. Above the fifth level, straight lines are completely abandoned with the highest terraces being oval platforms. Might not the galleries, then, represent stone-built terraces of *sawah* complete with outer retaining walls? I re-read Raffles' description hoping to find mention of rice seedlings sprouting from what were then in effect raised beds, suitably filled with water-logged mud. But no such luck.

Like most visitors, Raffles was more intrigued by the panels of sculpted reliefs which line both sides of the five main galleries. Like cartoon strips running clockwise round the monument, these tell in pictures the main stories contained in certain Buddhist texts, the most readily identifiable being those concerned with the Buddha's own life story. Interpretation depends on such audio accompaniment as monks, or now more commonly guides, may provide. The sculptures were therefore teaching aids designed to engage the interest of visitors while the necessary perambulation of the galleries won them spiritual merit.

No less important than this horizontal activity was the vertical ascent from gallery to gallery by way of the elaborate staircases at the four cardinal points. The climb is usually taken to signify a gradual progression from the realm of worldly desire, at the bottom, through that of righteous conduct to the formlessness of the unadorned terraces and open panoramas at the top. Here within the lattice of each bell-shaped stupa sat, like a bird in a cage, a cross-legged boddhisattva deep in meditation. As well as being a teaching aid for the laity, the monument was thus also a paradigm for the ascetic striving towards enlightenment.

But 'this is theorizing after the event and on false premises,' according to Michael Smithies. The frequent redesigning of the monument simply did not allow for such a comprehensive master-plan.

'Yes, I agree,' said Dr Soekmono. 'Perhaps it is Buddhistic but it is not Buddhist.' Soekmono was the man who oversaw the Unesco supported restoration of Borobudur in the 1970s and 1980s. We had met in Jakarta soon after the work was completed when the first yellow-robed monks were taking up residence. According to Soekmono, they and nearly all the other Indonesian pilgrims were 'neo-Buddhists' who had espoused their religious identity in the bloody aftermath of GESTAPU, the '65 Communist coup attempt.

'It's funny actually. I happen to know several of these neo-Buddhists and, well sometime back, they asked me for advice. What would be most proper for a Buddhist place of worship? With stupa or without? And what should be the proper form of ritual? They did not know even the form of ritual. So they ask me. Well, I am a Muslim. Not fanatic Muslim. But they ask me because I am an archaeologist. And you know, I think that perhaps we have always been like this.'

Apparently Java is dotted with Hindu and Buddhist sites which were subsequently appropriated as Muslim graveyards or incorporated into mosques. Numerous tombs revered as the last resting places of Muslim saints turn out to be the erstwhile pedestals of Hindu temples. There is one such in the middle of Jakarta 'near the fishmarket'. It all makes the archaeologist's job a very delicate one; it also makes one wary of religious labelling.

'You see, it turns out that for Indonesians the site is much more important than the construction itself. So there is a mosque but within the mosque is incorporated the remains of a *candi* [temple] and on the very same site we find also prehistoric remains. So when I lay stress on the fact that Borobudur is actually a stacked pyramid with a Buddhistic covering, I mean that it is actually a place of ancestor worship and these ancestors were pre-Hindu and Hindu as well as Buddhist. So it is in fact a national monument, a symbol of Indonesian syncretism.'

After Borobudur comes Prambanam, a sprawling complex of temples on the other side of Jogjakarta. Though only a decade or two later, it could hardly feel more different. While Borobudur crouches toad-like amid low-lying *sawah* near the confluence of two rivers, at Prambanam the principal temples rear into a merciless sky from a dry and lizard-infested plain.

Snake charmers, coca-cola vendors and skinny youths brandishing sun hats led the marketing offensive. A departing tour group conveniently drew their fire and I slipped through the entrance into open parkland across which a fairground tractor hauled carriages full of perspiring pink flesh from one mountain of masonry to the next. Fiery red carpets of casuarina blossoms dotted the parched ground on which acacia thorns lay in wait for bare feet. It was almost cactus country. As the noonday sun spat its venom on this shimmering semi-desert I plotted a course between the oases of shade offered by trees, portals, sanctums and the occasional workman's awning.

Borobudur had suggested Burma where, at Pagan, the idea of transforming small hills into stepped stupas had been taken up in the 11th century and pursued to the spectacular architectural effect which Borobudur sadly lacks. But Prambanam's links are unmistakably with India. I thought of those other great temple complexes at Bhuvaneshwar, Khajuraho, and in the Tamil country. Few predate Prambanam's temples and rightly Ananda Coomaraswamy included Java's master-works in his seminal analysis of India's temple architecture. The subtly exaggerated perspective of their soaring *sikharas* (main towers) with tier upon dwindling tier of subordinate towerlets is as typically Indian as the famous *Ramayana* frieze or the generous anatomical detail of the surviving statuary. Typical, too, are the emphatic horizontals of courtyard, outer wall and plinth which deceive the eye into over-estimating the vertical thrust of the main structures. Above all, Prambanam, like its Indian counterparts, is a celebration of stone which, though used for other purposes in India, was reserved solely for sacral buildings in ancient Indonesia. All the rarer for it, the mastery of this demanding material is a matter for wonder and uncritical delight.

The finest temple stands hard by the main road from Jogjakarta (or Jogja) to Surakarta (or Solo) and though then ruined and over-grown, was not unknown to the Dutch. But the first description dates again from 1812 and owes much to British familiarity with Indian architecture. It comes from the pen not of Raffles but of Colin Mackenzie, most illustrious of the numerous scholars who explored and surveyed in Java during the British occupation.

Improbably Mackenzie, the son of the postmaster in Stornoway in the Outer Hebrides, had first gone to India to study the Hindu system of logarithms. War interrupted his mathematical researches and during the East India Company's long tussle with the Sultanate of Mysore Mackenzie won a reputation for gallantry which eclipsed even that of this friend and fellow officer Arthur Wellesley. In the Peninsular War Wellesley would greatly regret the absence of Mackenzie and, as Duke of Wellington, would no doubt have appreciated his support at Waterloo. But by then Mackenzie's career had taken another turn. Deploying his mathematical talents, he had conducted an ambitious survey of Mysore and, in the process, become obsessed with India's classical past. In travels throughout the Indian peninsula he scoured the countryside for manuscripts, inscriptions and antiquities, amassing the greatest collection of Orientalia ever assembled by one man. Now an authority on the Buddhists and the Jains, indeed suspected of being a Jain, he immersed himself in Java's antiquities and was just the man to unravel the mysteries of Prambanam.

But Raffles, for reasons unknown, also sent a Captain George Baker to survey the site and Baker soon begged to differ with Mackenzie. Seeing numerous statues and reliefs of a cross-legged figure deep in meditation, Mackenzie had declared Prambanam Buddhist. But Baker, on the authority of one of his Indian NCOs, was persuaded that they could equally well be Hindu ascetics. Thus began a long controversy which, like that over Borobudur, is still unresolved. For what it is worth, both men were probably right. The two earliest temples at Prambanam are now thought to date from about 780AD and to be Buddhist, although their construction coincides with the earliest, Hindu, period at Borobudur. Fifty years later, when Borobudur had just been clad in Buddhist iconography, work began at Prambanam on the main, unmistakably Hindu, temple. An inscription suggests that this was built to celebrate the victory of a Hindu king over his Buddhist rival. Yet another inscription indicates that the adjacent and contemporary Buddhist temple was built to gratify his wife. It is, to say the least, confusing.

'Ah, but you see they are the same,' said Dr Soekmono. 'Some texts say Buddha and Siva were brothers. But the *Sutra Somar*, that is a manuscript of the Majapahit period, says they are different only in human eyes but that in fact they are one and the same, *Bhinneka Tungal Ika*. It is also the motto on our Indonesian coat of arms. It means, in Sanskrit, 'They are many, they are one'. Or we say 'unity in diversity'. So these two religions, they were different in India but in Java they were practically one and the same.'

Soekmono was evidently one of those who felt that antiquarian studies in Indonesia had suffered from a surfeit of Indo-centric appraisal. Smiling mischievously he recalled 'Greater India', an imaginary entity conjured up by British and Indian scholars which embraced all those countries with a Hindu-Buddhist heritage, including Burma, Cambodia, much of Vietnam and most of Indonesia. Also Central America. According to Soekmono, a group of Indian archaeologists had taken one look at Candi Sukuh, a curious truncated pyramid east of Solo, and declared it the missing architectural link between Hindu Java and Mayan Guatemala. 'I think that maybe they were confused. Because they are called 'Mayan Indians' they think they must be part of Greater India and so they looked for shared architectural style and they find this at Candi Sukuh.'

Sukuh, high on the slopes of Mount Lawu east of Solo, is one of several hundred Hindu and Buddhist sites in Central and East Java. In most cases the temples are considerably smaller than those of Prambanam and few have been subjected to such ambitious restoration. Nor are they as accessible. But the rewards are commensurate with the exertion.

Slogging up a near vertical trail in search of Gedong Songo ('the Nine Buildings') I was reminded of Borobudur as the desirable realms of cassava, cinnamon, maize and mango gave way to righteous rows of carrots, onions and beans framed in arabesques of pumpkin and roses. Amaryllis lilies grew wild in parterres cobbled with cabbages as big as footballs. Finally breathlessness brought formlessness as open sward fingered into the forest on the shoulders of Mount Ungaran. Frogs croaked a welcome. There was dew on the grass and pine scent in the air. Parting the webs of mist below, the rising sun turned the distant waters of Rawa Pening a fresh flamingo pink.

Feeling like the morning's first mushroom-picker, I ranged over the hillside from one clump of temples to the next, pausing only to sample a hot-spring. Amid such pristine delights the gloom within the tiny temples defied the day with a reek of bat and the must of ages. Siva should have been meditating here in timeless serenity but someone had removed the statue. On an outer wall Ganesh, his son, danced alone in the morning sun, his joy both impudent and infectious. As Merapi puffed a sullen plume of smoke into the flawless sky, I thought I heard a flute and half expected to see the youthful Mata Hari come pirouetting down the path, dark-nippled beneath diaphanous veils. Instead there appeared a couple of New Zealanders in Nepali caps, Rajasthani waistcoats and Punjabi pyjama bottoms.

'Hi.' said the girl. 'We thought we were the only ones here.' She had a ring in her nose and bad blisters. 'Haven't seen anyone since we got here. You reckon we're staying at the wrong place?' I reckoned they were and recommended the next bus back to Jogja.

'The Nine Buildings' predate Prambanam and, along with other temple clumps on the nearby Dieng Plateau, are the oldest in Java. They date from the early 8th century. By way of contrast, Mata Hari's beloved ruins in the Malang district of East Java are 13th century and Candi Sukuh, the Mayan lookalike, is 15th century. The Javanese were thus building temples of stone, and sometimes brick, for a good seven hundred years. During this time there is evidence of some structural modification, of an increasingly earthy and exaggerated style of sculpture, and of a definite devotional switch away from major deities like Siva to lesser figures like Arjuna and Bima from the Hindu *Mahabharata*. But since such developments were invariably associated with new sites often great distances from their chronological predecessors, there is some uncertainty about whether one can talk of a continuous tradition.

'An expanding cloud of localized, fragile, loosely interrelated petty principalities' is how Clifford Geertz has characterized the political make-up of pre-colonial Indonesia. The Mataram dynasties known to historians as the Sanjaya and Sailendra, either of whom could have been responsible for Borobudur and/or

Prambanam, certainly conformed to this pattern and so did the East Javanese kingdoms of Kediri and Singosari. But the great mystery is why, sometime in the 10th century, the cloud of petty principalities shifts from the middle of the island to its eastern extremities, why suddenly temples and inscriptions abruptly cease in Mataram only to reappear 200 miles away. Had Merapi erupted with devastating effect? Had some rival power, perhaps Sumatra's Srivijaya or Sunda's Pajajaran, intervened? Or had Mataram's precocious principalities simply collapsed, exhausted under the weight of their own masonry? It's anyone's guess.

Meanwhile in East Java the new cloud of petty principalities continued to shower the countryside with temples until in the 14th century the Majapahit kingdom south of modern Surabaya achieved a rare supremacy over most of Java and then laid claim to the only pan-Indonesian sovereignty in the pre-colonial era. It lasted less than 150 years during which the arrival of Islam proved disruptive. But it was the absence of an accepted system of succession that destroyed the kingdom.

Succession problems seem to have dogged Indonesia's dynasties; and they remain an abiding concern to this day if one may judge by the bloody fall of Sukarno and now the hysterical speculation over Suharto's successor. But an open mind about inheritance does have the advantage of throwing wide the net of legitimacy. If kinship with some illustrious antecedent is enough to establish a legitimate right to rule, then a new leader is liable to pop up anywhere. Back in Jogja no one seemed in the least bit surprised that, according to the newspapers, the next leader of one of the very few political parties countenanced by Suharto's New Order was likely to be Megawatti Sukarnoputeri, a lady with, apparently, absolutely no credentials for the job other than her electrifying name and her parentage. For she is, as Sukarnoputeri implies, the daughter of Bung Karno by his marriage to Fatmawatti, the Bengkulu beauty. ('No,' said old Dr Sartono, 'I don't think Megawatti has a daughter herself. Where did you hear of this Kilowatti?')

By a similar process of conductivity, c1600 a new dynasty claiming descent from Majapahit established itself back in Central

Java. After a hiatus of 700 years the cultural splendour of Mataram was about to be revived. Combined with claims to Majapahit's extensive sovereignty, it endowed the new kingdom with impeccable national credentials which neither three hundred years of colonialism nor fifty of republicanism have extinguished. To this day Jogja stands apart from the rest of Indonesia as the touchstone of Javanese culture and the guarantor of a national identity impervious to the brash internationalism of Jakarta. It is also, apart from Jakarta, the only *daerah istimewa*, or special district, outside the Republic's administrative system of provinces, answerable only to the central government and still under the governorship of its erstwhile Sultan.

In *Max Havelaar*, Douwes Dekker likens coach travel on the old Java *postweg* to a process of 'assimilation' between the passenger and his seat. Eventually, he claims, one no longer knows where the seat ends and the ego begins. In fact a touch of cramp may then easily be mistaken for 'moth in the cloth [of the cushion]'; or vice versa.

Sitting through a night-long performance of *wayang kulit* I recalled this idea of assimilation. The show was being held beneath an awning of hessian in someone's yard and the chairs were collapsible triangles of tubular steel with protruding seats of uncompromising rigidity. Rolling from buttock to buttock or sliding from cocyx to thigh brought only temporary relief. Without the benefit of cushion, cloth or even moth, flesh and steel remained irreconcilable. In an atmosphere thick with heat, humanity and clove-smoke, the only escape lay in hypnosis.

Mercifully *wayang kulit* could have been devised for precisely this effect. *Kulit* means leather, this being the material from which the cut-out puppets are cut, and *wayang* means shadow, the medium being shadow theatre. It is thus a black and white shadow puppet show. It is also unconscionably long, usually lasting from 8pm until 5am and, to any but a Javanese, almost totally incomprehensible. Add to this the mesmeric accompaniment of a gamelan orchestra and the sonorous monotony of the *dalang*'s (puppeteer's) delivery and it is small wonder that all accounts agree on the dream-like qualities of Java's most celebrated dramatic experience.

I don't know whether I slept and dreamt or whether I merely hallucinated. But for quite a few hours I lost track not only of where the seat ended and the ego began but of where the artistry ceased and trance took over. Before a performance the *dalang*, a highly respected artist, must undergo a period of meditation and abstinence. He is the medium in both senses of the word and his performance is as much about exorcism as art. Similarly his puppets, though not exactly worshipped, are treated with extreme reverence and accorded talismanic qualities. Many represent deities since the repertoire for nearly all performances is drawn from stories in the Hindu Sanskrit epic, the *Mahabharata. Wayang kulit* thus, like Borobudur, combines art and instruction with spiritual purpose and transcendental encouragement. The audience is conducted into a twilight zone between the real and surreal. One can enjoy the horizontal narrative about righteous conduct and refined etiquette or one can soar towards formlessness and enlightenment in a hallucinogenic haze of clove-smoke.

The origins of *wayang kulit* are unknown. In the relief sculptures of Borobudur and Prambanam gongs similar to those in a gamelan are much in evidence but no theatrical performances are illustrated and it is not until the 15th century that sculpted figures, like those at Candi Sukuh, begin to assume the sharp profiles, elongated noses and stick-like limbs of *wayang* cut-outs. On the other hand, the *Mahabharata*, like the *Ramayana*, was certainly familiar to classical Mataram and may well have inspired dramatic treatment as well as sculpture.

When in the 17th and 18th centuries Mataram at last revived, stone was no longer worked and styles had changed. But through the *wayang* the stories, the motifs and their centrality in Javanese life remained much the same. And this in spite of the fact that Mataram's new rulers were nominally Muslim. Even today the stories of the Sanskrit classics are better known, and their characters better loved, than those of the Qur'ān and the early Caliphate.

'I have been watching the *Mahabharat* on television,'

announced Dr Sartono. He had required guidance locating a chair on his own verandah. I wondered how one now so tragically blind could watch anything, let alone the 104 episodes into which Bombay's movie moguls had distilled one of the world's longest epics.

'Very interesting. It tells us much about our culture. I asked my wife to read the subtitles and, you know, these Indian characters are quite different to our Javanese characters. Arjun for instance. There he is a warrior, very righteous. But in the *wayang* stories he is a lady's man, a lover. A Don Juan, yes? And Bima. In India he is the strong man, very strong but not very clever. But here he is the mystic and ascetic whose strength comes from his austerities. It is very interesting.'

Pretty interesting too, I suggested, were the pictures in Jogja's first McDonald's. It had just opened and, as I tried to explain to the venerable historian, McDonald's was a company which prided itself on consistency, guaranteeing an identical product in identical surroundings all over the world.

'Like the Dong Son culture,' said Sartono in a reference to the identical bronze age drums found all over South-east Asia.

'Just so. But in the Jogja McDonald's two things are different. One is a sign on the menu board saying "100 percent halal". OK, so they offer the same reassurance in all Muslim countries. But what about the pictures? There they were: Ronald McDonald and his pals, Hamburglar, Birdie and so on; and right in among them, Arjun, Semar, Bima and the whole *wayang* gang. *Mahabharat* comes to McDonald's. Let's not exaggerate. But could there be a better example of *wayang*'s place in Javanese culture?'

'Very interesting,' said Sartono, groping for his notepad and then writing 'McDonald' with the wrong end of his pencil. 'I will go and take a look.'

The new McDonald's is on a busy retail thoroughfare called Jalan Malioboro which name could, like that of Bengkulu's fort, be a corruption of 'Marlborough' and may have been conferred by Raffles in honour of the Duke. Other explanations hark back to a Sanskrit phrase meaning 'flower-bedecked' and forward to the last

Sultan's preference for the big country brand of cigarettes. More apt is the Dutch word for a 'fortress built of limestone', Jalan Malioboro being in effect Jogja's Mall leading past the old Dutch fort and on to the walled *Kraton* or palace. As such it is the city's principal axis and so a prime candidate for rededication. On the map the section now graced by MacDonald's red and yellow arches has accordingly been renamed, like main streets everywhere, after General Ahmed Yani of the Crocodile Hole.

No doubt other sections will be renamed as and when the New Order throws up more heroes. They will be in good company for, apart from Malioboro, the street names hereabouts read like a dynastic roll of honour. Running east from Malioboro beneath the palace walls, Jalan Panembahan Senopati is named after the Majapahit descendant who actually founded the new Mataram dynasty. Beyond the palace, his street becomes that of his grandson, Sultan Agung ('The Great Sultan') whose long reign (c1613–46) saw Mataram extend its authority throughout central and east Java and run up against the first Dutch merchants in Batavia. A century later, in one of those interminable succession disputes, the intervention of the now rampant Dutch brought about the division of the kingdom into two more or less equal halves. One eventually settled on Solo (Surakarta) as its capital and there both court and ruler (often known as the Sushunan) flourished in state. The other, represented by a breakaway uncle known as Prince Mangkubumi, chose Jogja and the title of Sultan Hamengkubuwono I (ruled 1755–92). The palace was his creation and so was its ceremonial approach down Jalan Malioboro, the far end of which is duly called Jalan Mangkubumi.

Like the Batak king Sisingamangaraja (here banished to a radial road in the suburbs), Hamengkubuwono is a name worth getting the tongue round, if only because there have been nine of them, the present incumbent being Hamengkubuwono X. On no account, however, and for obvious reasons, should one attempt to pronounce Ngayogyakartahardiningrat. This was the new dynasty's name for Jogja (and hence sometimes 'Yogya'). Its interest lies solely in the first three syllables which represent a Javanese rendering of 'Ayodhya'. The Thais got nearer the original with 'Ayuthia', their pre-Bangkok capital. In both cases the idea was to substantiate and legitimize a new dynasty and a new court by equating it with that of Lord Rama (or Ram) who, according to the *Ramayana*, had ruled from the city of Ayodhya.

Though now an unattractive town in India's Uttar Pradesh notorious for its exhibitions of Hindu nationalism, Ayodhya under Rama and queen Sita had been a veritable Utopia. Beloved of the gods and at one with the cosmic harmony of creation, its just and ordered government represented the highest possible political ideal. To it, all Javanese dynasties aspired. But appreciating the spiritual finesse which must underlie such perfection, many spurned the chores of day-to-day administration to concentrate on creating a favourable and symbolic framework within which, if they got it right, the new Ayodhya would materialize as if by magic.

The consequent emphasis on external minutiae, on symbolism, on etiquette and on ritual, endowed court life with the mannered qualities of a tableau. It was also what prompted Clifford Geertz to characterize the kingdoms of Java and Bali as 'theatre states'. His meaning becomes obvious the moment you enter the walled precincts of Hamengkubuwono I's *kraton*.

'So where exactly is the palace?' asked a polite American expecting, no doubt, banqueting halls, ballrooms and state chambers all sumptuously accommodated behind a stately façade of architectural distinction.

'All is palace,' said the guide as he graciously waved his party through another fine gateway into another walled courtyard empty but for another raised *pendopo*. Resembling a stage with random bits of furniture as props (including mirrors, occasional tables and chandeliers of European make), a *pendopo* has no walls but a high pitched roof supported on pillars. It and the courtyard are the basic architectural elements of all Javanese palaces and to their groundplan of adjoining rectangles any domestic accommodation is subordinate and incidental. Replicated *ad nauseum* they provide a variety of venues for the main business of Javanese royalty, namely the performance of the countless ceremonies that fill the state calendar.

Such ceremonies, though resembling tableaux, are rather more than dramatic presentations for on their correct and lavish performance depends the well-being of the whole kingdom. The palace dancers dance exquisitely, the royal gamelan plays interminably, the sultan's accoutrements are paraded and the dynasty's regalia displayed. It looks like a colourful but conventional piece of royal theatre. But, like the *dalang's* puppets, every instrument, every dance, every state coach and every royal *kris* (dagger) has a mystical personality. As in legend, the trappings of royalty have become the talismans of royalty, imbued with formidable powers that must be regularly propitiated and re-enlisted in the service of the state. Handling these forces is sultan's work. He alone stands between the kingdom and the disasters, physical and political, waiting to overtake it. A priest-king if not a god-king, he presides over the delicate relationship between public affairs and divine sanction.

All this conforms to Hindu-Buddhist ideas of kingship and, though now given an Islamic veneer, has probably changed little since the days of Borobudur. In the Ayodhya ideal the order and stability of the kingdom were further strengthened by the rigid social structuring of caste. Greatly modified, caste distinctions are still evident in Bali but it is uncertain to what extent they were ever adopted in Java. There was, though, and there remains an obsession with hierarchy and social status. The Javanese language, for instance, has not only several different modes of address but several different vocabularies and several different intonations depending on the status of the speaker and whether he is addressing an inferior, an equal or a superior. Conversation thus becomes more like artistic composition, as rich in nuance as gamelan and ideally suited to the subtle characterizations, the courtly dilemmas and the 'in' jokes of *wayang kulit*.

In India caste identity depends on parentage and profession but in Java hierarchy hinges on the mastery of an exceedingly refined code of conduct which includes not only language but posture, dress, demeanour and expression. Across the *kraton's* courtyards glide small zombie-like retainers, bare-footed and stony-faced, while from faded portraits sultans gaze with statuesque composure. By such exquisitely delicate conduct the prestige of king and court are manifest.

The Javanese hierarchy embraces all creation from the coarsest of wild beasts to the most detached and exalted of deities. It governs mankind's position in the cosmic order; and it finds symbolic expression in that ubiquitous mountain shape call the *gunongan*. The 'mini mountain' is in fact Mount Meru (Sumeru, Mahameru), the axis of the universe in Indian cosmology. But like the cross in Christian tradition, it assumes various dimensions and serves numerous functions. Every *wayang kulit* performance begins with a lacy *gunongan* occupying the centre of the screen. The offerings of rice and fruit which those inscrutable retainers bear through the *kraton* may be heaped into mini Merus. With its peaked roof, each *pendopo* is also a *gunongan*; and so is the layout of the whole *kraton* with its elevated central focus. The tiers of Borobudur and the towers of Prambanam tell of the symbol's antiquity while the soaring profile of Merapi serves as a primordial prototype, its plume of smoke a reminder of hierarchical fragility.

But lest one get too carried away by the symbols and symmetries of ancient India, within the *kraton*'s mile-long walls the whole south-western section defies all architectural order. This is, or was, *Taman Sari* ('the fragrant garden') and appears to have been laid out by Hamengkubuwono I at the same time as all those formal courtyards; but for a very different purpose. For here the Mataram sultans turned their backs on both Islamic and Indic modalities to consort with the indigenous supernatural as represented by Ratu Loro Kidul, the goddess of the Southern Ocean. If an Islamic dynasty can be said to have a tutelary deity, it is she. Neatly linking all three of Java's greatest dynasties, her legend tells of a Pajajaran prince of Sunda who received her support to found East Java's Majapahit kingdom whence his distant descendants were eventually to return to the Southern Ocean to receive her blessing and instruction on the founding of the Mataram dynasty. All she demanded in exchange was marital union with each of the succeeding sultans.

Mindful of her watery realm, Hamengkubuwono seems to have planned *Taman Sari* as a suitable environment in which to enter-

tain the ever youthful goddess. Though now a dusty wilderness of
ruins scattered among bijou colonies and busy bazaars, most of it
was once under water with poolside pavilions and island mansions
linked by submarine passages and flanked by irrigated gardens.
Here were pioneered the swim-up couch, the water-cooled bed
and the sub-aqua seraglio. Pergolas broke the surface of the lake
at regular intervals to provide light and air to the labyrinth
beneath. Above, gilded barges forged through the lotus beds to the
trickle of gamelan and the sway of dancers.

Sylph-like and irresistible in her pale green *kebaya*, Ratu Loro
Kidul must have thought well of her earthly consorts. If less
impressed by the ruinous state of *Taman Sari* today, she still has
the consolation of regular visits by the Sultan to the shores of her
ocean at Parangtritis (south of Jogja) plus the thoughtful provision
of a permanently reserved suite in the best hotel at one of the south
coast's few resorts. Here, at Pelebuhanratu, fishermen appease her
stormy temper with the annual sacrifice of a buffalo. Yet should
some Jakarta belle venture into the breakers wearing a pale green
swimsuit, not even buffalo's blood can save her from the jealous
undertow and a speedy oblivion.

11. Surabaya Sue

Excluding the English East India Company's precarious and largely forgotten tenancy in Banten (1601–45), British participation in the history of Java has been short and reputedly sweet. The occupation during the Napoleonic Wars lasted five years (1811–16) and that after the Second World War just one year (1945–6). In both instances Britain's role is usually seen as that of a disinterested trustee for the Netherlands during her temporary incapacity courtesy of Napoleon and Hitler. Except in Raffles' ambition-crazed estimation, there was never any question of hanging on to the jewel in the Dutch crown once the crown itself was a free agent. Additionally the reforms introduced by Raffles and the encouragement given to the independence leaders by Mountbatten have afforded liberal British consciences no little satisfaction. Laurens van der Post's verdict on the post-war episode – 'a repeat performance in contemporary dress of the piece of high history enacted at the beginning of the 19th century round Raffles' – echoes such sentiments.

It also echoes the sentiments of Indonesia's nationalists although they see things somewhat differently. The 'piece of high history' did indeed repeat itself, though not for them in a display of even-handed conciliation and concern for Javanese well-being but in a couple of decidedly high-handed and bloody assaults on the nation's integrity. Historical amnesia being highly selective, neither of these features much in British mythology. The potential of 'With Raffles at Jogja' somehow escaped even G.A. Henty's eager eye for imperial heroics; and though I then scaled the 'War' shelves from floor level to the library ladder's topmost rung, the battle of Surabaya seemed also to have gone unchronicled.

Of the two, Raffles' storming of the Jogja *kraton* is the less explicable. In 1811 it was occupied by Hamengkubuwono II but disputed by his several brothers plus his son. The rival court at Solo was out to destabilize its neighbour in Jogja; and the Dutch had just demoted both courts to an inferior feudatory status. All these slights Hamengkubuwono II met with a still loftier detachment and a still grimmer insistence on the finest points of court etiquette, a response which the Dutch had found exasperatingly contrary to their assumption of sovereignty.

So did the British. That Hamengkubuwono II was also scheming to overthrow colonial rule, Dutch or British, was unsurprising and not especially relevant. But at an audience in the *kraton* Raffles and his entourage felt themselves slighted by the seating plan and snubbed by the Sultan's *hauteur*. This was insupportable. There could be no question but that treachery was planned. Unswayed by his regard for Javanese culture, Raffles resolved to reward the Sultan's 'insolence' with a pre-emptive strike.

In June 1812 he returned to Jogja with 1,200 British Indian troops. After an artillery bombardment, the massive but ill-defended walls were stormed and the butchery began. 'The loss on our side,' says his airy report, was 'very inconsiderable and comparatively nothing; on the part of the enemy dreadful.' Java's equivalent of Peking's 'Forbidden City' was then looted, the state archives burnt and the state treasury emptied. It was a misunderstanding, claimed Raffles; the hot-headed Rollo Gillespie, his military commander, was responsible. Yet the summary nature of the affair, perpetrated by one who considered himself Java's liberator from Dutch oppression, could not be excused. 'This was the only time in Javanese history when a court was taken by storm by the forces of a European government' (M.C. Ricklefs). The Sultan was deposed in favour of his son and half the kingdom was hived off as a subordinate fief for one of his brothers.

Defeat and division were nothing new in Mataram but the humiliation heaped on the earthly Ayodhya had far-reaching consequences. Disgusted by the *kraton*'s impotence in the face of colonial encroachment, Prince Diponegoro, the eldest son of the man who was now Hamengkubuwono III, withdrew into the countryside. In a charisma-building exile similar to that endured by Arjuna in the *Mahabharata* and much evoked by later leaders like Sukarno, Diponegoro meditated, listened to the grievances of the people, studied Islamic mysticism and won the decisive support of the lovely Ratu Loro Kidul, queen of the Southern Ocean.

Thus fortified, he bided his time until in 1825 a well-intentioned Dutch initiative back-fired and threatened to bankrupt the local aristocracy. Assured now of their support as well as of that of the oppressed peasantry and of disgruntled Islamic leaders, Diponegoro at last raised the standard of revolt. The ensuing Java War (1825–30), though essentially a prolonged guerilla campaign, cost thousands of lives and ended in ignominious defeat. Diponegoro was betrayed, captured and exiled to Sulawesi, a fate soon to be shared by the Imam of Bonjol. But like the Imam, the Prince had set a vital precedent for armed struggle against the colonial oppressor. In the pantheon of nationalist leaders, he was the first and thus takes precedence over the Imam, Teuku Umar, Cut Nyak Dien and all the rest.

More significantly his movement, part *jihad* (holy war), part peasants' revolt and part nationalist struggle, had briefly achieved the sort of consensus on which Indonesian independence would eventually be constructed. To encapsulate exactly the same elements Sukarno coined his 1950s acronym of NASAKOM, the NAS standing for nationalism, the A for *agama* (ie religion) and the KOM for Communism, an ideologically updated version of peasant revolt.

It was also significant that the pioneer of this consensus and the leader of the first anti-colonial struggle was a prince of Mataram and a legitimate claimant to the Sultanate of Jogja. No one could now dispute the primacy of Jogjakarta among the princely states of Indonesia. Combined with that costly defiance of Raffles, it elevated the Jogja *kraton* to the status of a national shrine and the Jogja state to a hushed eminence as the focus of Javanese and Indonesian identity. Later Hamengkubuwonos, though shorn of

their political autonomy, enhanced this reputation by the preservation and patronage of Javanese culture and scholarship. Jogja
became the Isfahan of Indonesia as well as its Persepolis. Here and
at Solo were, and still are, the most accomplished gamelan orchestras, the finest batik painters, the most delicate of dancers and the
most popular of *wayang* shows.

In the early 1900s it was also at Jogja that the first signs of a
modern nationalist consciousness became apparent. *Budi Utomo*,
the 'High Endeavour' movement, was essentially Javanese and
aristocratic while Muhammadiya had mass appeal and an Islamic
character. But both were founded in Jogja and both laid great
stress on the need for more educational facilities to arouse and
instruct the coming generation. In due course it was the bene-
ficiaries of these movements who founded in Jogja the vast Gajah
Mada University. Initially Hamengkubuwono IX, a thoroughly
modern sultan as well as a key figure in the independence struggle,
actually accommodated the university in a section of the *kraton*.
This was in 1946 when Jogja, as well as hosting the nation's first
university, was also playing host to its first government.

Sukarno and Hatta's flight from Jakarta to the comparative
safety of Jogja had strong religious associations. To the faithful it
mirrored the *hijra* of the Prophet Muhammad from Mecca to
Medina, thus enhancing the religious credentials of the new
government and the national credentials of the Jogja sultanate.
For three turbulent years, until overwhelmed by Holland's last
gasp offensive in 1949, Indonesia's first nationalist government
continued to operate from Mataram's ancient capital. If there was
irony in the 'Jogja Republic' enjoying the patronage of a monarch-
ist sultan, there was also enormous kudos in being seen to succeed
to the mystical powers and the political legitimacy of a dynastic
lineage that stretched back to Majapahit and beyond.

But as well as having a legitimizing bonus, the removal of the
nationalist leaders was an essential precaution. Although Jakarta
was nominally under British command, by early 1946 the Dutch
flag had already replaced the *merah-putih* on many public buildings and Dutch vigilantes were already gunning down nationalist
youths. The British were supposedly neutral. Go-betweens like

Laurens van der Post continued to pressure the Dutch into recognizing the strength of nationalist sentiment and making concessions. But after what had just happened in Surabaya, the Nationalists had good reason to distrust British tutelage.

There is a train direct from Jogja to Surabaya. It loops round the base of Mt Lawu to Madiun where, in 1947, Nasution would put down the PKI's first bid to ditch the NASA in NASAKOM and turn the Jogja republic into a people's republic, an incident graphically portrayed in one of those glass cases at the Crocodile Hole museum. Sidestepping another volcano, the railway continues east down the Brantas river past ancient Kediri and then Trowulan, the site of Majapahit's capital. Along this thoroughfare, between the Kendeng Hills to the north and the portico of volcanoes that screen Java's south coast, have passed those threads of empire, those filaments of faith and cords of struggle which, plaited together, comprise Javanese identity.

With a heavy concentration in the almost continuous towns and villages of this corridor, the Javanese constitute well over 60 percent of Indonesia's total population. Such demographic preponderance prompts the resentment of the outer islands and of other ethnic groups. They see Javanese names outnumbering all others in the bureaucracy and the armed forces. The crack regiments recruit in Java, graduates stream from its universities, and from its ports and airports, its studios and its presses radiate the archipelago's communications. Over-weighted and over-represented, Java is seen as the greedy centre and the Javanese as Indonesia's nearest thing to a master-race. Outward migration from Java becomes aggressive colonization while inward migration to Java becomes a cruel necessity forced on the disadvantaged periphery by Java-centrism.

These are emotive issues liable to cloud the clearest heads. Those who condemn the government's *transmigrasi* programme see only the ill effects of Javanese settlement in the felled forests and corrupted tribes of the outer islands. They take no account of the equally cruel necessities – over-population and minuscule land-holdings – which oblige the Javanese peasant to forsake his homeland or starve. They also take no account of Indonesia's peculiar status as a pelagic state. Were its islands joined together in a single landmass, movements of labour and patterns of settlement might go unnoticed. But because migration invariably involves a sea crossing it invites pejorative associations with European colonialism. The fact that such migrations have been going on for centuries and indeed provide the common language, the shared beliefs and political currency on which the nation has been built, goes unnoticed.

Finally, and this was why I rejected the direct route to Surabaya, anti-Javanese sentiment hinges on the idea that Java's population is a single homogeneous entity. The Sundanese would of course object to this and so would the people of densely populated Madura, the island off Surabaya. Furthermore there is in Java, as in nearly all the other islands, a great difference between the traditions and peoples of the interior and those of the coast. Java's coastal plain, essentially that stretching the length of the north coast, is known as the *paisir*. After plummeting down from the dewy alps of Gedong Songo, I aimed to strike it at Semarang which is both a major port and the capital of Central Java province.

My bus, a local bone-shaker of unpainted steel sheet and very few rivets, free-wheeled down deep Devonshire lanes collecting the blind, the halt and the lame like a highly rated evangelist. Evidently it doubled as an ambulance. Blood seeped from a bandaged head beside me and a man with one leg dangled from the luggage rack. Another, minus a forearm, was wedged across the aisle. Only a field surgeon could have been unembarrassed in such company. To the conductor's questions I therefore responded by indicating chronic deafness. I couldn't understand him anyway.

On the outskirts of town my fellow patients spilled on to the verge in a tangle of crutches, slings and dressings, thence to hobble into hospital. No one got on, but a scalding blast of sweat-soaked air invaded the bus, converting it into a leaky pressure-cooker. We must have reached sea-level. This was the *paisir*.

It occurred to me afterwards that the conductor had only been

trying to establish my destination; his route, it transpired, bypassed downtown Semarang to head direct for the docks. There,
thoroughly disorientated, I was deposited in a hall straight out of
hell. A sea of humanity surged aimlessly amid concrete benches
piled high with unwieldy bundles and cages of livestock. I fought
through the scrum from one bus bay to the next, handicapped by
a heavy case and a cherished umbrella. Whole villages were in
transit. A granny struggled with an assortment of hoes, her arms
as skinny as their handles; toddlers were borne aloft. Circuitously,
more by chance than direction, a few families found their way
down a ramp to a rusty steamer and eventually, since this was
transmigrasi in action, to a challenging new life in some forest
clearing on a distant shore.

Already the courtesies of their old life were being discarded.
Like cattle in the ring, they stampeded this way and that, wide-
eyed and near demented. Gone, too, were the certainties of home
and the reassurance of the familiar. If they were from the hills, the
dripping humidity would be as stressful a novelty as the dockland
stench. They spoke little. But the heat and the anxiety were
deafening. They didn't look much like a master race.

On the way back into town the heavens opened and the *becak*
driver halted to don a sou'wester and swathe my legs in polythene.
Lorries sped by, squirting muddy water from their much
remoulded tyres. We were stranded in a wasteland of high wire
fences and oil storage tanks, a forlorn trio of passenger, pedaller
and *becak* in the middle of nowhere. I loved it. No doubt the transmigrants were also heading east. Perhaps our paths would cross
again in Jayapura or Merauke. But theirs was a journey of forced
exile and horrific uncertainties, mine of purely selfish indulgence.
'*Saya sendiri*', 'I am alone', topped my list of handy phrases. I
trotted it out to waiters, to ticket clerks and to casual enquirers. It
was a password to privacy, proof of disengagement. Any traveller
worth his salt would have booked on that rusty steamer and
embraced the chance to investigate the *transmigrasi* experience. I
had shied from the ring and felt nothing but relief.

'*Saya sendiri*,' I told the receptionist when he asked if I wanted a double or a single. The hotel, a dismal place with flimsy rooms opening on to a noisy courtyard, was used by commercial travellers. Night would be disturbed by the clatter of high heels and the grunt and giggle of room service sex. It was run by a Chinese family. Prominent in all the port-cities of the *paisir*, the Chinese are said to constitute nearly half of Semarang's considerable population and to have been here for at least 600 years.

West of the city, Gedung Batu ('Stone Building' but actually a cave with shrines) commemorates the spot where the most illustrious of their forebears first came ashore. This was Zheng-Ho (Cheng-Ho, Zhenghe), the great Ming dynasty admiral and navigator whose several voyages to the archipelago, India, Arabia, East Africa and probably Australia anticipated by nearly a century those of Vasco da Gama and Alfonso da Albuquerque. With some 300 vessels, some of them treasure ships far larger than anything dreamt of by the Portuguese or the Dutch, he ranged the seas exacting tribute and collecting curiosities – a giraffe from Africa, a king from Sri Lanka – for his celestial masters. But in 1433 the mandarins tired of his novelties, of 'his exaggerations of bizarre things' and of the colossal expense of his voyages. Zheng-Ho fell from favour and China repudiated his expansionist policies, thus leaving the Eastern Seas wide open to European endeavour.

Only in Java's *paisir* did Zheng-Ho's memory continue to be revered and nowhere more so than at Semarang where he was deified as Sam Po Kong or Sam Po Tay Jin, 'The Three-jewelled Grand Eunuch'. For the Chinese, most of whom set up shop in Semarang during its Dutch development as a major seaport, the three-jewelled eunuch's shrine became a focus of Confucianist and Buddhist worship. More surprisingly it also continued to attract large numbers of Javanese Muslims. For by a happy if painful coincidence, the great Zheng-Ho was not just emasculated but circumcised. He was in fact a Muslim from Yunnan and, though it is doubtful whether he combined evangelism with imperial business, the Javanese proudly claim him as one of Islam's pioneers in the archipelago.

Such anomalies are not uncommon in the cosmopolitan *paisir*.

As the rainswept streets emptied for the cinema's last performance of the evening. Semarang's reputation for a hectic and very un-Javanese night-life became apparent. It recalled that scene in 'The Year of Living Dangerously' when, scenting dollars, Jakarta's whores smother a car-load of journalists by spread-eagling themselves on the bonnet and filling the windscreen with their gaping cleavages. Semarang's sirens were not quite so importunate but neither were they unobtrusive. Indeed, anatomically they had little choice in the matter and I wondered what exotic bloodlines must have crossed to produce such *belle tournure*. Plumped to a scarcely credible tumescence and precariously balanced on sharply tapered legs, their sensational upholstery completely blocked the pavement. Normally these and other sidewalk hazards – gaping man-holes, recumbent figures – can be avoided by walking in the road. But roads also serve as storm drains and, every shower being a storm, Jalan Pemuda was tonight in spate.

To contain such spates Indonesian pavements are raised to about knee height above the road. Clambering down and then up at each intersection makes for arduous street-walking. It also makes kerb-crawling awkward. The girls, obliged to negotiate with their patrons at calf level, tilted back their umbrellas and, prevented from squatting by already stressed mini-skirts, bent double at the waist like a retreating chorus line. Between the shop fronts and this row of stately buttocks it was just possible to squeeze. But in a society where the only part of the female physique normally visible is that above the collar, such a parade of stocking seams, multi-coloured knickers and taut upper thighs was disquieting.

I strode out nevertheless, intent on the night skyline. It fooled no one. Sensing an advantage, second string harpies groped from darkened doorways. For several previous blocks I had had the feeling of being followed. There was an air of menace about the place and, as the rain continued to empty the streets, I began to have second thoughts about being *sendiri*. As well as sex, Semarang has a reputation for violence. At the end of the war its *pemuda* (nationalist youths, after whom Jalan Pemuda is named) fought a ferocious battle with the Japanese to acquire their weapons and then used them to brutal effect first on Dutch prisoners of war and then, responding to events in Surabaya, on British troops. Here too, back in the 1920s, was founded Indonesia's first Communist party. Bad labour relations and massive under-employment still blight the city; cosmetic initiatives, like banishing all *becak* from the main thoroughfares to the warren of ill-lit lanes behind, deceive no one, least of all a *becak*-addicted foreigner.

When around my umbrella-supporting arm another, brown and bangled, locked with an intent more rapacious than affectionate, it was again time to shy from the ring. Discovering something that required immediate attention on the other side of the street, I wrenched myself free and leapt into the road. The flood was only ankle deep but the tussle had taken its toll. Instead of an umbrella, I was carrying a bedraggled totem resembling a dead cormorant.

'This Demak,' confided my neighbour, 'very holy place.' We were Surabaya-bound in one of the express mini-buses that ply the *paisir* route, linking its port-cities. Demak was the one whence Muslim rule spread along the coast in the 15th century, east to Majapahit and west to Cirebon, Sunda Kelapa (Jakarta) and Banten. Briefly it became the successor to Majapahit's maritime power and the focus of another of those trading zones, this one linking the north coast of Java with the south coasts of Kalimantan (Borneo) and Makassar (Sulawesi). But, as at Banten, tide and trade soon deserted Demak. Java is on the move, edging northwards with every flood which pushes its estuarial mud fans further into the shallow Java Sea. Port and city in these port-cities soon become detached. It had been a fair ride from Semarang's docks to its downtown but Demak is six miles from salt water. Mocked by its maritime past, it now trades only on its Islamic orthodoxy.

'Seven pilgrimages to *Mesjid Agung* is same as one *haj* [to Mecca]'.

'What about seven times round this roundabout?' We were stuck in heavy pilgrim traffic right in front of the great *mesjid* (mosque). My neighbour returned a look of withering contempt. In skull cap and shirt tails he at least evinced the gravity of the orthodox. I was less sure about the Great Mosque, the holiest in

Java. With a *pendopo* and tiered *gunongan* roof it seemed to belong to an older tradition and I was not surprised to read that, for the rulers of Demak, descent from Hindu-Javanese Majapahit mattered quite as much as their adoption of Islam. More surprisingly, Raden Patah and Raden Trenggana, the ex-Majapahit founders of Demak, appear to have been Java-born Chinese. They and Sunan Kalijaga, one of the nine *walis* or apostles of the new faith, are buried here. Hence the city's sanctity.

'This Kudus, very holy place.' We had travelled barely ten miles. Kudus seemed a good bit bigger than Demak and distinctly more prosperous. A sweet aroma of clove, 'that odoriferous pistil', according to Marsden, invaded the minibus. Here *kretek* are made, the quintessential Javanese smoke. But the mosque, as well as Javanese features, stands surrounded by brick portals and pavilions typical of a Balinese temple while its name, al-Aqsa, appears to be borrowed from that of the great mosque in Jerusalem. This fits with the etymology of 'Kudus' itself which is an approximation to 'al-Quds', the Arabic name for the city of Jerusalem. Had Abraham, like Zheng-Ho, also fetched up in Java? One got the feeling that, with more time, the *paisir* would lay claim to Sinbad and shed new light on the *Odyssey*.

After so many puzzling connections, it was a relief at last to follow the empty coast, here bleached to dazzling opacity by a merciless sun. Instead of vegetation and *sawah*, broad vistas of salt pans and prawn ponds flanked the road which was more like a causeway. Tiny donkeys, their coats encrusted with brine, were sandwiched between saddle sacks bulging with salt; their tails twitched to ward off the sand-flies. White-washed cottages strayed far from the villages and were strung about with pale blue fishing nets. A pony and trap brought the children home from school. Three minuscule cows and some scrawny sheep filed from the saline scrub that passed for pasture. It felt more like the Red Sea coast than Java.

At Tuban we swerved back inland to climb gently through silent plantations of teak saplings. Palmyra palms, taller than most coconuts, top-tufted and somewhat moth-eaten, dotted the landscape and declared the drier climate of East Java. When the *dang-*

dut, Indonesia's Islamic rock music, ran out on the casette, Radio Surabaya came over loud and clear. They were pronouncing it as 'Suroboyo' which sounded jauntier and more appropriate to the 'City of Heroes'.

Round Gresik, another once important port, we must have taken a bypass. I thought my companion was sleeping but on cue came a drowsy 'very holy place'. Two of the nine *walis* are buried here. I was still on the look-out for their graves when satanic saw mills and sugar refineries abruptly shut off the view. The industrial sprawl of Indonesia's second largest city, its eastern entrepôt and the capital of East Java, closed around us.

Back in 1945 Surabaya's troubles began at the Hotel Oranje in the colonial city's business centre. It is now called Hotel Majapahit and is screened from the street by a modern and ferociously air-conditioned annexe which serves as a lobby. Behind this, little has changed. In a typically colonial arrangement, wooden verandahs front the two-storey accommodation which ranges round three sides of a well-kept garden. In its midst a more imposing building contains the original dining room, reception hall and dance floor. Even the side doors here were locked but through their leaded panes of mauve and pink glass I saw mahogony banisters and dusty chandeliers glinting in shafts of sunlight.

In September 1945 the doors were open. No orchestra played and the potted plants had disappeared along with much of the furniture. But there was beer and there was Bols and in the middle of a hostile city, after forty months of internment and starvation, it must have seemed an oasis of normality and plenty. Here, then, soon after the Japanese surrender, the first Dutchmen to secure their release congregated to await developments. They were sick but sanguine and in between ridiculing native pretensions to self-government, speculating on when the British would arrive, and anticipating the juicy contracts which post-war reconstruction promised, they drank too much and talked too loud.

Or so thought the mysterious 'Miss Manx', who claims to have elicited details of the planned British deployment from one such *habitué* and to have passed them on to the Nationalists' intelligence. That a single woman of doubtful nationality, with bright red hair, practically no Dutch, and a rather unconvincing war record was not immediately recognized as a spy is surprising. She certainly thought so and quickly moved elsewhere, thus missing the first nationalist victory. It came after the Dutch hoisted their flag over the hotel. Youth groups (*pemuda*) promptly stormed the place, killed a Dutchman, captured others, and chopped the band of blue from the flag. The now *merah-putih*, the 'red and white' of Free Indonesia, was hauled back up the flagpole whence today still flies the most immaculate ensign in the city.

By early October British warships were off the harbour. Word of more atrocities reached them there but no move could yet be made against the city. 'Java is in a mess,' declared *The Times* of London. Jakarta and Bandung, though far from safe, had already been occupied; but for Surabaya more troops and more support were urgently needed. Thirty thousand prisoners of war were thought to be at risk in East Java. Yet the city was completely in the hands of the *pemuda* whose ranks were swelling daily as more *jihad*-minded radicals and Nationalist guerillas poured in from outside. They were well-armed; the Japanese had surrendered to them both the rifles and the artillery of what had been one of their main bases. And they were highly motivated by a charismatic young revolutionary called Sutomo ('Bung Tomo').

On 25 October, though still in no position to tackle the city, the British landed. Brigadier Aubertin Walter Southern Mallaby, a stooped and careworn 45-year-old, but a dedicated soldier, commanded 6,000 men of the 49th Indian infantry. The most he could hope to achieve was the safe evacuation of nearby prisoner of war camps and to this end he opened negotiations. On 27 October planes from Allied Command in Jakarta dropped leaflets on the city demanding the surrender of all weapons. Mallaby claimed to know nothing of this but the *pemuda* were unconvinced and sensed betrayal. Fighting broke out next day. Mallaby lost two of his officers and his Indian troops, hopelessly outnumbered, were soon in trouble.

To avert a catastrophe, two days later the British flew in

Sukarno and other members of his government. Perched nervously on the bonnet of a Buick, Mallaby and General Sudirman, Sukarno's military commander, toured the city; Sukarno himself broadcast appeals for calm over Radio Surabaya. A ceasefire was agreed in principle and the Republican leaders were flown back to Jakarta the same day. Mallaby was left to sort out the details. It was not, he must now have realized, going to be a formality.

Of perhaps 140,000 combatants in the city, only 20,000 were regulars in the Republic's army, itself a force barely cobbled together from various militias created by the Japanese. The rest, the loosely termed *pemuda* struggle groups, owed no particular allegiance to Sukarno whose record of co-operation with the Japanese and now the Allies smacked of compromise. They preferred the fiery rhetoric of Bung Tomo, a man like them in his twenties who habitually wore battledress and brandished a gun. It was his Radio Pemberontakan, 'Radio Revolution', to which they listened and it was his screamed defiance that would sustain them in the terrible weeks ahead.

On the afternoon of 30 October Mallaby and an escort drove into the centre of town. Fighting had broken out between some of his Maratha troops and Indonesian regulars near the Oranje Hotel. It was soon quelled and he then set off on another tour of the city. What happened next is disputed. But it seems that on Jembatan Merah, the 'Red Bridge', he was halted by a large crowd of armed *pemuda*. Pressing round the escort, they demanded the surrender of all weapons. Mallaby probably hoped to get a message back to the Marathas. He stuck his head out of the car window to say something and was instantly shot dead at close range. His escort replied with a hand-grenade and then escaped by jumping into the river.

'Mallaby Murdered,' read the London headlines on 1 November. 'Almost War In East Java.' An entire armoured division was now on its way to Surabaya. Mosquito fighters were being flown in from Jakarta and, unless the murderers were surrendered forthwith, the city could expect to be 'crushed' using 'the whole weight of sea, land and air forces with all the weapons of modern warfare'. These apparently excluded the atomic bomb only because the

British did not have one. More pamphlets were dropped, more appeals made by Sukarno. But Bung Tomo's Radio Revolution continued to crackle with defiance and it now introduced English language news broadcasts. Colourfully written and read with feeling by a woman with the remains of a Glasgow accent, they were meant to influence the world's media, especially the USA's, and to counteract the propaganda of Allied broadcasts from Jakarta. But they were also heard by the British and Indian troops now converging on the city and it was they who, in the tradition of 'Shanghai Lil' and 'Tokyo Rose', dubbed this surprising voice 'Surabaya Sue'. At last 'Miss Manx', for it was she, was publicly identified with the Indonesian cause.

'Right from the start Bung Tomo and I got on famously . . . His luminous eyes shone with inward fire . . . He could charm the ducks off the water.'

Reading, weeks later, Miss Manx's somewhat breathless narrative I would have difficulty reconciling the characters with the events. The heroic red-head ('Miss Minx' my Balinese informant would invariably call her) and the fiery revolutionary who was 'such a brilliant conversationalist' seemed to have stepped from the pages of *Woman's Own.* Yet here they were, conversing brilliantly while they inspired a revolution, risked the destruction of a major city and contrived the turning point of the Indonesian revolution. There may even be substance in the heroine's claim to have provoked a mutiny in the British Army. Taking their cue from Surabaya Sue, men of the West Yorkshire Regiment apparently expressed their misgivings about the bombardment of a city with whose population they were not officially at war and with whose unanimous desire for self-determination they had no quarrel.

The West Yorkshires having been moved elsewhere, on 10 November, henceforth *Hari Pahlawan* ('Heroes' Day') throughout Indonesia, the battle for Surabaya began. It lasted twenty days. From the sea Allied ships bombarded the city, overhead Mosquitoes strafed and Thunderbolts bombed, on the ground tanks, howitzers and 25-pounders shelled. Resistance was stiff. To save face General Mansergh let it be known that his painfully slow progress was designed to save lives. It did. Allied casualties were modest, 'comparatively nothing' as Raffles would have put it. But on the receiving end of this blitzkreig it was a different story. In the clapboard *kampungs* fires raged for days. Streets in the vicinity of supposed targets were obliterated. Ten thousand, mostly civilians, is a conservative estimate of the fatalities. More died in the street fighting. By the end of the month the city had been 'cleared' and the enemy, including the fiery Tomo and Miss Manx, dispersed.

For the Allies it had been a technical victory but for the Indonesians a massive psychological triumph. In all but Dutch eyes, the strength of Nationalist sentiment and the determination to resist the reimposition of colonial rule were now beyond dispute. On British insistence the Dutch were dragged to the negotiating table and, four years and two broken accords later, on American insistence they at last relinquished their claim to the archipelago. Surabaya had indeed been the turning point.

By an odd coincidence, my visit to the 'City of Heroes' coincided with a lesser battle that was under way in the correspondence columns of the English language *Jakarta Post*. It seemed that the events of 1945 were subject to revisionism. One writer, claiming that the battle of Surabaya had been 'blown up out of all proportion', proved conclusively that the Allies had no bombers within range of the city and that therefore it could not have been blown to smithereens. Another, besides wondering whether bombs required bombers, quoted extensively from a guide book and a recent history, both published in the USA, to the effect that the city had nevertheless been 'levelled'.

Lying in bed with a cup of tea, I read with growing disbelief. It was not, after all, that long ago. The old boy in *peci* and sarong who brought the tea had probably lived through it. Newspapers of the day had been full of it. Some of the old Dutch warehouses near the station looked as if they still bore the scars. Yet such sources had been implicitly discounted by the paper's correspondents. It was as if they must be suspect simply because they were readily

available. Better to stick to something which, published abroad
and in English, must be of less questionable authority.

While examining my own conscience in this matter, a light
shower of paint flakes and strawy plaster landed on the newspaper.
I looked up just in time to see a small crack in the ceiling bulge,
open and fall, closely followed by a tabby cat. It was very thin and
it landed lightly on my knees. There it paused just long enough to
get covered in dust and then shot through the window. That
seemed to solve the problem of the bombers. If a feather-weight
cat could bring down the ceiling, a stick of hand-grenades dropped
from above would surely blow the roof off.

There remained the mystery of Miss Manx. If she was
'Surabaya Sue', was she also then K'tut Tantri, the Balinese
princess turned freedom fighter who had reappeared in the Hotel
Indonesia sometime in the 1980s? Who else was she? And how
come this Balinese princess had red hair and a fair grasp of
Glaswegian patter?

The ex-Governor of Surabaya, who was supposed to have all
the answers, was not at home. Nor was his home where he said it
was. He had given me the address on the phone but neither the
hotel reception nor the taxi driver had heard of it. After an hour's
futile enquiries we settled for his office as given in the directory.
There an elderly clerk brought coffee. His Ex-Excellency, he
explained, was in Jakarta for the day. The address he had given me
was correct; he would be expecting me about now. So what, asked
the clerk, was I doing in Surabaya?

Not for the first time I had fallen foul of metropolitan pre-
sumption. Foreign visitors are presumed to be Jakarta-based, to be
ringing from Jakarta, and to be conducting in Jakarta whatever
business concerns them. So what was I doing in Surabaya?

'Ah, you mean Sudara K'tut.' His eyes did not exactly light up.
Sudara, he said, was the female equivalent of Bung. And yes, she
had certainly joined Bung Tomo as a radio announcer. After
Surabaya she went to Jogja and worked with the Republican
government. He had also heard her called Miss Manx. She was
American, he thought. Or possibly Australian. But she had lived
in Bali before the war. That was why she had a Balinese name. It

was a great pity that I was not in Jakarta. There so many people would be able to help. Of course I could try in Bali. He was not very hopeful; but I would like Bali and then I could fly back to Jakarta. More coffee?

12. Paradise lost

One easily forgets, when so much among slight and graceful figures, what an ungainly lot the rest of us are. After 2,500km in the company of various peoples who nevertheless all shared this typically Malay physique, I had come to take it for granted; so I was quite unprepared for my first Melanesian. Crouched by the roadside in a jumble of elbows and knees, he was waiting for the bus which during a protracted circuit of the Surabaya suburbs conveyed passengers from the old terminus to a new one from which, unbeknown to anyone but the drivers, long distance buses now plied.

Perhaps the Melanesian was also in the know for he boarded last, carried a guitar, and immediately essayed 'Auld Lang Syne' in a voice that was never meant to sing and in a language, presumably one of the 250-odd spoken on Irian Jaya, of which no one understood a word. Taller than most and blacker than all, he had close-cropped curly hair, butterfly nostrils and teeth like tombstones; below the waist incredibly thin hips in skin-tight jeans were ideally fashioned for busking one's way down a packed bus aisle.

I called him Dick because he reminded me of Raffles' Dick. In 1816, between his stint in Java and his 'exile' to Bengkulu, Raffles returned to England accompanied by 'a lad who came into my service under very peculiar circumstances'. The circumstances were peculiar presumably because Raffles, a sworn enemy of slavery, had had to purchase Dick. Science occasionally obliged a man to stifle his scruples. But Dick, who much preferred this name to the alternative 'Papua', seems to have been rewarded with whatever freedom a total dependant could hope to enjoy plus his passage to London. There, though only ten years old, he 'excited some curiosity as being the first individual of the woolly haired race of Eastern Asia who has been brought to this country'.

'The buttocks are so much lower than in the negro,' opined Sir Everard Home in the course of a detailed examination, 'as to form a striking mark of distinction'. On the whole Sir Everard thought that the Papuans were not related to the negro races of Africa although others argued for some ancient linkage and pointed to Dick's protuberant lips, especially the lower one which 'projects forward from the lower jaw to such an extent that the chin forms no part of the face, the lower part of which is formed by the mouth'. Dick bore all this scrutiny with admirable patience and appears to have stayed on in England after Raffles' departure. His chinless profile attracted several artists, one of whose canvases was engraved for Lady Raffles' *Memoir* of her husband. It was this picture of a winsome Dick, posed against a backdrop of beach and palm trees, that was brought to mind by the busker on the bus.

By the time his tadpole hips were level with my seat he had finished 'Auld Lang Syne' and was on to Dylan.

'From Jayapura?' I asked.

'It's all over now,' he croaked, 'Fuck-Fuck Baby Blue.' The language was still incomprehensible but I recognized the tune and realized that 'Fuck-Fuck' was an interpolation. While waiting to board the *bis malam* for Bali, I found it on the map. Spelled Fakfak, it bulged like a full crop just below the Bird's Head (Vogelkop) peninsula on one of Irian's western extremities.

Between Surabaya and Fakfak was mostly sea. Though only half way down the arc of the archipelago, I was a lot nearer journey's end than the longitude suggested. Crinkly hair and low slung buttocks would become progressively more commonplace. Indo- was about to peter out; ahead lay the watery world of -nesia. But first came Bali and Lombok whose considerable celebrity owes much to their unique location on this cultural cusp. Hybrids of mysterious Asia crossed with easy-going Oceania, they may be

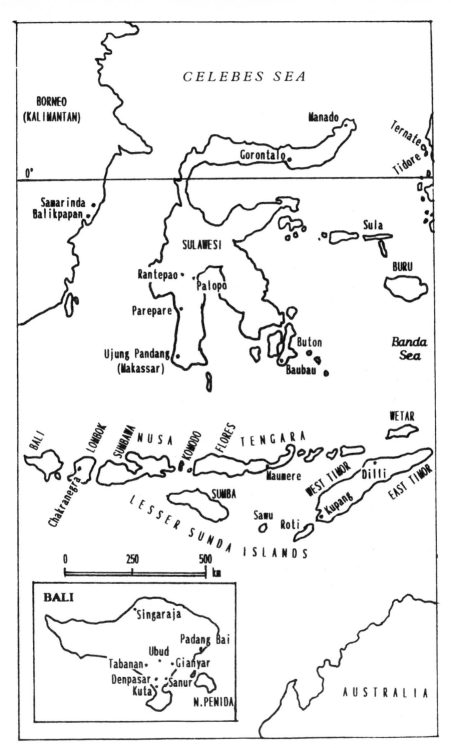

BALI, SULAWESI AND NUSA-TENGARA

the only places in the world where Exotic East and Pacific Paradise are packaged as one.

It was not always so. In 1815, during the briefest of visits, Raffles found the Balinese backward and much less civilized than their Javanese neighbours. Far from being any kind of paradise, he identified the island as the archipelago's main source of slaves. Indeed it was here that he acquired Dick. The majority of Batavia's slaves came from Bali, Balinese women being especially sought after by the Chinese community who appreciated their willingness to cook pork as much as their comely appearance. Later, when acquainted with the slavers' ravages on distant Nias, Raffles was inclined to equate the Balinese with the Niha; on the ladder of civilization both occupied the same rather lowly rung. They were robust, independent and hard-working peoples whose untutored ways might render them more amenable to European influence and Christian values than their more effete neighbours. That Bali is now credited with one of the world's more sophisticated and durable cultures and Nias with one of its more primitive and endangered would have surprised him.

Perceptions of Bali changed when the world became better acquainted with it; and they were much influenced by the direction from which outsiders approached the island. Coming from India by way of Penang and Java, Raffles never doubted that Bali belonged to Asia and that, however primitive, its culture was unmistakably and, for South-east Asia, uniquely Hindu. Its caste system and its principal deities he greeted like old friends unexpectedly encountered in improbable surroundings. He encouraged his Bengali servants to tell the Balinese how comfortable their co-religionists in India were under British rule; and to the consternation of the Dutch, who had as yet shown little interest in the island, he hatched numerous schemes to bring it under British jurisdiction. These, like others, came to nothing; once again his only reward was a sharp rap on the knuckles from London.

More significantly, as the first visitor to the island with any claim to scholarship, Raffles advanced the idea that Bali provided the vital clue to Java's history. 'What they [the Balinese] now are, it is probable that the Javans once were.' In Java, Hinduism survived only in the tumbled ruins of places like Prambanam and amongst a few marginalized social groups such as the Badui and even the Tengger highlanders whose mountain retreat my *bis malam* was even now flying past. But in Bali Hinduism still governed the lives of 90 percent of the population. 'The present state of Bali may be considered, therefore, as a kind of commentary on the ancient condition of the natives of Java.'

Such statements made the study of Balinese culture eminently respectable. From the anthropology syllabus, where most of Indonesia's ethnic minorities still languish, the Balinese were promoted to the arts faculty. Here was a place apart, an archive of pre-Islamic beliefs and customs miraculously preserved in a forgotten Asian basement. Insights into Java's and perhaps even India's classical past were anticipated. But when eventually European scholars took up Raffles' challenge, they were easily seduced from their textual studies by the vitality of Balinese culture. So were the Americans. Coming to Bali after field trips to Samoa and New Guinea, the formidable Margaret Mead and her associates saw the island in a Pacific context. An ethnographer and social anthropologist, Mead concentrated on human behaviour from the toilet to the temple but had little time for the tenets of Hinduism or the subtleties of the East. Coming via Polynesia, Hollywood followed suit; Crosby and Hope donned grass skirts in *The Road to Bali*; 'Bali Hai' was seductively located in the *South Pacific*.

Coming from Surabaya I was still thinking of Sue, alias Sudara K'tut. It so happened that the seat beside me had been allocated to a Balinese girl who, with almond eyes and a flawless complexion to satisfy the most exacting tourist fantasy, could herself have been a princess. We had exchanged smiles on boarding since when, appalled no doubt at the prospect of spending the night with an *orang putih* (white man), she had found friends at the back. Miffed, though grateful for the extra space, I went to sleep.

It was the bus's manoeuvres on boarding the ferry at Banyuwangi that woke me. Much smaller than the roll-on-roll-off monsters of the Sunda Strait, this ship received traffic from the side and accommodated it on deck. A turntable would have helped, failing which buses were obliged to advance and reverse with precision at the frantic behest of a gang of loaders. Only dimly aware of all this, I quickly registered a closer presence. My companion had not only reclaimed her seat but, as is the way with Indonesians in buses, had fallen asleep sprawled across her neighbour.

It was like having some exquisite butterfly alight on one's chest. The idea of disembarking to explore the ferry and savour the sea at night was unthinkable. I lay back, petrified lest the slightest movement rouse her. A numb arm and the tickle of a raven curl barely registered. I closed my eyes and, breathing as lightly as lungs permitted, savoured her fragrance. It was that of the dusk, a mixture of jasmine, something tart rather like apple, and the tang of earth just after rain.

She was still sleeping when we bounded off the ferry. Even Bali's tighter bends and sudden declivities failed to wake her. Approaching Tabanan a small patch of the night sky dead ahead burnished to a coal-scuttle lustre. The patch grew and the copper faded to purple and then to a pale grey which gradually overspread the sky. My companion stirred. But as if reluctant to concede, the stars now shone more brightly than ever and the black of night inked the overhanging palms. Dawn doesn't come up like thunder; Kipling got it wrong. It goes to work like a cleaner, laboriously sweeping away the night and then buffing up the day with a duster.

Where the copper had first shown, a flush of salmon pink now suffused the horizon. It too then paled as a pillar of cloud defied the sun. Alert at last, the girl rose. She flashed no farewell smile but, as she turned, a disconcertingly yellow light flooded the bus. The sun was up, the *sawah* shone, Bali beckoned.

It was smaller and more cluttered than I remembered. After Java's stately vistas its immediacy was almost fussy. Bamboo thickets brushed against the window as the bus dashed and danced along switch-back lanes like the scatty but loveable *barong* whose hairy advent is bad news for troublemakers in Bali's mythological dramas. While we stopped to let the girl off, a bent crone rested her besom brush and on her well-swept threshold placed a small raft-like offering bearing a single vermilion blossom. She was so bent that she scarcely needed to stoop yet she grounded the offering with both hands as if tentatively launching a paper boat. Small boys returned from some communal bathing place, their hair still flattened and their shoulders freckled with drips. Dew glistened on a spider's web and smoke billowed from a kitchen door. Of all the epithets heaped on Bali, Nehru's 'the morning of the world' seemed the most apposite.

Though now the best known island in Indonesia, as much visited as Hawaii or Majorca, until this century Bali was among the least known and the least visited. In a reversal of Java's geography, it has mountains to the north and arable to the south thus, as it were, turning its back on the busy trade routes of the Java Sea. Apart from a long-standing interest in Lombok, whose high and hazy profile they confront, the Balinese traditionally devoted their labour, structured their society and managed their devotions in the interests of irrigated rice production on minute and vertiginous terraces. They shunned the sea and the sea shunned them. With no spices and no traders, they were bypassed by the spice trade and so ignored by Islam as it swept east through the ports of the archipelago. The Portuguese rated rain-starved Timor a better bet than Bali; at least it had sandalwood and willing converts. And the Dutch, in spite of Raffles, preferred to die for the doubtful prize of Aceh before pocketing the paradise on their doorstep.

In the early centuries AD, Hindu and Buddhist influences had presumably reached the island from East Java. A mere three miles wide, the Bali Strait impeded neither ideas nor armies. Balinese rulers occasionally laid claim to Java's eastern extremity and eventually claimed descent from Majapahit's rulers. Javanese rulers, particularly those of Majapahit, often laid claim to Bali and may have eventually sought sanctuary there. Links were close and until the 18th century Bali still had a Hindu neighbour in East Java's Blambangan peninsula. But the political monopoly engineered by Holland and the spiritual monopoly enjoined by Islam severed these links and isolated Bali as never before. Left for 200 years to its own already anachronistic devices, it was not well placed to face the challenges of the 20th century.

★

Dr Ide puffed on his cigar.

'My great grandfather, you see, he was still a sovereign power here. He had unlimited power, absolute power, and this power is surrounded by a kind of holy appearance and complete allegiance of the people. When he went out he never walked. He was always borne on a palanquin and there were always thirty or forty bearers, you see, accompanying him.'

An ancient retainer poured the coffee as sparrows hopped about the table. Otherwise the *puri* ('palace' but actually a series of stone courtyards barely distinguishable from a Balinese temple) was as deserted as ever. We sat in an airy *pendopo*, facing each other across the sparrows, me on the sofa, he in an armchair which his watch chain, impeccably tailored jacket and chestnut sarong somehow transformed into a throne. Dr Ide Anak Agung Gde Agung is no longer raja of Gianyar and no longer the wielder of absolute power. But with a name which, if not an incantation must surely be some form of gamelan notation, he remains a Balinese institution, as unaccountably immune to change as was his great-grandfather's absolutism.

'That is also a riddle for me, you see. The Dutch appointed a Resident in the northern part of Bali in about 1870, in Singaraja, and for them it would have been a very easy walk-over to conquer the main Balinese principalities here in the south. But they waited, you see, 36 years, until 1906. It's a riddle.'

Presumably his great grandfather was Dewa Manggis Disasteria VII who, anything but a disaster, had made Gianyar the most powerful of the seven to nine principalities into which the island was divided. 'Power served pomp and not pomp power,' writes Geertz in his analysis of these 'theatre states'. If Jogjakarta went in for spectacular rituals, Bali went in for ritual spectacles whose magnificence and drama confirmed the ruler as a cosmic icon and provided the only true measure of political ascendancy.

When Disasteria VI had died in 1847, his cremation attracted crowds estimated at 50,000. The eleven-tiered tower on which his body, wrapped in white linen and guarded by men carrying fans, was borne from the *puri* up the lane behind to the cremation ground required 500 bearers. It was preceded by pikemen and lance-bearers, numerous orchestras, and thousands of gaily dressed mourners carrying gifts of gold and silver, weapons and ornaments, fruit and fried rice. There were priests, princes and yet more orchestras and, behind the towering hearse, there followed three lesser towers, also gorgeously caparisoned. In each sat a young woman, dressed in white like the corpse of her master. Their hair hung loose and with comb in one hand and mirror in the other they seemed oblivious to the world as they carefully arranged their tresses for a celestial rendezvous.

The pyre was more like a pit, walled with brick to contain the flames and provide a back draught. These walls supported a pavilion with crimson pillars and gilded roof wherein stood a lion with trappings of purple and gold. The lion was the coffin. Through a panel in its hind quarters the corpse, after the necessary rituals, was placed in its belly and the faggots beneath set to burn.

To one side and considerably above this soon blazing pit, two towers of bamboo scaffolding, 20ft high, were connected by a bridge from which a small gantry reached towards the flames. The bridge was wrapped in wet banana fronds to stop it catching fire and provision had been made for a small waiting area beside the gantry. There the three women assembled after venturing from their towers on to the bridge. The flames rose higher, sparks showered among them and the crackling vied with the music. 'Still they showed no fear,' wrote a Dutch traveller who happened to observe the ceremony, 'still their chief care seemed to be the adornment of the body . . .' At last the moment was judged right and a plank was pushed from the end of the gantry to serve as a diving board. On each head was placed a dove and as each bride walked the plank she joined her hands above her head, encircling the dove as with a cage. The bird, like the carefully combed hair, flew free as, one by one, the women leaped soundlessly into the inferno.

Having to hand a copy of the Dutchman's description of this spectacle, I showed it to Ide. It was eloquent testimony to his ancestors' authority and also reassuring evidence of the continuity of Balinese culture. For two days earlier, at the cremation of a celebrated wood carver in a nearby village, the ritual had been repeated down to the last detail save that for a woodcarver the towers were not so high. Also the attendant crowd included about 300 tourists plus a film crew; and there were no suicides.

'No, that is not suicide, that is not suicide at all.' insisted Ide, 'that is *sati*. It is the belief by my compatriots, you see, that it is better to die than to lose your honour. Or to dishonour the king. It is the same with *puputan*.'

Puputan means 'ending' and is the equivalent at national level of a royal cremation. In the latter half of the 19th century, with the Dutch apparently content to restrict their interference to the north coast, the Balinese kingdoms were free to indulge their passion for spectacle and status while welcoming their first scholarly attention. H.N. van der Tuuk, an eccentric philologist, began compiling a dictionary of the Kawi language and in his employ a young Javanese schoolmaster met and married a Balinese girl. Their son was named Kusno Sosro Sukarno who, though born in Java, seems to have been conceived in Bali. He later dispensed with the first two names but made much of his Balinese pedigree.

Under van der Tuuk's patronage there also came to Bali a Dr Julius Jacobs, 'the man who discovered the Balinese female breast' (A. Vickers). This was in the 1880s. Bare breasts and the sexual excesses of the Balinese nobility, unworthy of remark in Raffles' day, now added a titillatory dimension to the image of Bali. Jacobs disingenuously clothed his observations in ethonographic jargon laced with Latin and German; but word nevertheless got out. There was definitely something different, as well as public, about Balinese breasts. Full and firm, they had an unsupported innocence which, following the sort of examination to which Dick had been subject, Jacobs ascribed to pectoral development just below each orb.

He also hinted at the prevalence of abnormal sexual practices plus a high degree of sexual licence. Bali, in short, was ripe for prurient celebrity. But in 1894 Dutch-Balinese relations received a serious set-back when in neighbouring Lombok a Dutch expeditionary force, sent to support a revolt by the indigenous population, was routed by Lombok's Balinese overlords. Although

Lombok was of no strategic and little commercial value, such a blow to Holland's colonial prestige could not go unavenged. A second expedition laid Lombok waste, routed Balinese rule there and replaced it with Dutch supervision. To both parties it was clear that the same fate could easily befall Bali itself. Barbaric customs like *sati*, periodic famines and incessant warfare between the petty kingdoms provided ample justification for Dutch interference. Although attempts have been made to romanticize the last century of Balinese independence, it was no golden sunset; destabilized by the Dutch presence in the north and wasted by its own rivalries, the island lurched towards its nemesis not in a blaze of glory but in a wide-eyed daze of drama and excess.

Two unrelated incidents of slight but significant import began the crisis. The raja of Tabanan ignored Dutch protests about a particularly spectacular *sati*; and the raja of adjacent Badung (roughly the modern Denpasar) declined to compensate a Chinese ship-owner whose vessel was wrecked and then plundered on a reef off Sanur, now one of the major tourist beaches.

'It was a very small amount of money,' said Ide with a wave of his cigar, 'about 7500 guilders. But you see, the prince of Badung found it unjust. He thinks: 'I have no reason to pay you Dutch,' and so only for $700 there was a quarrel. The Dutch sent their expeditionary force and the prince died with his 2,000 people. It was a question of his honour, you see. He thought: 'I don't like to be put under pressure by these Dutch people; I like better to die'. So he marched through the gates of his *puri*, you see, followed by all his court, his wives, his sons, his nephews, his cousins, everybody dressed in white and the ladies with flowers in their hair as if they were going to a temple festival. And music and drums. And they marched through the gates. And the Dutch thought this is some kind of procession. But instead of a procession to the temple, they just marched into the fusillades of the Dutch forces, you see. Everybody was killed. And he who wasn't killed, killed himself. This is *puputan*, the ending. So it was unbelievable expression of defending honour.'

At Pemacutan the ritual repeated itself that same afternoon. Next morning a young noble presented himself to the Dutch saying he had been away the day before and had missed being killed with the rest so wanted to be shot now. 'When he was refused he drew his *kris* and stabbed himself before he could be prevented' (M. Covarrubias). Days later the Raja of Tabanan contrived a modest *puputan* in gaol; 18 months later Dutch gunners mowed down the royal family of Klungkung before demolishing Bali's finest *puri*. Klungkung's sole survivor, a female relative of the raja, who had fainted from her wounds, recalled 'the cool hissing of the bullets' in her ears, 'like music', she said.

It was April 1908. Bleriot was about to fly the English channel; Henry Ford was tooling up for the Model T. But from Bali came crisp photos of Dutchmen, looking indistinguishable from Boers in their wide-awake hats, firing their belt-fed machine guns indiscriminately into the flower-bedecked ranks of an ancient aristocracy processing to the music of gongs and armed only with ceremonial lances and daggers.

People were reminded of the Rajput *jauhar* when another ancient aristocracy chose death rather than dishonour. In a final act of reckless valour the Rajput warriors would charge into the line of fire while behind them their womenfolk leapt into the flames which engulfed their desert fortresses. But that was in the 18th century. Victor and vanquished were both Indian and, for a Rajput, defeat without death was never an option. This was the 20th century. The rajas of Badung and Klungkung could, like Dr Ide's grandfather in Gianyar, have negotiated favourable terms; their women were guaranteed immunity and their retainers would actually be freer under Dutch supervision. But they chose to die; and not just to preserve their honour but to spite the enemy with the guilt of their complicity.

Around and on top of the dead raja the bodies piled in a mortuary mound of the whitest garments and the reddest blood. Youthful limbs and melting smiles tangled with the bent and wasted forms of palace pensioners. To the stench of powder and death were added the boudoir scents of roses and gardenia. Jewellery of gold and finely wrought *kris* littered the grass. In carefully dressed tresses the now crumpled blossoms of red hibiscus and white champak anticipated the *merah-putih* of a new generation.

Such scenes, captured on camera, probably provoked as much revulsion against colonialism as any incident this century. From them even the Dutch combatants reeled in disgust. Henceforth they readily conceded that Bali was different and that, like a child orphaned in ignorance, it deserved the mildest form of tutelage.

'But it was not the last *puputan*,' said Ide. 'It happened again in 1946 during the revolution. The Balinese opposed the return of the Dutch after the war, you see. But Ngurah Rai – he was the leader – was eventually surrounded in the environs of Badung by a huge Dutch force with modern weapons and so on. Instead of just escaping to the mountains as guerillas, he too chose to face the Dutch and again it was a kind of *puputan*. He thought it is better that I die with all my forces than to surrender. So he sacrificed them; he died with all his 150 people. You will have seen his statue near the airport. The airport itself is named after him.'

As a martyr to the nationalist cause, Ngurah Rai was quickly co-opted into the Indonesian pantheon alongside Diponegoro, Imam Bonjol, Teuku Umar and the rest. By emphasizing his revolutionary and anti-colonial credentials rather than his obsession with Balinese precedent, Rai and so Bali were firmly lashed to the raft of mainstream Indonesian experience. Twenty years later the success of this policy was painfully evident when in 1965–66 the island enthusiastically subscribed to the pan-Indonesian pogrom against Communism provoked by the GESTAPU coup attempt and the Crocodile Hole massacre.

For this latest holocaust Ide suggested the figure of 70,000 Balinese fatalities, say 5 percent of the then population. Unlike in Java the army played no part; the Balinese simply massacred one another. Although Communist ideology may have been seen as a threat to Hindu culture, the PKI's General Secretary had sought to allay such fears by ostentatiously worshipping in a Hindu temple; most of Bali's so-called Communists probably knew no more of Marxism than they did of macro-economics.

It was more a question of ancient caste and family rivalries having become politicized in the heavily charged atmosphere of Sukarno's era. To his mother's homeland, Sukarno brought patronage and international celebrities like Jawaharlal Nehru, thus inaugurating the modern tourist boom. Expectations were heightened and loyalty to a party, any party, seemed to offer an exciting alternative to the old allegiance to raja and *puri*. But when from Java there came word of the PKI's proscription and of the immunity from prosecution for those who eliminated this 'enemy in their midst', *parangs* were sharpened; the 'enchanting' Balinese, 'the happiest people on earth', cheerfully steeped themselves in blood. 'Communists' who last year diverted the water from your *sawah* to theirs were hacked to death in their beds; others, for declining their labour or marrying above their status, were burnt in their homes or butchered at their bathing pool. Many, it is said, donned sacrificial white and presented themselves *en masse*, with their women and children, for an honourable death.

'Yes,' said Ide, 'for the Communists too it was a sort of *puputan*, an ending with honour.'

Above Gianyar deep gorges, now choked with bamboo and banyan, have been gouged by the streams which drain the island's mountain spine. The ridges which divide them descend gradually in broad flights of *sawah* which contour round their flanks into long sinuous ledges of cultivation. Here ducks guddle among the water-logged rice seedlings while cinnamon cattle graze the embankments, their white stockings and hind-quarters more antelope than cow. A tinkle of music is borne on the breeze. Cloud clings to the slopes of Gunung Agung ('the great mountain') but below, where the terraces sink towards the sea, panes of water reflect a flawless sky. In the distance coral sands and turquoise depths fringe the Lombok Strait.

Unmarked on the map, tiny roads run interminably north-south. Arcadian villages embowered in flowering shrubs line their narrow strip of tarmac over which hang, from bamboo poles like street lights, the corn-dolly blossoms fashioned for the Galungan festival. Beneath them women, immaculately groomed and tightly girt in blouses of lace and *kains* of batik, file towards the temple, salvers piled with bananas and mangos on their heads, fresh blossoms in their hair. Their menfolk crouch at a wicket gate, each cradling his rooster, the essential fashion accessory of the Balinese male. A youth of radiant beauty straddles his motorbike while fondling a Cuckoo Marran with the eye of an osprey and the neck of a vulture. Over the fence a Rhode Island Red is being bathed in a bucket.

The cocks make no attempt to resist these attentions. On the contrary, they appear profoundly jealous of their keeper's affections. The solace is mutual and there is probably no closer bond between human and bird. As a baby is to a mother, a fighting cock is to man, wrote Margaret Mead, 'something to play with, to titillate and tease, to dawdle over, to carry about, to dress up and undress, to stroke and tickle.' Yet men have occasionally killed for cocks; and cocks still kill for men as often as they enter the pit. A casual blood-letting with all the trimmings of ritual, the cock-fight remains central to social life in most parts of Indonesia and nowhere more so than in Bali. Neither social reformers like Raffles nor Islam's injunctions against gambling have managed to outlaw it. Imminently these same affectionate roosters, with five-inch blades of razor-sharp steel spliced to their spurs with white thread, must kill or be killed. The masculine ego will settle for nothing less.

Cock-fondling of a more intimate sort was one of Margaret Mead's most satisfying discoveries. She had come to Bali with Gregory Bateson, her fellow field-worker and third husband, to honeymoon and to spend two years (1936–38) studying cultural aspects of schizophrenia. Since Balinese dancers so readily fell into a trance, it was presumed that much might be learnt about the schizoid condition.

Predictably, Mead was not disappointed. Like their ducks, the Balinese seemed to live in a daze of contented guddling, 'a rhythmic, patterned unreality of pleasant, significant movement, centred in one's own body to which all emotion long ago withdrew'. It began in the cradle when maternal fondling and tugging of the infant's genitalia suggested 'the idea of the separate penis.' Recalling Freud, the Batesons maintained that such stimulation must be indicative of cultural repression. This repression conditioned the Balinese to a life of gregarious harmony interspersed with periods of complete abstraction and outbursts of culturally controlled hysteria and excess. In Balinese idiom the sexual imagery is always that of the assassin or the cock-pit. The penis is a *kris*, a blade, with which to pierce the woman or to prod her ovum. In the acts of male homosexuality portrayed by Balinese artists this imagery is even more explicit, the passion and the pain being equally apparent. That savage and apparently uncontrollable eruption of violence which elsewhere in Indonesia is characterized as *amok* is thus in Bali sanctioned by culture, to some extent ritualized within dance dramas, and epitomized in the cultural cataclysm of the *puputan*.

The Batesons' two years in Bali in the late 1930s coincided with the island's first flush of popularity as an exotic international destination. Cruise liners took to anchoring off Sanur whence a fleet of small boats and crowded jalopies whisked passengers into Denpasar for four hours of indifferent dance performances, frantic souvenir hunting, and sumptuous lunching in one of the two new hotels. In more leisurely style here stayed such celebrities such as Barbara Hutton, Charlie Chaplin and Noel Coward. Quipped Coward: 'As I said this morning to Charlie,/ There is far too much music in Bali . . .'.

All visited Ubud where the suave and charismatic Walter Spies, a German aristocrat and noted painter, had assembled a menage of local musicians, dancers, painters, and other decorous disciples. Taking their cue from Spies' insights and contacts, the precious and privileged international set enthusiastically portrayed the Balinese as denizens of an artistic Elysium. In a wider world soured by recession and menaced by totalitarianism people needed a paradise myth and Bali provided it. 'The nearest approach to Utopia that I am ever likely to see,' cooed Geoffrey Gorer, one of Mead's recruits. 'Everybody in Bali seems to be an artist,' noted Miguel Covarrubias and it was this 'effervescence of artistic activity and the highly developed aesthetic sense of the population' that was so conducive to harmony and happiness.

But in 1938 the Batesons moved on and in 1939 the idyll

abruptly ended. A Dutch crack-down on homosexuals, spies, and other undesirable aliens led to Spies's arrest and the speedy departure of many of his friends. Others heeded the call to fight Hitler in Europe. By the time paradise was finally lost to the Japanese, practically the only survivor of the halcyon Thirties was the woman whom Dr Ide insisted on calling 'Miss Minx from the Isle of Wight'.

Considering that Ide had just cited, as the worst possible example of cultural exploitation, the showbiz wedding in a Balinese temple of 'Mike Jogger', lead singer of the Rolling Stones, I was prepared to accept that 'Miss Minx from the Isle of Wight' must be Miss Manx from the Isle of Man.

'That book. So much rubbish. You see, she hood-winked the Raja of Bangli. He felt sorry for her and found her a house. But she says he adopted her. So much rubbish. You have read the book?'

I hadn't even heard of it. But later I found a copy and, rubbish or not, the pieces at last fell into place. *Revolt in Paradise* by K'tut Tantri is, according to a timely reassurance in the author's blurb, 'in all essentials factual'; only inessentials, like the author's real name, her parentage, circumstances and motives are omitted or obviously fabricated. It is enough for her readers to know that, though born in Scotland, she considered herself the great-grand-daughter of a Manx witch and that she spent part of her childhood in the Isle of Man. Hence 'Miss Manx' or 'Minx'. Another alias was 'Muriel Pearson' but the name in which her birth was registered in Glasgow and by which she was known in Scotland seems to have been Vanneen Walker.

Losing a father and then a step-father, Vanneen accompanied her mother to the USA after the First World War. 'We settled in Hollywood . . . I myself was really an artist.' But good money was to be made in writing profiles of tinseltown's stars and it was as a journalist, according to Ide, that she appeared in Bali. The year was 1932. She had seen a film called *Bali, The Last Paradise* and had 'become entranced. It was as if fate had brushed my shoulder.' With a two-year supply of paints and canvases, she had sailed from New York.

Chance encounters play no small part in her story. Crossing

Java by car, she picked up a youth who later, as a guerilla leader in the independence struggle, would help to rescue her from the Japanese and sponsor her as a propagandist for the Nationalists. Similarly, on arrival in Bali – it was, of course, 'sheer enchantment' – her car ran out of petrol on the threshold of what proved to be the Raja of Bangli's palace. A dashing prince with large dark eyes and fluent English promptly scooped her up and introduced her to the raja. He not only insisted she stay but also acknowledged her as his adopted daughter.

'He was a silly man,' snorted Ide. 'But there was no adoption. She was not a princess, just a guest.'

Adopted or not, she acquired a new name. 'K'tut' signifies that she was the raja's fourth child (Wayan is first-born, Nyoman second, Made third); and 'Tantri' indicates one versed in Balinese culture, perhaps a reference to her ambitions as an artist. Naturally her privileged situation was the envy of people such as Spies and the Batesons, but she soon tired of royal attentions and hankered after earthier insights into Balinese life. She now spoke Balinese, wore a sarong and, red hair notwithstanding, was 'accepted as a Balinese throughout the island'.

While touring the villages in the south she happened upon a particularly fine and deserted stretch of beach near the *kampung* of Kuta. In her bungalow at Bangli she had already been taking paying guests; at Kuta she now resolved to build a hotel. Partnership with an American couple called Koke provided the cash and in due course her Kuta Beach Hotel became the first of the now perhaps 3,000 hotels and homestays that have reduced Kuta to the status of Indonesia's most crowded resort.

A second hotel at Kuta, built for her by her Balinese friends when she fell out with the Kokes, proved an even greater success. She narrowly avoided deportation when Spies and the rest were flushed out by the Dutch and she was still there when the Japanese arrived off Sanur.

'Why she did not leave like all the other foreigners?' asked Ide. 'Why the Japanese did not intern her? You see, I think she was collaborating.'

She claims that she was protected by her Balinese friends,

especially the dashing prince who wanted so much to marry her. He, already an Indonesian Nationalist, installed her in Surabaya where for an unspecified period she claims to have been part of a smuggling ring supplying arms to the underground resistance. This interlude ended with her equally unconvincing arrest and imprisonment by the Japanese. Torture led to hospitalization and suddenly it was the end of the War. She was immediately accepted by the Nationalists as a partisan, starred as Surabaya Sue of Radio Pemberontakan, and then joined the Republican government in Jogja. From there she accompanied Sukarno on several tours and became closely associated with his minister for defence, the Christian, and later Communist, Amir Sjarifuddin. In 1947, in ever mysterious circumstances, she left Java for Singapore and then New York, at which point her book ends.

'Don't read it,' said Ide. 'So much rubbish. She was not even very pretty.' Yet for the most part his aspersions had only heightened the mystery. K'tut, like Mata Hari, was undoubtedly given to excessive romanticization. But even if only half the 'essentials' were factual, it was still a remarkable story. Newsmen of the day sometimes called her 'the second Mata Hari'. She relished this billing and was no doubt flattered to be compared with such a noted beauty. No doubt also that she had earnt the title.

13. Ours The Land and The Water

In March 1946, when from Jogja K'tut Tantri was pleading over the radio waves for international recognition of the Republic of Indonesia and when in Bandung British troops were still under fire from Indonesian Nationalists, readers of the London *Times* were more exercised over whether it was appropriate for their newspaper to be countenancing use of the word 'Indonesia'. 'My encyclopaedia says it covers eight areas including Madagascar, Borneo and the Philippines,' harrumphed that enemy of jargon Sir A.P. Herbert. It was bad enough, grumbled another correspondent, that the word had just made its unwelcome appearance in *Whitaker's Almanack*.

The editor of the *Times* responded lamely. The term had been employed officially, he wrote, 'since the beginning of the disturbances' and was a convenient way of denoting 'a wider area than Java', though just how wide he did not say. A further correspondent came to his rescue with the news that 'although the choice of the word is not a happy one', the Dutch government had accepted its use 'for a number of years'.

This was not quite true. The Dutch carefully avoided the word and had in fact banned its use ever since Nationalists had adopted it in the 1920s. Dr Sartono, my sightless guru at Gajah Mada university, says it was invented by a 'Mr Logan' in about 1840; but it was little used in the 19th century and was unknown to Edward Douwes Dekker, the author of *Max Havelaar*. When Dekker wanted a term to describe the Netherlands East Indies which did not mention The Netherlands he came up with 'Insulinde'.

From the Latin, 'Insulinde' means exactly the same as the Greek 'Indonesia' (*Indos-nesos* 'Indies-islands'). But perhaps because Dekker was Dutch and perhaps because 'Insulinde' was adopted as a party label by a later group of mainly Dutch liberals, local Nationalists preferred 'Indonesia'. They adopted it to distinguish the Malay language as spoken in the islands (*bahasa Indonesia*) from that spoken on the Malay peninsula and, since the promotion of this common language became one of the main planks in the nationalist platform, the term quickly entered political dialogue; among the first to endorse it was Partai Komunis Indonesia (PKI). That left 'Insulinde', or in Laurens van der Post's parlance 'Insulinda', for the writers of precious prose.

As well as 'Insulinde' and 'Indonesia' there was yet a third contender. 'Nusantara', a Malay word meaning something like 'across (*antara*) the islands (*nusa*)' was coined by Ki Hadjar Dewantoro, a champion of native education in Java, in about 1920. Although it never gained wide currency it was favoured by some scholars as a suitably indigenous and neutral designation and is much used today as the equivalent of 'inter-island'.

Most nations can take themselves for granted; some – like Pakistan and Indonesia – have had to invent themselves. But while 'Pakistan', for instance, is territorially quite specific (the 'P' stands for Punjab, the 'K' for Kashmir, the 'S' for Sind, etc), 'Indonesia' is exceedingly vague. So are 'Insulinde' and 'Nusantara'. All imply an island identity but none defines it. A. P. Herbert therefore had a point. They could well include the Philippines, whose people are of the same racial stock, or even Madagascar with whom the archipelago has some linguistic affinities.

At the time of independence the main question was what they included to the east. Etymologically-minded Nationalists realized that whereas Sumatra, Java and Bali, all islands with an Indic heritage, were well covered by the term 'Indo-nesia', the same could hardly be said for non-Indic Sulawesi (Celebes), Timor and Irian, nor for most of the myriad islands in between them. Here the people were as much Melanesian as Malay; their languages exhibited greater diversity than anywhere else on earth and, more to the point, their political sympathies could not be taken for granted. In 1950 half of Timor was still under Portuguese rule; Irian had been withheld from the final independence agreement and was still under Dutch rule; and the rest of the eastern archipelago, including Bali and Lombok, had lately been constituted as a separate 'East Indonesian State'. This state was incorporated not within the Indonesian Republic but as a federated member of a wider 'United States of Indonesia'. Moreover it was no secret that within this sprawling East Indonesian State (*Negara Indonesia Timur*, or *NIT*) nationalist sentiment was weak and several of its more influential components wanted nothing to do with Jakarta.

In 1949 the prime minister of NIT had been my old Balinese friend, Dr Ide Anak Agung Gde Agung, the raja of Gianyar. He had also been Eastern Indonesia's spokesman at the final independence negotiations in The Hague and then served in the first cabinets of the United States of Indonesia (USI). But the USI lasted barely six months, Sukarno's Nationalists insisting on the unitary and centralized straitjacket which, supposedly, could alone contain the improbable jumble of peoples and places that was Indonesia. As a convinced federalist and the supporter of a multi-party system, Ide fell from grace.

Along with all the country's other assorted rajas and sultans he was deprived of land and authority during Sukarno's 'Guided Democracy' (i.e. personal rule) and in 1962 was accused, with the charismatic Sutan Sjarir, of plotting to overthrow Sukarno. Both were arrested and imprisoned in Java until Sukarno himself was usurped by Suharto's military take-over. As with Dutch attempts to foster federalism in West Java (Pasundan), the fact that NIT had been a Dutch creation had irredeemably discredited it in nationalist eyes which saw federalism as a poor disguise for separatism. Ide, though, and quite a few others in the east of the archipelago still feel that a looser federal arrangement would be more appropriate in the far-flung island realms beyond Bali.

Aboard the Lombok ferry as it churned out of Padang Bai (Bali) on the four-hour crossing to Lembar (Lombok) I began to understand his bitterness. Gunung Agung, Bali's tutelary volcano, rose peerlessly from its cushions of cloud to claw at the sky with its shattered apex. It looked as if some mountain-chomping monster had not just nibbled its nipple but snatched a great bite from its noble Balinese breast and then, perhaps, spat it seaward to where Nusa Penida lay low and unloved on our starboard. Ahead Rinjani, Lombok's less ruptured 'mountain of fire', was higher still and occupied half the island. Behind it, hidden from view on Sumbawa, the map showed Tambora The Destroyer from whose now gaping caldera there blasted in 1815 more moving matter than all the world's other volcanoes had produced in a century. Which of these, I wondered, was responsible for the shaggy skirts of coconut palm ringed by life-belts of beach and coral which, bobbing low in the water to the east, proved to be the sun-drenched Gili islands?

On the horizon a rakish schooner with what looked like a henhouse for a poop must be a Bugis *pinisi* homeward bound for Sulawesi. Astern, by way of contrast, the Benoa flyer powered towards us; a futuristic hydrofoil, air-conditioned throughout, it cuts the journey time from Denpasar to Lombok by hours. To relieve the diesel-choked highways of south Bali and the over-taxed sewers of its resorts, mass tourism is being encouraged to relocate on Lombok. Over the straits pass frequent flights and the ferries get more like pleasure steamers.

I leant on the rail and watched strange slicks of dead calm water, rich in tropical detritus, alternating inexplicably with fields of a darker blue ploughed by a slow and heavy swell. The Lombok strait is really a trench with some of the deepest water in the archipelago. Down it the naturalist Alfred Russel Wallace drew his famous line. Here elephants, tigers and most other mammals stopped and opossums, cockatoos, and megapodes started. If you went by the fauna, it was where Asia ended and Australasia began.

The Wallace Line ran neatly north-south splitting Sulawesi from Borneo (Kalimantan) as well as Lombok from Bali. Comparing the distribution of species on either side of it, Wallace found strong corroboration of his own evolutionary theories which anticipated those of Charles Darwin and contributed crucially to them. Based on these studies he also advanced ingenious ideas about the archipelago's geological history which have since been revised. So has the Wallace Line, thus named by T.H. Huxley. Wallace himself moved it east to leave Sulawesi as a transitional zone and Weber, a German, and then Lydekker, an Englishman, pushed it still further east till only Irian and the Aru islands were awarded to Australasia. But so curious and distinctive were the species in between that nowadays the whole area between Bali and Irian is considered a transitional zone of sufficient interest in its own right to be known in scientific circles as 'Wallacea'.

This, with the inclusion of his own Bali and the exclusion of East Timor, is also what comprised Dr Ide's short-lived East Indonesian State (NIT). It had a certain logic. In the trickle of attenuated 'South Eastern Islands' (Nusa-tengara) which from Lombok straggle away towards Darwin for a thousand miles, in the insignificant speckle of the Spice Islands, and in the tortured configuration of Sulawesi, NIT epitomized geography's capacity for the exotic just as Wallacea did zoology's.

Most of it, of course, was water and it was not inappropriate that its capital was located at Makassar, the great entrepôt on Sulawesi's most southern arm. Makassar's maritime and commercial tentacles, typified in that Bugis *pinisi* on the horizon, extend throughout the eastern archipelago. In pre-colonial times the fleets of the Makassarese and their Bugis neighbours repeatedly intervened in the affairs of Nusa-tengara and the Moluccas; their settlements are still evident today in Sumbawa, Flores, Ternate and Banda. As boat-builders, traders and pirates, they would maintain a healthy challenge to Dutch monopolism. And Makassar, redesignated as Ujung Pandang, is still even now the communications and business hub of the region, in fact the Piraeus of the eastern archipelago.

Thinking of Piraeus, it suddenly occurred to me that plumping for the Greek 'Indonesia' rather than the Latin 'Insulinde' or the Malay 'Nusantara' had been an inspired idea. Had those early Nationalists scoured the atlas for examples of another nation state comprising scattered islands and a lot of sea, they must surely have paused on the page for the Aegean. Like the Greeks, Indonesians cherish tales of questing argonauts, odysseys of sea-borne adventure and memories of maritime 'empire'. Like the Greeks they view the intervening waters and channels of their archipelago, not as dread frontiers but as corridors of commerce, highways of intercourse and hunting grounds for their fishing fleets. And like the Greeks they resent talk of open seas and unrestricted access to these precious and vulnerable 'wet lands'.

'*Tanah Air Kita*' is the Indonesian equivalent of 'This Sceptred Isle' or 'The Land of The Free'. It means simply 'Ours The Land and The Water'. Like Greece, Indonesia includes the intervening seas within its national borders and, on this basis, can claim to be one of the world's largest states as well as one of its most populous. And like Greece, over the several decades during which the United Nations' Law of the Sea has been under discussion, Indonesia has staunchly insisted on this 'pelagic' or archipelagic concept of its territorial sovereignty.

The argument goes as follows. Take, they say, a country like Australia. The centres of settlement and population are scattered round the periphery while the interior is largely inhospitable desert, uncrossable until the rail, road and air links of the 20th century. Yet no one disputes Australian sovereignty over these intervening wastes, no one claims unrestricted access across them and no one presumes a right to whatever minerals or proteins they may yield. Now take Indonesia. The centres of settlement and population are again scattered, but less so than in Australia. And while mountain and jungle have effectively isolated peoples like the Batak or the Badui, the intervening seas have never been a barrier to intercourse. On the contrary, like trails across the prairies, they have facilitated contacts since as far back as history goes. For a maritime, or pelagic, nation the sea is just such a prairie, criss-crossed by innumerable trails, worked by those who live beside it and uniting all who share its bounty.

The value and scope of maritime commerce in pre-colonial south-east Asia is well attested by Portuguese, Dutch and English pioneers. To see the anchorages of Aceh, Banten or Makassar crammed with the vessels of so many different nations, all trading amicably thanks to a sophisticated financial infrastructure, had been a real eye-opener. But as well as this international commerce, the new-comers had also noted, and would soon exploit, the local or 'country' trade of the archipelago. The Moluccans could only concentrate on producing spices, or the Timorese on sandalwood, thanks to Java and south Sulawesi providing their rice and textiles. This trade depended on Chinese capital and on Malay, Bugis, and Makassarese shipping which in turn depended on timber supplies from Borneo and central Sulawesi. Whether it was Bali's slaves or Sumbawa's sulphur, every island contributed to this network and was dependent on it. Thanks to the ease of maritime commerce, the archipelago was an economic unit, or perhaps a series of such units; and it is on the basis of this economic interdependence that, in the eyes of many Indonesian apologists, their nation state is premised.

By now the Lombok ferry was edging into Lembar while the Benoa flyer was half way back to Bali. Wallacea as represented by south Lombok looked drier. Tufts of trees punctuated an empty horizon above tawny hills. The only forest lay tucked away in their folds. Underfoot, sharp grit and thorny twigs recalled the rock and acacia scarps of West Timor. Eucalypts wilted among the coconut palms along the roadside.

While I was still wondering what on earth could have attracted the Balinese to this place, Outback abruptly ceased and Bali began again. Green baize sheets of *sawah* shelved to the roadside in a flight of billiard tables. Water gurgled into the pockets and bird-scarers whizzed and tinkled overhead in an untidy web of home-made streamers. As the *bemo* rattled into Chakranegara, 'city of the wheel (of *karma*)' in Sanskrit, the split portals of Balinese temples boxed in a main street which could have been Gianyar's.

All that night from an adjacent temple there emanated the most excruciating noise ever devised. It was like a heavily amplified dialogue of the dying.

'*Kedong*,' said a witless Balinese from whom black revenge had made me order tea at 3am. Worse even than Cambodia's classical theatre, it was perhaps some part of Bali's *gambuh* cycle. 'Curiously dissonant and archaic, with great contrasts of deep voices mingled with high falsettos, whines and loud cries,' says Covarrubias, forgetting only to mention that each syllable is indefinitely prolonged to afford full scope for the pitches of pain being endured by the two ancient protagonists. They fell silent, hopefully dead, at dawn only to clear the airwaves for the boisterous hallelujahs of several thousand school children marching down main street to salute the New Order on behalf of Lombok's evangelically-inclined Christians.

Next night at Suranadi, a forest retreat where spring water bubbles copiously through the pebble floor of Indonesia's coldest swimming pool, the Balinese ballyhoo resumed. Again there was an adjacent temple in which this time they were sacrificing a buffalo. It crumpled to the ground at 4am without so much as a gurgle. But the gamelan players, who had struck up at sunset, paused not once during the whole night and were still wearily hammering away at their instruments when I left at noon next day.

Should the Muslim Sasaks of Lombok take advantage of Indonesia's next civil upheaval to massacre their Balinese neighbours it will be no surprise. Javanese decorum suddenly seemed rather appealing. So did Islamic sobriety. I resolved to miss out on the 'South Eastern Islands' and tack north, like that Bugis *pinisi*, to resume my west-east progress from Muslim Makassar. Travelling the length of Java had meant by-passing Borneo; now following the spice trail would mean cutting out Nusa-tengara.

It meant missing the giant lizards of Komodo and the coloured lakes of Keli Mutu, five-star attractions on the back-packers' trail to Maumere, Kupang and Darwin. I would see nothing of Sumba or Sumbawa, Flores or Alor, nothing at all of the province of Nusa-tengara Timur and, shamefully, nothing at all of Indonesia's 27th province, its newest and most notorious, otherwise TIM TIM (Timor Timur) or East Timor.

'You really have to go to Dilli,' said the BBC's Jakarta newshound scribbling down addresses. 'It's the one big story. The only story. Bloody terrible. They need all the publicity they can get.' An almost incredible 200,000 East Timorese, 30 percent of the total population, are said to have been killed, starved, or tortured to death since the Indonesian takeover in 1976. Resistance continues; it is the one Indonesian news story that still achieves international coverage. Yet I was heading off to Makassar.

When in 1950, within months of the Dutch recognizing Indonesia's independence, Sukarno abolished the federal United States of Indonesia (USI) in favour of the centralized Indonesian Republic, there was considerable disquiet in Dr Ide's erstwhile East Indonesia State (NIT). Open revolt in both Sulawesi and the south Moluccas taxed Jakarta's resources and for a time the prospects of a pelagic super-state succeeding to all the colonial possessions in the region and so fulfilling the promise contained in the term 'Indonesia' looked highly doubtful.

Even after these outbreaks were suppressed and NIT secured, a big question mark still stood over the status of Irian. The Dutch had at one point acknowledged nationalist claims that this vast but largely unknown territory should become part of the new nation. But at the final Round Table Conference in the The Hague, Irian was withheld, its future to be decided in subsequent negotiations between Holland and the USI. Sukarno's prompt abolition of the USI provided conservative Dutch politicians with the excuse they needed. They reneged on the promise of negotiations and determined to hold tight to this sole surviving remnant of the Dutch East Indies.

During the late Fifties Sukarno responded by mounting a strong bid for the territory at the United Nations. When this failed, he nationalized all Dutch concerns, and threatened to invade Irian. Other distractions, like the PRRI in West Sumatra and the *Permesta* revolt in North Sulawesi, kept Jakarta occupied until in 1962 Indonesian troops at last began to infiltrate Irian. The operation was commanded by a hitherto unknown general called Suharto and was a dismal failure. But later in the same year, with Sukarno now clearly bent on seizing the province, the Dutch caved in to American pressure. Under a face-saving arrangement brokered by the Americans, Irian was handed over to the United Nations for six months and then passed under Indonesian control pending an act of free choice by the Irianese which was to be held before 1969.

Considering that even by 1969 much of Irian was still unexplored, let alone administered, it is hard to see how anything like a plebiscite could have been held. But Indonesia did arrange a consultative process in which a thousand carefully selected Irianese duly pledged their support for incorporation into the Indonesian Republic. This failed to satisfy the UN although, twenty-five years on, its continued refusal to endorse Indonesia's sovereignty may appear academic.

So by 1963, with NIT and now Irian secured, Indonesia had established itself as the sole heritor of all the Dutch East Indies. The Dutch East Indies were not, though, all the East Indies. Pockets of territory within the archipelago remained as yet un-liberated from the colonial yoke. True, the yoke in question was now Portuguese or British, but to a nationalist way of thinking, that was merely an accident of history. 'Indonesia' as a territorial definition could, reasonably, be taken to include them all. No sooner, then, had Sukarno got his way over Irian than he turned his attention to the extremities of Kalimantan (Borneo).

Here Sarawak and Sabah (North Borneo), were about to be integrated into the new state of Malaysia while Brunei was to go it alone. Sukarno claimed that Malaysia was just a neo-colonial dis-guise for continued British supremacy and that the people of Borneo had not been consulted about joining it. Indonesia there-fore opposed the integration and declared not war but *konfrontasi* (confrontation); 'Crush Malaysia' became the slogan of the day as infiltrators crossed into Sarawak and the British embassy in Jakarta was sacked.

Observers suspected that, as with Irian, Sukarno was manu-facturing a foreign crisis to distract attention from the country's desperate economic and social plight. But he was also pursuing the logic of 'nation-building', a term which he interpreted in an acquisitive as well as a figurative sense. For although he made no territorial claim to Sarawak etc., there is good evidence that he subscribed to the idea of a 'Greater Indonesia' which might even-tually include the Malay peninsula as well as all Borneo. It was to this end, perhaps, that some forces infiltrated even mainland Malaya.

In the event, this aggressive posture against another emerging nation cost Indonesia the support of many non-aligned powers. It was a serious miscalculation and it eventually came to nothing when the policy, along with its instigator, was quietly dropped in 1966. This, of course, followed that great climacteric in modern Indonesian history, the abortive 1965 Communist Coup (GESTAPU), the Crocodile Hole and the subsequent holocaust. Ten years later those same cataclysmic events, and the fears they had unleashed, combined disastrously with the precedents of NIT and Irian to propel Indonesia into yet another territorial adventure, this time in East Timor.

Though *konfrontasi* with Malaysia had failed, Indonesia's expectations of monopolizing the archipelago in accordance with its pelagic imperative remained. When in 1974 the Portuguese signified their intention of leaving East Timor, it was widely assumed that Indonesia would, and in the case of such a minuscule territory, should move in. Nehru had done the same in Goa. Australia and, crucially, the United States whose support had proved so decisive over Irian, indicated that they were resigned to such an outcome.

But Suharto's Indonesia was inclined to be more circumspect than Sukarno's. To maintain the foreign investment and the international esteem on which the New Order depended, it must display maturity, moderation and stability. Instead of inflammatory rhetoric and intimidation, reasoned diplomacy and propaganda were to be given a chance. This softly-softly approach was also premised on Jakarta's estimate of pro-Indonesian sentiment within East Timor. But when this proved to have been wishfully exaggerated and when Fretilin, the territory's increasingly popular pro-independence party, appeared to be taking its cue from the Marxist Frelimo movement in Mozambique, alarm bells sounded. Having at appalling cost eradicated all vestiges of the Indonesian Communist party, the nation was faced with the prospect of a left-wing People's Republic in its midst. The Americans had just been defeated in Vietnam; dominoes were falling as never before. Dilli, like Da Nang, could well become a Soviet naval base, affording dissidents in Irian and the erstwhile NIT a champion on their doorstep. It was an horrific, an unthinkable, prospect.

Needless to say none of this explains, let alone excuses, the Indonesian response. Cynical manipulation of the East Timorese situation gave way to an exceedingly brutal invasion and then flagrant disregard of human rights during the long years of repression. Apportioning blame to the US, Australia and other covert supporters cannot exonerate Jakarta. Doubts about the body count are irrelevant; and apologies about the blundering incompetence of the Indonesian armed forces are neither here nor there. The plight of the East Timorese, a brave and woefully wronged people, does indeed deserve unreserved sympathy. I just wondered how the usually charming and sensitive peoples of Indonesia could live with the knowledge of what had been perpetrated in their name.

The answer is, I'm afraid, very easily. Over several months and many miles the subject had seldom arisen; but, when it did, opinion proved unanimous in applauding the integration of TIM TIM. Christians, even Catholic co-religionists, had little sympathy for the East Timorese. Muslim spokesmen ventured no criticisms of the behaviour of the army; federalists and potential separatists saw no parallels with their own aspirations; political economists expressed no reservations about the legality of integration. The received idea that East Timor was 'raped' by the bellicose generals and Javanese bullyboys of a detested military regime found no support whatsoever.

Few Indonesians, of course, are well primed on Amnesty International reports and many know no more of the affair than their still far from free press vouchsafes. Perhaps, too, it was naïve of me to expect expressions of dissent from total strangers. But what was clear was that all considered the integration of East Timor as acceptable, logical, and inevitable. 'Ours The Land and The Water.' It was all down to that pelagic imperative. I just wondered where, if you claim both land and water, the line should be drawn. If neither sea nor mountain constitutes a natural frontier, what does?

'This concept of the Law of the High Seas. It was known to the Bugis and Makassarese of south Sulawesi long before Plautius.' According to Dr Andi Zainal Abidin, an awful lot of things were known to the peoples of South Sulawesi long before anyone else. They had settled in Madagascar long before the Portuguese 'discovered' it. They were in the habit of visiting Australia long before Captain Cook set foot in the country. They had charts and navigation laws long before Europeans considered such things necessary. And in *I La Galigo* – 'it is a 14th century epic about the origins of the Bugis' – they had the longest literary masterpiece in the world long before anyone else.

'Plautius, you see, he said the sea belonged to no one. But the Makassarese, they say that the sea belongs to everyone.' He paused to check something in his notes. 'To God, yes.'

We were sitting in an empty classroom at Ujung Pandang's Hasanuddin University. Chalk dust hung in the rays of a sinking but still vicious sun. There was no breeze, no fan. How could students possibly concentrate in such heat? Was Dr Andi having me on? And who the hell was 'Plautius'?

Ujung Pandang, or Makassar, had seemed full of Andis. Many were 'Doktors' and quite a few were attached to Hasanuddin University. So I was feeling pretty good about having tracked down, of an equatorial afternoon, this leading authority on Sulawesian law. In a place best known for producing a hair oil so damaging to Edwardian upholstery that our ancestors had to invent the 'anti-Macassar', and in an island so little explored that these same ancestors had thought it was an archipelago ('The Celebes'), I was not expecting to be ambushed by classical authors. Plautus, Plotinus, Plato, Pliny – sluggishly they came to mind. But 'Plautius'? Dr Andi's English pronunciation was erratic; perhaps I had misheard him.

'No, Plautius.' He was clearly appalled at my ignorance. 'Plautius, yes? The Dutch jurist, 16th century, who formulated the Law of the Sea?'

Oh, that Plautius. Of course. Dr Andi foraged in his notes again. I quickly changed the subject.

'So how does this tie in with Indonesia's insistence that the seas belong to the nation?'

'No, they belong to everyone, to God. That is Makassarese belief. So when the Dutch prevent all people to go on the high seas and call the Bugis pirates and smugglers, we say this is wrong.'

'But what about *Tanah Air Kita*, 'Ours The Land and The Water'? Doesn't the archipelagic concept amount to the same insistence on a monopoly of the seas as the Dutch tried to enforce?'

'No, is quite different. We say sovereignty over the intervening seas must rest with Indonesia, to ensure that everyone has the use of them. Because they belong to everyone. To God, yes?'

He flourished a wadge of typescript; I should read his paper on the subject. The Bugis and Makassarese, he added, were extremely stubborn; hot-tempered too. It was 'because they were sailors since olden times'.

Though none of this was crystal clear I decided against labouring the point. The trickles of sweat had now reached my ankles. Even Dr Andi's Terylene clung like a wet-suit. And, whether or not their law of the sea was heretical, he had made a good case for the Bugis and the Makassarese. There was no question that they, and the other maritime peoples of South Sulawesi (Mandarese, Bajau), had made a distinctive and important contribution to Indonesian identity.

For one thing it appeared that, uniquely among the people of the outer islands, these Sulawesians had a genuine tradition of historical writing. As well as the ancient and enigmatic *I La Galigo*, they had been committing to Lontar palm leaves chronicles, chronologies and king-lists since pre-Islamic times. We thus have an unusually full picture of South Sulawesi's history. That doesn't mean that it is immediately comprehensible. Anything but. But it may give some clues as to the fragmented and vulnerable nature of power structures elsewhere in the archipelago in pre-Islamic times.

True, pre-Islamic times were comparatively late in Sulawesi. According to Dr Andi, when the Portuguese had reached Makassar in the 15th century they found no Muslims of any consequence and quickly claimed for Catholicism four of south Sulawesi's numerous kings. It was not till 1603–5 that the kings of ancient Luwu (east of Torajaland) and of upstart Gowa (roughly Makassar) were converted to Islam. Bone, the most powerful Bugis kingdom (straddling the peninsula between Gowa and Luwu) followed suit, but continued to resist the challenge of its deadly Makassarese rivals in Gowa.

According to Andi, there was no great difference between the Bugis of Bone and the Makassarese of Gowa (sometimes, confusingly, spelled 'Goa'). Ethnically they were indistinguishable; both were heavily involved in maritime trade; and neither constituted a homogenous state, their power depending on alliances with other Bugis and Makassarese kings of which there were many. But their languages were different and, though the Bugis were more numerous, Makassar ruled the waves.

Strategically placed near the end of the spice route, Makassar in the early 17th century was probably the largest port-city in the archipelago. 'It was the same size as Paris,' said Andi. Here English and Portuguese vessels, after their exclusion from the Moluccas by the Dutch, found all the nutmegs and cloves they could carry. Good prices and a quick sale were attracting an armada of Moluccan spice smugglers and it was to stop this haemorrhaging of their monopoly that the Dutch in the late 1660s finally overwhelmed Sultan Hasanuddin (after whom both university and airport are named) and destroyed his capital. In this titanic struggle they were eagerly assisted by the Bugis of Bone, although they too would taste Dutch retribution in the 19th century and again in the early 20th when Holland finally extended its influence over the whole of Sulawesi. After the Second World War, both peoples suffered still greater torments in the independence struggle which, thanks to the notorious Captain 'Turk' Westerling, claimed more victims in South Sulawesi than Java.

For the vanquished the only consolations were Islam and emigration. Mosque-building has today become a major industry in South Sulawesi and civil grievances invariably acquire a religious complexion. Here too, as in West Java and Aceh, the *Dar-ul-Islam* movement found ready adherents during its resistance to Jakarta in the 1950s; and it could do so again. Indeed only in Aceh is greater orthodoxy evident.

Emigration, on the other hand, seems to have been a South Sulawesi imperative from the earliest times. Dr Andi thought he detected a diaspora in the travels of Sawerigading, the hero of *I La Galigo*, while Raffles had insisted that both the Minangkabau and the Malays of Johore were descended from Bugis adventurers. More certainly in the 17th and 18th centuries Bugis and Makassarese settled in Borneo, Java, and the Malay peninsula as well as all over eastern Indonesia. Bugis soldiers served the English at Bengkulu and in Tonkin while, by way of Thailand, some Makassarese entered French service; one was actually adopted by Louis XVI with the title of 'Louis, Dauphin de Macassart'.

As a staunchly Islamic and widely distributed entity, the peoples of South Sulawesi thus had much in common with the Minangkabau of Sumatra and they too proved to be ideal nation-building material in the struggle for independence. But far more than the Minang, the Bugis and Makassarese kept to the trade routes and the port-cities. Sailors rather than intellectuals, they lent substance to the idea of a closely integrated maritime nation. It was a pity that they could not also be credited with having inspired the pelagic conceit of *Tanah Air Kita*.

While in Makassar I forgot to enquire why the Indonesian republic had renamed South Sulawesi's capital after its old fort of Ujung Pandang. Perhaps it was to erase the unhappy memory of Makassar as the capital of Ide's short-lived East Indonesian State (NIT). There have since been efforts to reinstate the old name but, should they succeed, it will take more than the romance of one mighty Makassar to make it a tourist favourite. Reeling from the heat and the imagined hostility of an Islamic but hospitable people, foreigners invariably head straight for the short flight or the long bus ride to the mountains of Torajaland (Tanahtoraja).

If the Bugis etc. are the Minang of Sulawesi, the Toraja are the Batak. A largely Christianized hill people, ingenious and profligate builders, experts in the husbandry of pigs and buffaloes, and mighty connoisseurs of funerary ritual, the Toraja may even be ethnically related to the Batak. But, smaller of stature and sweeter of temperament, they are tainted with neither cannibalistic antecedents nor authoritarian ambitions and have thus enjoyed an extraordinarily favourable press. Only the Balinese have inspired so much affection. From Harry Wilcox's 1950s classic *White Stranger* about his 'six moons in Celebes' to Nigel Barley's 1988 account of inducing Torajan craftsmen to construct a traditional rice barn in London's Mayfair, the diminutive folk of Tanahtoraja emerge unscathed.

Few are innocent of the bounty which good English, a winning smile, a plausible tale and foreknowledge of local death feasts may elicit. The Toraja *tongkonan*, as elaborately decorated as a Minang house but with a roof heavier than that of the Batak and banana-shaped, has become an architectural cliché, conflated for churches and public buildings and miniaturized for the packable castings and carvings of the souvenir trade. There is even talk of Torajan rituals being scheduled and staged more for the visitors' convenience than the deceaseds' safe passage to Puya, homeland of Torajan souls. But somehow all this only makes the Toraja more endearing.

Even the Indonesian Ministry of Religious Affairs seems to subscribe to this indulgent and mildly patronizing attitude. In 1969, when in the post-GESTAPU panic everyone wanted to belong to a recognized religion to avoid being branded a Communist, the doctrinal arbiters in Jakarta recognized the traditional beliefs of the non-Christian Toraja as a form of Hinduism. Since Hinduism in Bali so delighted the visitors, perhaps this was also part of some oblique tourist promotion for Torajaland. It certainly took no account whatsoever of history, theology, cosmology, or culture. *Aluk to dolo*, the Torajan 'way of the ancestors', is rich in external ritual but its tenets are variously said to be too variable for generalization or too vague for definition.

It made me feel particularly sorry for Lombok's *Wetu Telu*. Another small and endangered sect, the *Wetu Telu* go in for a lot of rice and ancestor rituals like the Toraja. But they also acknowledge Allah and consider themselves Muslims; unfortunately no one else does.

'We pray five times a day in the mosque. They pray three times a year. On top of a mountain.' Nasr, an orthodox Sasak (i.e. Muslim) waiter, had slammed down my *ayam goreng Kentaki* with undisguised contempt. 'How can they be Mussulman?' They can't, according to The Ministry for Religious Affairs. Although victimized in the 1966 massacres, and in spite of requests for recognition, the poor *Wetu Telu* remain outside the pale. It was OK for my *ayam goreng* (fried chicken) to pass itself off as *Kentaki* (Kentucky) but not for those who made the Islamic confession of faith to pass themselves off as Muslims.

In Torajaland, when someone dies, the prolonged and lavish funerary arrangements include the construction of a life-size effigy of the deceased, lovingly dressed in the height of fashion and sometimes mounted on a horse. Nowadays the effigies are usually of cloth and bamboo and are dismantled at the end of the cere-monies. But formerly they were often beautifully carved from jack-fruit wood and were installed in the entrance to the cliff-face burial chambers where the Toraja finally deposit their dead. Although perhaps a hundred feet up a sheer wall of limestone, some of these *tau-tau* have been stolen for sale on the international art market but many, possibly replacements, remain.

The chambers, hewn by hand, appear from below like rec-tangular verandahs. Some have railings behind which the *tau-tau* stand, facing out across the valley; those pictures of the House of Windsor posing for the crowds on the balcony of Buckingham Palace give a fair idea of the arrangement. Standing in a pile of skulls and busted coffins at the base of the cliff, it occurred to me that some redefinition of what constitutes a religion was called for.

Pancasila, the five principles which pass for Indonesia's state ideology, include an insistence on the profession of a monotheis-tic faith. Islam, Protestantism and Catholicism thus qualify by right while Buddhism and Hinduism wangle a place thanks to ingenious arguments about all their deities being aspects of one godhead. But all these belief systems are of Asian origin, concoc-tions of revelation and rationalization as formulated by the peoples of the arid Middle East and the fickle Gangetic plains. All came from the West and all look to the West. They cater for the Indo-, but what of the -nesia? What of the revelations and rationalizations of peoples of the lush islands and the bounteous seas?

Someone needs to conduct a scrutiny of the belief systems of

Oceania to identify shared ideas about origins, life and death and shared characteristics like the celebration of ancestors. Perhaps they have. But they then need to formulate them, preferably in archaic language tastefully printed on thin paper and bound between leather covers. And finally they have to persuade the Indonesian Ministry of Religious Affairs to accord them its imprimatur.

NK

14. Islands of exile

Before they introduced TV screens, the departure board at Ujung Pandang's Hasanuddin airport used to take up a whole wall. Given time, a not inconceivable luxury in Indonesia's provincial airports, it could become boringly familiar; but to the newcomer it was enlightening and, to this newcomer, intensely exciting. There I first learnt to juggle with the syllables of Borneo's principle destinations – Banjarmasin and Balikpapan, Pontianak and Tarakan: big brown rivers clogged with bruised timbers swirled to mind. On Sulawesi the choice was between Rantepao, Palu, Gorontalo, and Luwuk; I heard mountain music. Or there was brassy Manado, the good-time capital of North Sulawesi, with a possible onward connection to Zamboanga on the Philippines' island of Mindanao. The piratical hijackers of the Sulu Sea used this link; so did the gun-runners of the Filipino *mujahedin*. Better still were the wild and wonderful locations to the east. Sorong and Manokwari sounded irresistible; Baubau and Fakfak must be the alarm calls of the bird of paradise.

Such musings transformed that departures board into something intensely challenging. I couldn't forget it. I pored over maps and I thought of Wallace, the naturalist, whose eight years in the archipelago (1854–62) enabled him to visit every island of any consequence plus quite a few of none. '11.4.60: [Wallace] leaves Matubela for Manawoka. 26.4.60: leaves Manawoka for Gorong. 27.5.60: leaves Gorong for Waru (Seram). 10.6.60: leaves Waru for Wahai etc.' Dr Bastin has managed to extract an itinerary from

Wallace's somewhat confusing narrative and if ever there was a journey crying out to be retraced, this is it. Later I fantasized in Dalton's *Indonesia Handbook*, a modest title for a marathon of research and travel which has since been more pirated than the Sulu Sea.

The message of these assorted classics, and indeed one of the great attractions of Indonesian travel, is that practically anywhere in the archipelago is accessible. Even places in the extreme east that look unthinkably remote on the map prove perfectly possible. The Kei archipelago? No problem; boat or plane from Ambon. Tanimbar? Ditto. Morotai? Plane from Ternate or ferry from Halmahera. Nowhere in the world is the wildly exotic so readily attainable. Coral sands and coconut palms? Unavoidable. Pig cultures and penis sheaths? Mostly in Irian. Snowfields and alpine crags? Ditto. A volcanic eruption? Nowhere are your chances better. An island to yourself? Choose from thousands.

Personally, I was not ambitious. I just wanted to visit the Banda Islands. And in particular I wanted to see the most far flung of this minuscule group, by name Pulau Run. The Bandas lie between Seram and Tanimbar in the middle of the Banda Sea which is an eastward extension of the Java and Flores Seas. They form a detached part of the south Moluccas but, because that name is anathema to the Indonesian government, the province is called Central Moluccas (Maluku Tengah); nowadays there is no 'South Moluccas' (Maluku Selatan) although there is a South-east Moluccas (Maluku Tenggara).

None of the seven Banda islets is much bigger than London's Hyde Park; their total population is given as 14,000. Only one island has a road; with spurs, it runs to about three miles of tarmac which is used by eight vehicles and a dozen or so motorbikes. A small power plant has recently transformed the lives of the islanders; with a satellite dish you can get two TV channels; marine batteries can be recharged; and beer, though comparatively expensive, is now served cold. Visitors are expected; sometimes they actually materialize. For as well as the electricity, and in addition to a historical interest out of all proportion to their geographical insignificance, the Bandas also have an air service.

Weather permitting and a full load guaranteed, it operates twice weekly from Pattimura airport on the island of Ambon whose town, also Ambon, is the provincial capital of Central Moluccas. To Ambon, then, I flew from Ujung Pandang, a busy sector on the main west-east axis from Jakarta to Jayapura.

As the plane dropped towards the Pattimura runway, while watches were being adjusted for Indonesia's third time zone, we passed low over the island of Buru. Quite big and densely forested, this is the least loved of the Moluccas. Its erstwhile speciality of catering for long-stay visitors, none of whom came from choice and many of whom never left, is not forgotten. I peered down expecting to glimpse forest clearings with barrack-like huts and perimeters of watch towers and razor wire. There was no sign of them; the inhumanities of Buru have another, more lasting memorial.

Anywhere less like Siberia than eastern Indonesia it is hard to imagine. Yet to these paradise islands the archipelago's rulers have traditionally exiled their enemies. The Dutch did it when they banished Hatta and Sjarir to Irian and Sukarno to Flores. The Japanese followed suit but preferred Ambon itself and neighbouring Haruku. Allied prisoners of war were shipped from Java to build air strips, Pattimura's included, for the Imperial airforce. Most never returned. Of the 1,500 removed from van der Post's camp at Bandung only 200–300 survived; they 'looked like pictures of the last inmates of Belsen on their day of liberation'. Sukarno himself, once in power, also packed his enemies off to Ambon, though not to hard labour. It was under Suharto's New Order, as recently as 1966, that the labour camps reappeared and Buru became one big penal colony.

Its inmates were mostly those suspected of Communist sympathies but who had somehow survived the post-GESTAPU massacres and could not certainly be identified with any conduct for which a sentence could be meted out. For such a non-crime the non-punishment of removal to a virgin island could be shown as appropriate. Additionally Buru's swamps and jungle guaranteed the complete isolation in which hardship, starvation and torture could go unreported. They also ensured that elimination by natural wastage, when unchecked by medical treatment, was colossal. And they made escape nigh impossible. Mere survival was the only priority as prisoners, many of whom were intellectuals and artists, toiled to turn forest into rice fields. There was no need for armed guards and elaborate security. Escapees collapsed from starvation long before they reached the coast. Only migrant birds and insiduous ideas came and went as they pleased.

'The novels were already in my head. But witnessing the state of my fellow detainees, I felt I had to do something to restore their morale. So that's how they came about.'

Pramoedya Ananta Toer (or 'Pram') was 40 in 1965, already a respected author and an authority on the history of the independence struggle. He had been imprisoned before, both by the Dutch and under Sukarno; he was never charged then and he had not been charged now. But this time he did not expect to get out alive.

'So I might as well enjoy myself. But paper was not given to me so the novels had to be composed in oral form.'

Buru was divided into several work units. Pram would relate each episode to his own unit and while toiling in the fields and the forest they would spread the tale to other units.

'Sometimes I would introduce a character, the woman Nyai Ontsoroh for instance, to tell my fellow inmates. "Look a woman can do this, so you too should be able to stand up for yourselves." And, yes, I think the novels did help build up their spirits.'

'The novels', composed amid the appalling tribulations of Buru, later appeared in print and were translated into English as the four-part epic sometimes known as *This Earth of Mankind* (the title of the first book). They tell of the national awakening in Java during the first half of the 20th century as reflected in the life story of the endearing Minke and half a dozen other central characters. Under the circumstances, just sustaining the subtle characterization and the complex thread of such an ambitious narrative was a major achievement. But this is also a work of universal appeal, so broad in its scope and so true in its detail, that, set almost anywhere else in the colonial world, it would surely have won a universal readership. Foreign universities would have vied for Pram seminars; his proud countrymen would have been pressing for his recognition by the Nobel committee.

He is, in theory, now free and for this he acknowledges the power of international opinion. But freedom, after fourteen years detention (1965–79), consists of a small room with an old typewriter, stacks of books and a blanket ban on all his writings. Just for possessing a copy of Indonesia's one undisputed classic there are people serving gaol sentences. Pram's movements are watched, his contacts logged, his voice silenced. He cannot travel; nor does he receive many visitors, anonymity in a Jakarta suburb being a condition of his release. A slight and wizened figure, white hair *en brosse*, only his drumming figures betray impatience.

He denies that he ever joined the PKI; 'as a writer I lack discipline in a political sense'. But he does confess to a more dangerous allegiance – a devotion to historical truth.

'Here official histories are written by the government while real histories are written through fairy tales. In the fairy tales, the feudal stories, kings always win. There is a great fear of power. We are taught to be afraid of power and so people are afraid of their own history. We are a people used to saying yes and taking orders. I chose the novel because it allows one to record society's failings and to show the weakness of power, both in victory and defeat.'

The notion that power becomes powerless in the face of history's inexorable progress is what riles the regime and constitutes Pram's sedition. 'Official' histories imply that the national awakening began in 1908 with *Budi Utomo* ('Great Endeavour'), a Javanese, aristocratic and essentially cultural movement. Pram dismisses this group as tools of the Dutch and traces the roots of the national revolution to indigenous associations that were independent of any patronage other than the spirit of the times. What happened in Java was happening all over the archipelago and all over the world. Nationalism in Indonesia was a popular and universal phenomenon to which ordinary Indonesians, like the characters in *This Earth of Mankind*, spontaneously responded because they had history on their side. Social justice and democratic rights are also universal phenomena. To them too, ordinary Indonesians must and will respond. History will not be denied.

As well as being Indonesia's 50th birthday, 1995 is Pram's 70th. While passing through Jakarta, I had phoned the man who had interpreted at our earlier meeting. 'No change,' he said; no let-up in the ban, no easing of his 'town arrest', and no change in Pram. His message is the same as ever. The main character of Pram's novels, says Max Lane, is not Minke but history. It was with history that he tried to restore the morale of his fellow detainees on Buru, with history that he continues to defy the New Order, and with history that he still challenges his fellow countrymen.

It was also with history much in mind that I was set on the Banda Islands. In Indonesia the lethal properties of this apparently harm-less commodity are such that, like nuclear waste, it needs a century or more of careful storage before it can be handled. But in Europe history has long since been made safe; the only trouble is that there is far too much of the stuff. We take it for granted; and we forget the best bits.

On the apron at Pattimura two small planes were parked. They were identical, in fact 'Twin Otters' according to the man from the control tower; one, he said, was the plane for Banda. I wondered whether it was wise to cross so much sea in something called an 'Otter' and I cursed my luck in having just missed the *Rinjani*. Missing the *Rinjani* and its sister ships of the national shipping line's fleet of sumptuous ferries is the lot of every visitor to the eastern archipelago. Eternally just a day or two ahead, they elude man's best endeavours like an overdraft that declines to be liqui-dated. Were it not for the pictures in every shipping office, one might take these stately liners for a figment of the eastern seas.

I thought of them a lot during the twenty-hour wait and then the forty-minute flight. How magnificent the *Rinjani* must look steaming sedately through those tight narrows into Banda Naira's welcoming anchorage. Would it glide gently to that little jetty? Or would it moor securely in the lee of Gunung Api? By now, with engines roaring, the Otter was bucketing furiously as it banked against the steep inside wall of what used to be a volcanic crater. Straightening out of this manoeuvre at sea-level, it skimmed the waves to touch down on a runway which, lapped by the tide, could have been a slip for boats. It was short enough – maybe 300m, that being the full width of the island. But it was also steep. The Otter hit the incline at speed and then, as if determined to take off again, raced agonizingly up the hill. Perhaps the pilot simply wanted to show how abruptly the cliffs plunged from the lip at the top; alternatively he needed every inch of the bumpy tarmac.

We turned from the abyss and freewheeled back down the hill to a cottage of low eaves and flower-laden trellis which proved to be the terminal. Thence the road into town, the only road, had the pretensions and dimensions of a driveway to some stately home. White lines and traffic signs would have betrayed its function as a public utility. Instead there were frequent and distinctly viceregal lamp standards. At carriage height their cast-iron shafts branched into elaborate candelabra whence fanciful tendrils twirled beneath the three little pagoda lanterns. They would not have disgraced the Tivoli gardens and looked especially fine running the length of a paved causeway which connected the pillared frontage of the Governor's residence with his island belevedere.

Set in the middle of the unfrequented Banda Sea, among a cluster of islands whose equatorial forest plunged untamed from a still smouldering volcano to a tousled shoreline of mangrove, coral and lava, such evidence of ordered living and gracious dalliance was unexpected. On the steps of the governor's mansion two Melanesian housewives sat hunched with their elbows on their knees; each held aloft a red and green umbrella and each dangled from the index finger of the other hand a big steely-blue tuna. Supper means fish in Banda and a Bandanese without a tuna feels as naked as a Balinese without a cock. Beneath the belvedere, brown-skinned boys, glistening like dolphins, somersaulted from dug-out canoes.

At closer quarters the anchorage looked too tight for liners. Small coves screened by fallen trees wherein timbered hulks rotted bespoke the age of piracy. From a hill above the tiled township the startled bastions of Fort Belgica, built in 1611 and still the largest structure in the Bandas, commanded the narrows. All that was lacking were the tall black ships. I imagined them dressed with

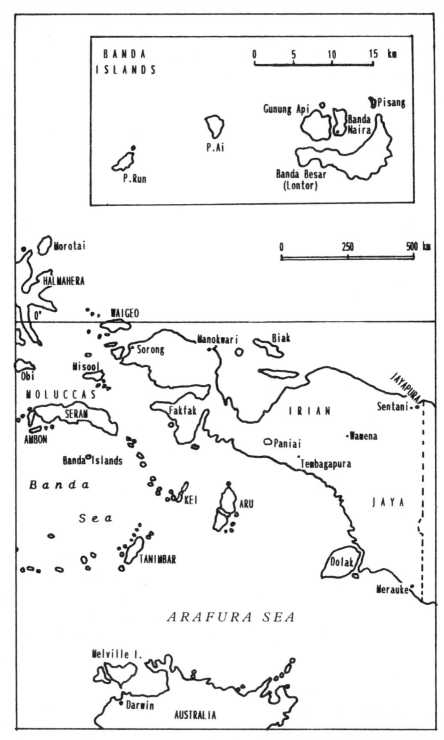

THE MOLUCCAS AND IRIAN JAYA

pennants and ensigns, their masts a web of cordage, their gunwales rows of cannon apertures and their poops all leaded
windows with scrolls of red and gold. That was how it had been in
the days when Banda Naira was the most sought-after anchorage
in the East.

I looked again at those preposterous street lanterns. Their cast
iron pillars were bedded in white-washed pedestals and where they
joined the pedestals they appeared to issue from a bright gold bud.
On closer inspection this bud turned out to be the split shell of a
nut, like a slightly open pistachio. And the base of each pillar was
swollen and rounded to fit into it snugly, like a kernel. Only the
gold paint was wrong; for this ingenious arrangement was
undoubtedly meant to represent the nutmeg, Banda's russet
bounty.

The prize for which Europeans first sailed round Africa, first
crossed the mid-Atlantic and ventured into the Indian and Pacific
Oceans was a share in the priceless spice trade of the East. Pepper,
cinnamon and cardamom they obtained in India, Sumatra and
Java. But cloves, nutmeg and mace were to be found only in the
Spice Islands proper, i.e. the Moluccas. And while cloves, though
now a specialty of Ternate and the north Moluccas, were to be
found all over the Spice Islands, nutmegs and mace came only
from the tiny Bandas. It was probably the most valuable and jeal-
ousy guarded monopoly in the world.

To the Bandas, specks so small that even modern maps habitually omit them, the Portuguese, Spanish, Dutch and English were
drawn as to a pot of gold. Throughout the hundred years of the
Spice Race (c1520–1620) the finest ships that Europe had ever
built, massive carracks, tall galleons and heavily-armed East Indi-
amen, homed in on this minuscule archipelago. Navigators and
supercargoes, the trail-blazers of their day, hailed the stern profile
of Gunung Api (Banda's 'Fire Mountain') as their Eldorado. And
beneath its shadow they traded, fought and died, all for the small
brown kernels of a russet nut.

Among the dead, in a long lost grave amid the forests of Ai

island, lie the bones of one Nathaniel Courthope. He was English, a servant of The Honourable East India Company and, if we may judge by his diaries, a good and just man. In 1616 he was summoned from one of the Company's outposts in Borneo to take command of the *Swan* and the *Defence*, both 400 tons, on a voyage to the Bandas.

For the past ten years English ships had been contesting Dutch claims to an exclusive trade with the Bandas. So had the Bandanese. On Banda Naira, centrally located and then as now the only township, the Dutch had built Fort Nassau and, when this was overwhelmed by the Bandanese in 1609, the more commanding Fort Belgica. They had also made good their claim to Banda Besar or Lonthor, the much bigger island which, like a high sea wall, shields Naira and Gunung Api from the south and renders the narrows between these three islands such a desirable harbour. Here, then, the Dutch were nigh invincible; but beyond this central cluster, eight and fifteen miles to the west, lay the outer islands of Ai and Run. Both produced fine nutmegs and for over a decade their best customers had been the English.

In 1615 the Dutch, having determined to close this loophole in their monopoly, overran Ai. The English retired to Run but not before a deputation of Bandanese had presented them with the most valuable object they possessed, a nutmeg seedling. It was a token of their trust in that, planted anywhere else, it could end the Bandas' monopoly; and it was also a pledge of fealty by which Pulau Ai and Pulau Run (*pulau* is island) were made over to the English crown in perpetuity. Later the pact was ratified by a document wherein James I was acknowledged as 'by the Grace of God, King of England, Scotland, Ireland, France, Puloway and Puloroon.'

James was doing well for someone who had started out with just Scotland, a country whose value, according to at least one contemporary, would certainly be exceeded by Pulau Ai and Pulau Run. But with Ai already in Dutch hands, these latest acquisitions clearly needed protection. That was where Courthope came in. His orders were to occupy Run and to hold it fast, come what may. On arrival he therefore took formal possession; 'we spread [the flag of] St George upon the island and shotte off most of our ordnance.'

Run is about two miles long and a mile across at its widest. Magnificent *kanara* trees, whose shade and protection is so essential to the delicate nutmeg, blanket its rugged profile and lean out from its cliffs giving the island a dishevelled and top-heavy appearance, like an overloaded flower vase. Nowhere is land visible except where the trees have been cleared round a bay to make way for the island's only village and where a sandy atoll basks on its coral reef at the island's eastern extremity. Here, commanding both the bay and a distant view of the other islands, Courthope landed his guns and constructed a makeshift fort.

Then, as now, the big drawback of the Bandas was that, nutmegs doing so well, they produced little except nutmegs. Tuna provided protein; fruit, including thirty-eight varieties of banana, provided vitamin C. But there was no cereal, no rice. And, in the case of Run, no fresh water outside the rainy season. Courthope was therefore dependent on outside supplies.

When the *Swan* was captured during a water-run to Lonthor and when the *Defence* also fell into enemy hands, his situation looked desperate. The Dutch offered to return the ships, now coralled in front of Banda Naira, if he would evacuate. No deal, said Courthope, peeling another banana. He could no more surrender King James's property than he could betray his faithful Bandanese supporters.

In March 1618 Gunung Api erupted, showering the Dutch with debris. The Bandanese said it was a good sign and, sure enough, before the month was out, Courthope spied two laden English vessels bearing down on Run. Relief at last. Unfortunately the Dutch in Naira saw them too. While Courthope and his men lined the shore for a mighty welcome, four sails raced out from behind Gunung Api. The two fleets were still exchanging broadsides when darkness fell. Next day the English ships were seen being escorted into Naira, their colours trailing from Dutch sterns. As he faced the prospect of a third year marooned on Run, Courthope managed to despatch a desperate appeal to Banten.

I have but thirtie-eight men to withstand their [the 'Holland-
ers'] force and tyranny, our wants extreame . . . They have here
at present eight ships and two gallies, and to my knowledge all
fitted to come against us. I look daily and howerly for them.
And I wish it [ie an attack], being not so much able to stand out
as willing to make them pay deare.

By now the dungeons of Fort Belgica were crammed with
English seamen who added their entreaties to the demands of the
Dutch. According to one of the prisoners, the Dutch 'pisst and
shatt upon our heads until we were broken out from top to toe like
lepers.' Courthope's 'arrogance' was responsible and he should be
made to pay for it. But still he refused to budge.

In 1618 the Dutch at last attacked; with Bandanese assistance
they were easily beaten off. Six months later there came a small
pinnace from Banten. It brought a few supplies and a letter
promising the eventual support of the whole English fleet; meanwhile Courthope was to 'proceed in your resolution'. He had little
choice. History had devised one of the most prolonged and hopeless blockades on record. El Dorado had become exile.

In 1619, with the Dutch and English companies engaged in a
final trial of strength off Sumatra, Dutch shipping was recalled
from Banda Naira and Courthope was free to obtain supplies from
the other islands. But the good Bandanese were 'spending their
gold and estates, beggaring themselves in expectation of the
English forces'. And still the fleet did not come. 'We have rubbed
off the skin alreadie,' he wrote in a final plea, 'and if we rub any
longer we shall rub to the bone. I pray you looke to it.'

But 1619 became 1620 and still no fleet. As a fourth year of
flag-hoisting, horizon-scanning and banana-eating drew to a close,
only Courthope's resolution did not waver. His thirty-eight Long
John Silvers had long since discarded hose and doublets; the ships'
boats had become fishing boats; and now of an evening, after tuna
suppers under palm-thatch awnings, there were Anglo-Bandanese
toddlers to tug at ill-kempt beards. Like Pram, the exiles 'might as
well enjoy themselves'; perchance Courthope rallied their faint
hearts with spirited yarns.

★

There is still no jetty at Pulau Run. Prahus of meagre draught can glide over its collar of coral but their passengers must then leap overboard into shallow water that looks, and feels, like soup; rich in nutritious matter and covered with a slight scum, it proved to be just off the boil but still too hot for sunburnt shins. The beach popped as the tide receded. Under the sun's midday inquisition, the village cowered in silent submission. Then someone started a chain saw.

'Boat-building', said the guide, 'many boat-building in Pulo Run.'

Between the houses which, fronting the main thoroughfare, backed on to the beach, half a dozen racy prahus, identical to that in which we had made the three-hour journey from Naira, stood propped on stocks over beds of shavings. No nails were used. The jointing and dowelling were faultless. Except for the engine mountings, they were just such boats as the one in which Courthope made his last voyage.

He was heading back from Banda Besar; perhaps he had been for water. It was 20 October 1620. Two Dutch vessels chanced to be in the vicinity. They closed and, eager as ever 'to make them pay deare', Courthope and his companions resisted. He was shot in the chest and, still refusing to countenance surrender, rolled, or fell, overboard. His companions were taken prisoner. The long siege was over. It was the Dutch who found Courthope's body. They dug a grave on Ai and 'buried him so stately and honestly as we could'; it was, they explained, 'only fitting for such a man'.

No such indulgence was extended towards Courthope's valiant Bandanese allies. With the English eliminated, the Dutch moved quickly to end local hostility by ending the locals. In what amounted to genocide they reduced the Bandanese population from 15,000 to 500. Many were horribly massacred, others were deported, and the rest fled. The nutmeg plantations were then farmed out to Dutch planters to be worked by imported slaves. Only on Ai and Run were there no plantations; for there the nutmeg trees were clear-felled, partly as the ultimate retribution and partly because of nagging doubts about the legality of that transfer of sovereignty to the English crown.

I don't know when the trees were replanted. But from Run's forest canopy of giant *kanara* there comes again the boom and bark of the Banda's giant pigeon, a magnificent bird with a big buff chest and emerald-black wings which feeds almost exclusively on nutmeg fruit. Much like apricots, the fruit were hanging heavily from slender branches in the forest shade. And below, along the carefully swept lane that passes for the village street, what appeared to be fiery paving turned out to be a patchwork of russet nuts and scarlet mace drying on mats in the sun.

The mace is the caul or membrane which is left clinging to the nut after the fruit has rotted, or been pecked, away. More valuable than the nut, it is also much lighter and more perishable. Nowadays the fruit itself also has its uses. Crushed, the juice is decanted into bottles as an unappetising cordial and boiled it makes a sickly jam for the visitor's breakfast table. But both fruit and mace lack the preservative qualities of the nut.

'No canned stuff can last more than nine months without using nutmeg. I mean they try everything. You know, Americans, Europeans, Japanese. It might not even be in a can. Maybe a plastic container or something like that. Still needs the nutmeg. Your Irish stew, let's say, or your steak and kidney, ya? It will not last more than six months without the nutmeg.'

Today's undisputed 'Mr Nutmeg' is an expansive entrepreneur called Des Alwi. He owns the only hotel in Banda Naira plus several of the planters' paved and pillared mansions which have now been turned into guest houses. For the electricity and the airport he was principally responsible. And it was he who first alerted me to the triumph of diplomacy which would be Courthope's least expected legacy.

'Next time you come, bring a metal detector. We go back to Pulau Run, together ya? Canons, coins, some buried treasure. Ya, maybe Courthope buried some treasure. Why else would the Dutch buy it for Manhattan?'

If 'Puloway and Puloroon' had originally been ceded to the English East India Company, their conquest by the Dutch might have ended the matter. But because in its infancy the Company had no legal right to territorial sovereignty, they had been accepted on behalf of the English crown. In fact they were arguably the crown's first overseas possessions. They were therefore rather precious and it was the crown, rather than the Company, which doggedly pursued English claims for the next half century. Even Oliver Cromwell was mindful of English rights to Run and with his encouragement a couple of attempts were actually made to resettle the island.

These failed and, in the Treaty of Breda, Charles II finally surrendered all rights to both islands. It was part of a much wider adjustment with the Dutch which included a reciprocal surrender of Dutch possessions in the New World, the most notable of which was New Amsterdam. This thriving township was promptly renamed New York and did indeed include the island of Manhattan. But as the first English colonial possession in the East, Run also deserves a place in history as the seed from which would grow the world's mightiest empire. A shipload of Cromwellian settlers destined for Run were eventually redirected to St Helena which thus became the first actual settlement in the East; it was soon followed by Bombay, Bengal, India and Empire. Run, then, is to British imperial history much as Runnymede is to British constitutional history. Courthope had been vindicated.

For the return journey from the Bandas there was a ship. It was not the *Rinjani* and, without life-boats or life-rafts, radio or radar, food or drink, it was not an altogether convincing ship. The *Waisamar* was more than a boat, though. It had a funnel, albeit it of two roughly symmetrical iron sheets bolted either side of the sort of vertical exhaust fitted on tractors; it did not seem overcrowded with about a hundred passengers; and there was a crew of six, one of whom kindly made his cabin available for what was to be an all-night voyage.

I felt mildly guilty about this for, among the steerage passengers sprawled over their possessions just forward of the engine, I recognized several distinguished vocalists. All week Banda Naira had been rocked by blasts of wildly amplified music as contestants rehearsed for the 'All Indonesia National Karaoke Finals'. These

had been held on the previous three evenings in the grounds of the
Governor's one-time residence and had drawn, for Banda, a massive and attentive audience. I attended once and decided that the
event could not possibly be a national final; perhaps it was a
regional qualifier, a Central Moluccan final.

Elsewhere the pop video of the moment was of an Indonesian
star on a beach singing in English 'I can't stop loving you'. None
of the 50 or so Banda contestants had ventured into English but it
was pretty obvious why the old Ray Charles number was going
down so well. Grief and nostalgia, the pangs of separation and the
agony of unrequited love were seemingly the only themes that
appealed. To the same ponderous beat, tune after tune, many of
them repeated, soared to crescendoes of anguish and subsided
into troughs of despair. There were no 'songs for swinging lovers'
in the Moluccas. Nor was anything like self-consciousness allowed
to betray the songsters' dignity. It was as solemn an occasion as the
Aceh Qur'ānic Contest. Ladies in party frocks, gentlemen in
casual chic, none of them under twenty-five, they had advanced
across the stage without so much as acknowledging the audience
and then, focusing hard on some distant constellation, launched
into another lovelorn melody.

Now they waved a final farewell as the *Waisamar* chugged and
spluttered between portals of tumbling vegetation and out into the
Banda Sea. Astern, a pair of crimson parakeets streamed screech-
ing from the slopes of Gunung Api and headed for a Fort Belgica
bathed in the gold of sunset. I thought of the parakeets' bazaar
cousins, chained to perches and crammed in cages, from whom
these calls of the wild invariably prompted a chorus more poignant
and despairing even than the Karaoke repertoire. I thought, too,
of Courthope's men in the Fort's pit-like dungeon, 'broken out
like lepers'; and of Courthope himself marooned on Run. Banda
had been as much a Siberia-on-Sea as Buru. That such spectacular scenery could host so much misery and evoke so much sadness
still seemed contradictory.

Away to the east, basking in the evening glow, two more outlying islands (formerly Pisang and Rosengijn) have been renamed
Sjarir and Hatta after yet other exiles. In 1934, when Sukarno was

banished to Flores during a Dutch crackdown on nationalist activity, Mohammed Hatta and Sutan Sjarir had been packed off to the notorious death camp of Boven Digul near Merauke in what was then West Irian. But a year later they were moved to a less strenuous detention in a planter's villa in Banda Naira and there they stayed until the Japanese arrived in 1942.

During this time Sutan Sjarir, the most eloquent and endearing of the independence quadrumvirate, adopted a Banda-born child. Sjarir had been partly educated in Holland and wanted for his foster-child the best possible education. But during the War, while Sukarno and Hatta pursued nationalist objectives in co-operation (some would say 'collaboration') with the Japanese, Sjarir went underground to lead a nationalist resistance. He had seen fascism at work in Europe and, as a convinced socialist and democrat, feared its influence on Indonesian nationalism. His adopted child, none other than Des Alwi, the future nutmeg king, was therefore himself sent abroad, another exile.

This background detail I owe to Dr Ide in Bali who became a close associate of Sjarir. At the end of the War, Sjarir, with his unblemished record of resistance, was more warmly entertained by the British than were Sukarno and Hatta and played a crucial role in pacifying Jakarta and opening the road to Bandung for Allied forces. He pleaded the case of Indonesian independence at the United Nations and thrice served as Prime Minister. In his wake, the small boy from Banda acquired international tastes and contacts.

But in the 1950s Sjarir, like Ide, recoiled from Sukarno's increasingly autocratic 'Guided Democracy' and in 1962, while attending the cremation of Ide's father in Bali, he with Ide was arrested for supposedly hatching a coup against Sukarno. Both were imprisoned in Madiun in Java. Sjarir was released for medical treatment in 1965 and died the following year.

At his funeral his fellow Minang exile, Hatta, made one of his now rare public appearances to sing the praises of Indonesia's best-loved socialist and declare him more wronged at the hands of the Indonesian Republic than ever he had been by the Dutch. Perhaps to make up for this, Des Alwi has been given a surprisingly

free hand in Banda. With his private plane, his unbounded enthusiasm and his manifold interests he typifies the entrepreneurial
wizardry so vaunted by the Suharto regime. In the phraseology of
the past, the foster child of a dedicated socialist has become an
exemplary capitalist.

It was not until next morning, as the *Waisamar* swung uncertainly
into the fjord-like maw that is Ambon Bay, that our lack of speed
became apparent. Small prahus with outboard engines shot past,
their commuters not even deigning to wave. Atop the cliffs of
feathered greenery a solitary palm had no difficulty keeping pace
with us; when it did finally stoop from view, successive headlands
disclaimed all knowledge of Ambon's busy harbour. It was all
deeply provoking to un-breakfasted passengers with a dwindling
day's work ahead of them. And when at last port and city, coffee
and breakfast, stood waiting behind an empty quay in the mid-
morning glare, the *Waisamar* perversely slewed away to sidle up to
a rank of rustbuckets across whose oily decks, rich in the reek of
cloves, passengers and luggage were obliged to clamber ashore.

Another city, another litany. Ambon's street plan featured old
friends like General Ahmed Yani and Prince Diponegoro, Teuku
Umar and Imam Bonjol. But who was this 'A.J. Patty'? And who
cared anyway?

There comes, I suppose, a point on every journey when time
and patience run out. A slow boat to Ambon might dull the keen-
est curiosity; it could even waken thoughts of home. I was ready to
turn back. But this was Ambon, ancient entrepôt of the spice
trade, scene of the infamous Amboina Massacre and latterly a
focus of international terrorism. A last effort was called for.

Though the better for brunch, I was still scandalously undis-
mayed to learn that Fort Victoria was closed to visitors. Here in
1623 fifteen servants of the English East India Company were tortured, and ten of them executed, by their Dutch counterparts on
the dubious charge of plotting to take the fort. It was a sequel to
the Pulau Run affair and effectively ended English attempts to
claim a slice of the spice trade. But the manner of the massacre,

and the tales of torture told by its survivors, prompted much colourful pamphleteering and provoked near-riots in London. Because of 'this crying business of Amboina', England and Holland teetered on the brink of war throughout 1625; and when, under Cromwell, there were Dutch wars aplenty, the memory of the Amboina Massacre was evoked with telling effect. It was another instance, as Pram would have it, of history triumphing over power.

The fort had originally been built by the Portuguese who had made Ambon the last of their fortified bases on the long trail that constituted their *Estado da India*. They had also converted many of the Ambonese to Catholicism. Subsequently under Dutch rule for longer than almost anywhere in Indonesia, Ambon witnessed further conversions, now to Protestantism, and by the 19th century had the most Christianized and literate population of any island in the archipelago.

This shared faith, plus a warlike disposition towards Muslims, recommended the Ambonese as recruits in The Royal Netherlands Indies Army. Like the Manadonese (of Manado in North Sulawesi which had undergone a similar process of Christianization), most Ambonese thus became closely identified with Dutch rule and loyal subjects of the Dutch crown. Used in this capacity to suppress nationalist outbreaks, they were badly placed in the run-up to independence. Dr Ide's East Indonesian State offered their best security and when this was wound up, their position within an Indonesian republic dominated by Muslim, Javanese and nationalist majorities was unenviable.

It would be wrong, though, to suggest that the Ambonese were unanimous in supporting the Dutch and opposing integration into the new Republic. South Moluccan society was nothing if not fragmented with a strong Muslim minority and numerous aristocratic and *adat* loyalties. In a curious sequel to the British occupation during the Napoleonic Wars, Thomas Matulessy, a former sergeant-major in the British forces, had opposed the reimposition of Dutch rule with a spirited guerilla campaign conducted from the neighbouring island of Saparua. Under the name of 'Pattimura', 'the generous one', his memory is cherished as one of rather few Ambonese with impeccably anti-Dutch credentials. Both Ambon's airport and its university are named after him. 'Jalan A.J. Patty', the city's busiest shopping thoroughfare, evidently recalls a later phase of anti-colonial struggle when the eponymous Patty, said to have been a moderate nationalist in the 1920s, won the rare distinction for an Ambonese of being incarcerated in Boven Digul.

But these were the exceptions. And for every such anti-Dutch Indonesian Nationalist, there was also a pro-Dutch Moluccan Nationalist who rejected not only Jakarta's pretensions but even those of Ide's East Indonesian State as far too radical for loyal subjects of Queen Wilhelmina. Such *Belanda Hitam* ('Black Dutchmen'), mostly soldiers and civil servants, floated the idea of an independent *Republika Maluku Selatan (RMS)* or South Moluccan Republic (which is why the term is now anathema to Indonesian officials). The RMS, like Irian, was to be outside even a federal Indonesia and would retain close links with Holland.

Its moment came in 1950 as soon as Jakarta moved to abolish the East Indonesian State. Federalists wavered and, as more disillusioned Ambonese soldiers drifted home, supporters of the RMS issued a unilateral declaration of independence. This precipitated the incursion of units of the Republican army, precisely the danger which it was supposed to pre-empt. Ambon city was bombed and heavy fighting ensued. It lasted three months with the outcome never in doubt. But some RMS units fought on in Seram and eventually escaped to still Dutch Irian. They and other Ambonese units of the erstwhile Indies army then demanded protection from Holland and duly won their case in the Dutch courts. In 1951, 35,000 Ambonese, all soldiers and their families, were evacuated. It was on the understanding that they would be supported by the Dutch state for a period of six months and then repatriated, hopefully to an independent and internationally secure South Moluccan Republic.

No such entity materializing, the Moluccans stayed on in Holland for more than six months. They were still there in 1966 when an RMS leader was executed in Java, a blow to which the Moluccans responded by setting fire to the Indonesian embassy in

The Hague. And they were still there nine years later when, to the world's considerable surprise, a commuter train was hijacked by dark-skinned Che Guevaras in the middle of the wintry Dutch countryside and held for twelve days. In 1977 another train and a primary school were held at gunpoint for two weeks. Moluccan patience was exhausted. Few of them were in good jobs and many were still living in refugee accommodation. But it was their children, brought up in camps, fired by a sense of injustice untempered by residual loyalties to the Dutch monarchy, and wise in the ways of the Red Brigade, who had taken the initiative.

Whether anyone outside Holland and Indonesia grasped the gist of their protest is doubtful. But it was enough to spur the Dutch government into rehabilitation measures, cultural exchanges and job creation. It was also enough to put the wind up Jakarta whose troops remain in Ambon, most conspicuously in and around Fort Victoria. Enquiries elicited the information that it may be some time before the fort is open to visitors.

Epilogue

Before moving on to Irian I took a taxi to the north coast of Ambon island where only a wide channel separates it from Seram, its larger and less frequented parent. On hills sunk deep in forest the dainty clove trees stood side by side with the darker nutmeg. A mightier giant had strewn the ground underfoot with crisp leaves of dinner plate dimensions. It was like walking on papadums.

Nearing the coast, we stopped to watch the harvesting of a sago palm. The whole tree had been felled, and from its hollowed trunk the pith was being hacked out, then pounded and sluiced with water from an adjacent stream. One tree and a week's work would produce enough to feed a family for the best part of a year. True, sago cakes and sago dumplings make dull eating; the grey goo is not especially nutritious and saucers of the stuff, provided gratis on the counter of Ambon's post office for sticking up envelopes and improving the adhesion of stamps, seemed to attract no diners, only a few flies. But where else do people eat trees?

The sago consumers lived mostly along the coast. Green paint and the rust of a tiny tin dome denoted a Muslim village; yellow stucco and a stubby spire meant Christian. Some villages were both, an invisible line of custom and faith dividing the Friday worshippers and their wispy goats from the Sunday worshippers and their rootling pigs. The beach was shared by all. At the far end the four stark walls of another fort, once Portuguese then Dutch, had been colonised by the writhing progeny of a giant banyan. There must be as many forts in the Moluccas as castles in Syria. Having crusaded in vain for the Holy Lands, Europe had fared better in reclaiming the Spice Islands for Christendom. But neither Prophet nor Saviour could, it seemed, be totally confident of the hearts and minds of a people who lived on trees.

It was in a Christian village that the taxi driver insisted on trying the telephone.

'Direct dialling,' he said, 'but only to west Seram.' He summoned an old man wearing nothing but a sarong, and together we all approached a not very old tree. It appeared to be an evergreen, but not one I could identify.

'It is telephone tree.'

The taxi driver was now whispering. He motioned to me stay back as the old man advanced on the tree deferentially and extended his silky lizard-skin fingers over a slight irregularity in the bark at about head height.

'See, he dials,' said the driver. The fingers scarcely moved but in no time at all the patriarch was pressing an ear to the same bit of bark.

'He remembers. Now not working. But he remembers. Every night he hear news from Seram. It was first telephone in Ambon.' The suggestion of a smile puckered the corners of the old man's eyes. Perhaps he was remembering; perhaps he was just relieved that the demonstration had gone off so well. I gave him 500 rupiah.

'He is collecting for the church,' said the driver.

Ancient *adat* allegiances link the peoples of Ambon and west Seram. The adjacent islands of Saparua and Haruku are part of the same network and no doubt have their own 'field telephones'. Similar affiliations, based on shared migration myths, trade links and unexplained alliances reach further abroad to the coasts of Irian and Halmahera. For these extensive but little understood networks, the wonders of modern technology have provided a new vocabulary and a retrospective credibility. It can only be a matter of time before someone claims a suitably scooped rock as a satellite dish.

Such technology transfers are the modern equivalent of the

cargo cults which once swept through Oceania and are still current in parts of Irian and neighbouring Papua New Guinea. The novelties and the luxuries which materialized so bounteously from the white man's uninvited craft naturally inspired great awe amongst their fortunate recipients. Respect was shown to the needs and opinions of the strangers who accompanied this largesse and everything possible was done to ensure a continuity of supply. Hence the cargo cults with their strange mix of propitiating traditional powers, humouring the newcomers with deferential borrowings from their liturgies, and indulging the universal passion for acquisitive consumerism.

'The sago palm,' said the driver, 'it is our Tree of Life, our Milk of Kindness.'

Sophisticated peoples, like the villagers of Ambon and their coastal neighbours in Seram and Irian, have long since abjured cargo cults. Yet they do not accept that imported verities, whether religious or technological, are necessarily inimical to *adat*. On the contrary, such novelties may, as with the telephone and the Tree of Life, endorse traditional beliefs or, as with the sago adhesive, actually improve on them.

After the all-pervading Karaoke and the ubiquitous 'Kentaki' chicken, this more robust attitude towards imported tastes seemed admirable. In Torajaland they have been known to decant Coca-Cola into the bamboo pipes used for carrying water and palm wine. It goes flat but the bamboo pipes make it more acceptable at funerary feasts. The further east I went, the more I sensed a pragmatic and unpolarised attitude towards acculturation. Perhaps it had something to do with the waning influence here of Islam. The rigid rejection of all things 'western', as symbolised by the Muslim veil, was as much a novelty as the slavish imitation of imported novelties by the blue-jeaned followers of fashion. I looked forward to Irian and possible corroboration from its penis-sheathed highlanders.

But winging east on the final leg from Ambon to Jayapura, I conceded defeat. Below lay a land that coincided so precisely with the map that it could have been an aerial photo. Big brown rivers wound snake-like and capriciously across a background of un-interrupted green which ended only where blue sea bit into its borders. The forest cheated the land of all character, blanketing hills, habitations and trails in an impenetrable fog of greenery that stretched from the horizon in front to that behind. Even scars of deforestation would have been a relief to the eye; but there were none. And a wisp of smoke proved to be only a trail of stray mist. No roads were visible and, sure enough, but for four unrelated squiggles which stopped within an inch or two of the coast, no roads figured on the map. There was more in the way of airfields. In fact, nearly all the few place-names were those of airfields. But a strip of grass in a sea of trees doesn't show up well from 17,000 feet.

The land, like the map, was a blank waiting for someone to fill it in, waiting for someone to take advantage of it. One of those squiggles of road runs from the south coast through 90 kilometres of malarial swamp, forest and mountain to Tempagapura, 'Copperville'. Thence the world's longest single span cable wires carry 17-ton cars 2000 metres up into the clouds where whole mountains of copper are being mechanically excised. At current prices the enterprise is said to earn its operators, the American owned Freeport Indonesia Corp., over two million dollars a day. One of the largest copper mines in the world, it is thought also to contain some of the world's largest single deposits of both silver and gold. And in Tembagapura, a company town closed to all but the friends of Freeport, it has spawned one of Irian's half a dozen modest population centres.

What copper and Freeport have done here, petrochemicals, timber and their respective multi-nationals are doing on Irian's satellite islands and along its coastline. Upriver the wretched *transmigrasi* vainly try to turn scrub and forest into irrigated rice *sawah* while, further inland, missionaries, many attached to the obscurest of denominations, labour to win this last frontier for Christendom. They have had a fairly free hand in the interior ever since they were among the first to penetrate it in the 1930s. Many of those airstrips on the map are theirs; to reach them it helps, as with Tembagapura, to be a friend of the company. The lives saved by God Inc. with free antibiotics are rivalled only by the souls saved with free catechising. This is noble work and should no more be disparaged than the job opportunities created by Freeport or the informal economy generated by transmigrants. Likewise the incriminating film and the notebooks bulging with indignation which eco-righteous guardians of endangered societies and species diversity accumulate so readily in the Irian interior. For them, as for policy makers, anthropologists, and adventure writers, Irian provides a field-day every day. As a land to take liberties with, only Amazonia and Borneo can touch it.

I wanted none of this; yet I couldn't see how to avoid falling into the same trap. The place was just too big and too unmanageable, too new and too vulnerable. I was not even sure that it was relevant.

Although Irian Jaya accounts for nearly a quarter of Indonesia's total land area (and perhaps a tenth of its land-plus-sea area), it supports less than one per cent of its population. As quite a few of these are *transmigrasi* peoples from Java and Bali, native Irianese make up only about half of one per cent of Indonesia's population. They are outnumbered not only by major groups like the Batak and the Bugis but even by the peoples of minuscule homelands like Tanahtoraja and the Moluccas. And amongst these native Irianese, there is such a profusion of languages, customs and presumed ethnic affiliations that no single group can claim more than 250,000 adherents and most no more than 20,000. To its 800 different types of spider, its 100,000 insect species, 3000 fishes, and a greater plant variety than any other comparable region in the world, Irian thus adds a human diversity every bit as abundant and, in some areas, just as conjectural.

Aboriginal Papuan groups related to Australia's native peoples have evidently been residing in the island since very early times. But from their supposed arrival circa 40,000BC until the missionary push into the interior after 1938, practically nothing is recorded of them or by them. This is a land without an intelligible history. No doubt new crops, new agrarian techniques and improved tools and weapons wrought their own revolutions in

Irianese society; perhaps one day scholars will be able to piece together a full chronology of migrations and inventions. But for the time being the past is as successfully obliterated by the riot of nature as, from the air, is the land itself.

Away in the distance, where pinnacles of black rock rode above the clouds, what appeared to be a fairy-tale mirage of snow and ice held greater promise of a recognisable reality. But this too proved to be part of the Irian enigma. In Puncak Jaya, previously Carstenz Top, Irian boasts the highest peak in Australasia. To swamp, forest, savannah and mountain, equatorial snowfields add a final flourish of superfluous exotica.

In Jayapura, having for the most part scorned sea-side resorts, I went out to the beach. It was about eight in the evening, but a full moon gave the palm fronds a gun metal gleam and turned each breaking wave into an explosion of foaming shrapnel. The beach, about five miles out of town, is known as 'Base G'. You reach it down a sandy track through what looked in the headlights like dense forest. In spite of the name it was indistinguishable from a million other castaway's havens between the slumbering forest and the restless sea. There was no one around and not a light to be seen; I had the place to myself.

Five thousand kilometres away at the other end of Indonesia, every foreshore and freighter had reminded me of Joseph Conrad. Here it was James Cook who sprang to mind. I could see the dreaded *kora-koras*, the war canoes of the Pacific, being rushed down the beach by a hundred naked paddlers; and I saw their sharp bows snatching at the moon as they reared over the rollers to stab into the swell beyond.

Cook did visit Irian and received just such a reception. From Tahiti and New Zealand, in the course of his first voyage, he made his famous landfall at Botany Bay and then, after nearly perishing on the Great Barrier Reef, turned his attention to New Guinea. But as his object was to confirm the existence of the Torres Strait, it was along Irian's south coast that he sailed, receiving his 1770 rebuff from the Asmat people north-east of Merauke. Nearly two hundred years later Michael Rockefeller, the son of the Governor of New York, disappeared in the same region while on an expedition to collect Asmat wood-carvings. His fate remains a matter of sensational report and wild conjecture. Seemingly a simple drowning is too prosaic a demise for a Rockefeller.

Of such random incident is Irian's modest celebrity composed. Only once has it grabbed the headlines with matters of greater moment and that was in April 1944 when the sands at 'Base G' got their name. For it was here that General Douglas MacArthur, four months before Mountbatten's men landed at Sabang at the other end of the archipelago, began his island-hopping blitzkreig round the Pacific rim. It would push the Japanese forces back to Japan enabling MacArthur to fulfil his promise of 'I will return' to the Philippines.

Relying on the devastating over-kill that would characterize this whole campaign, he struck first at Jayapura, then known as Hollandia, with 1200 planes, 200 ships and over 80,000 men. At 'Base G' and other neighbouring beaches, throughout the night of April 21, every wave brought ashore another chevron of landing craft, jeeps and GIs, churning the sands and flattening the forest. At the airport, built by the Japanese on a scale that now looks wildly profligate for a place of such modest consequence, 300 Japanese aircraft were destroyed. Nearby, on hills overlooking Lake Sentani, where naked spearsmen now as then stand poised in their canoes, MacArthur established his headquarters. From the airport Superfortresses were soon blasting Japanese bases in Biak and Ambon. Jayapura became the unlikely launchpad for further amphibious landings along the Irian coast and onward to Morotai in the north Moluccas. Thence was mounted the final strike at the Philippines.

In this corner of the eastern archipelago the rusted remains of sunken ships still litter the loveliest of bays. Abandoned tanks protrude from the forest and a forlorn chassis serves as a climbing frame. At Biak, an island off the north coast of Irian, the US advance was nearly halted when over 7000 Japanese died in its defence; many were scorched to death as flame-throwers were directed into the network of caves which they used as air-raid shelters. But here too war left a bonus in the acres of concrete run-way and hangar. For trans-Pacific passengers from the US west coast, Biak frequently provides the first transit stop on Indonesian soil, the first cup of black *kopi* and the first sweet whiff of *kretek*.

Paddling in the moonlight at 'Base G' I wondered how it would be to approach the archipelago, like MacArthur or Margaret Mead, from the Pacific. And how it would be then to reverse my progress by travelling from east to west. In so vast a country that begins in teeming Asia and ends at the crossroads of empty Australasia and unbothered Oceania, perceptions must be radically altered by one's starting point. That pelagic idea, for instance, which seemed so presumptious in the Asian context of continental states and precious sea-boards, here seems far less contentious. Or instead of tracing those threads of Indian influence to their uttermost limits, how would it be if one arrived in Irian clutching different threads paying out, perhaps, from Polynesia or Adelaide? How long then before one lost track of all that was familiar, and began noticing Sanskrit place-names and Islamic sobriety?

Across the mouth of Jayapura's harbour and round the next headland lay the Papua New Guinea frontier. Like Aceh, it is closed to incoming visitors, and the same is true of its whole 600 kilometres of dead straight perpendicular line. It ends at Merauke, a place of no consequence and such expensive access that I felt even less guilty about ignoring it than I had about Sabang. Most of this neat frontier is un-policed, unmarked and practically inaccessible. Like the guards in Buru's labour camps, Indonesia here relies on the hostility of nature to discourage unauthorised passage. The world's largest pelagic state ends in a wall of forest.

I faced about and, for the first time in months, flew into a setting sun.

Further Reading

Anderson, J., *Mission to the East Coast of Sumatra in 1823*, London, 1826

Barley, N., *Not a Hazardous Sport*, Viking, London, 1988

Bastin, John, *The British in West Sumatra 1682-1825*, Kuala Lumpur, 1965

Baum, Vicki, *A Tale from Bali*, OUP reprint, Singapore, 1973

Bogarde, Dirk, *Backcloth*, London, 1986

Coast, John, *Recruit to Revolution*, Christophers, London, 1952

Covarrubias, Miguel, *Island of Bali*, Cassell, London, 1937

Dalton, Bill, *Indonesia Handbook*, Moon, Chico, 1977

Dumarcay, Jacques, *The Temples of Java*, OUP reprint, Singapore, 1986

Dunn, James, *Timor: A People Betrayed*, Jacaranda, Milton, 1983

Furneaux, Rupert, *Krakatoa*, Secker and Warburg, London, 1965

Furnivall, J.S., *Netherlands India*, Cambridge UP, 1939

Geertz, Clifford, *The Theatre State in Nineteenth Century Bali*, Princeton, 1980

Kahin, A.R. (ed) *Regional Dynamics of the Indonesian Revolution*, U of Hawaii, Honolulu, 1985

Keay, John, *The Honourable Company; A History of the English East India Company*, HarperCollins, London, 1991

Keay, Julia, *The Spy Who Never Was; The Life and Loves of Mata Hari*, M Joseph, London 1987

Legge, J.D., *Sukarno, A Political Biography*, Allen and Unwin, Sydney, 1972

Marsden, William, *History of Sumatra*, London 1783

Modigliani, Elio, *Un Viaggio a Nias*, Fratelli, Milan, 1890

Mossman, James, *Rebels in Paradise*, Cape, London, 1961

Multatuli (E. Douwes Dekker), *Max Havelaar Or the Coffee Auctions of the Dutch Trading Company*, U. of Massachusetts reprint, Amherst, 1982

Oey, Eric et al (eds), Periplus Guides to *Sumatra, Java, Sulawesi* etc, Periplus, Singapore, 1991-

Parkin, Ray, *Out of the Smoke*, Hogarth Press, London, 1960

Pramoedya Ananta Toer, *This Earth of Mankind, Child of All Nations* etc, Penguin Australia, 1988-

Raffles, S., *Memoir of Sir Thomas Stamford Raffles* etc, Murray, London, 1830

Raffles, T.S., *History of Java*, London, 1817

Reid, Anthony, *The Conquest of North Sumatra*, Kuala Lumpur, 1969

Ricklefs, M.C., *A History of Modern Indonesia*, Macmillan, London, 1981

Schnitger, F.M., *Forgotten Kingdoms in Sumatra*, OUP reprint, Singapore, 1991

Shibeth, Achim, *The Batak*, Thames and Hudson, London, 1991

Smithies, Michael, *Yogyakarta*, OUP, Singapore, 1986

Szekely, Ladislao, *Tropic Fever* OUP, reprint, Kuala Lumpur, 1979

Van der Post, Laurens, *The Seed and the Sower*, London, 1963; *The Night of the New Moon*, London; 1970, *A Walk with a White Bushman*, London, 1986.

Vickers, Adrian, *Bali, A Paradise Created*, Periplus reprint, Berkeley, 1989

Vlekke, B.H.M., *Nusantara; A History of East Indian Archipelago*, Harvard, 1943

Wallace, Alfred Russel, *The Malay Archipelago*, OUP Reprint, Singapore, 1989

Wilcox, H., *White Stranger; Six Moons in Sulawesi*, Collins, London, 1949

Zain'uddin, Ailsa, *A Short History of Indonesia*, Cassell, Melborne, 1968

Index

Abidin, Dr Andi Zainal, 240-1
ABRI (*Angkatan Bersenjata Republik Indonesia* – Armed
    Forces of Indonesian Republic), 96-7, 144, 147, 237,
    268
Aceh, 8-10, 11-28, 30, 54, 65, 79, 121, 136, 234
Adat, 53-5, 80, 89-91, 92, 273
Afro-Asia Conference, see Bandung
Agam, West Sumatra, 90
Agus Salim, Haji, 93
Ai, Pulau, Banda, 257-8, 261
Alexander the Great, 81
Alwi, Des, 262, 265-6
Amboina Massacre, 266
Ambon, 27, 250, 251, 254, 266-9, 271-3, 277
Anderson, John, 30-1, 41, 45
Anjer, West Java, 120, 121, 127
Architecture, 53-4, 59, 68, 71, 74-5, 86-7, 132, 186-7,
    201, 245
Army, Indonesian, see ABRI; Dutch, see Netherlands
Arnold, Dr Joseph, 102, 112
Aru Islands, 233
Asahan, North Sumatra, 30, 38, 46
Asmat tribe, 276-7
Asoka, emperor, 80

Badui tribe, 138-9
Badung, Bali, 219, 221
Bahasa Indonesia, 4, 91, 122, 230
Bakauheni, Lampung, 117, 121
Baker, Captain George, 178
Bali, 2, 4, 62, 110, 151, 207-8, 210-27, 231-2, see also
    Denpasar, Sanur etc.
Balikpapan, Kalimantan, 249
Banda Aceh, 8-10, 11-28, 41-2
Banda Besar (Lonthor), 258
Banda Islands, 233, 250, 254-66
Banda Naira, 254-7, 258, 262, 265
Bandung, 137, 157, 158-70
Bandung (Afro-Asia) Conference, 166-8
Bangka, 127
Banjarmasin, Kalimantan, 249
Banten, West Java, 105, 129-33, 138, 140, 191, 234, 260
Banyuwangi, East Java, 213
Base G, Jayapura, 276-7

Batak peoples, 22, 41, 42-4, 46-59, 61-2, 80, 136, 141,
    244
Batak church, see HKBP
Batam, Pulau, 5-8
Batavia, 116-7, 120, 131, 138, 161, see also Sunda
    Kelapa and Jakarta
Bateson, Gregory, 223-4
Bawomataluo, Nias, 71-7
Belawan, North Sumatra, 30
Bengkulu, 30, 85, 99, 103-113, 116, 244
Betawi, see Batavia
Biak, 277-8
Blambangan, East Java, 215
Bogarde, Dirk, 161-3
Bogor, 139, 157
Bone, Sulawesi, 242-3
Bonjol, West Sumatra, 88, 90, 97
Bonjol, Tuanku Imam (see Imam Bonjol)
Borneo (Kalimantan), 2, 135, 200, 238, 244
Borobudur, 6, 103, 154, 173-7
Brastagi, North Sumatra, 50, 61
Bromo, 122
Buchari, Dr Mahmud, 169-70
Buddhism, 27, 40, 41, 174-9, 198
Budi Utomo, 194, 253
Bugis, 233, 240-44
Bukit Barisan, 44, 47, 101, 116
Bukit Lawang, North Sumatra, 62
Bukittinggi, 80, 82-8, 90-4, 96-7
Buru, 251-3

Celebes, The, see Sulawesi
Chakranegara, Lombok, 235
Chinese community, 161, 198, 212
Chola kings, 39
Cik di Tiro, 21
Cilacap, Central Java, 127, 171
Cirebon, 200
Cloves, see Spice Trade
Coen, Jan Pieterzoon, 118
Coffee, 31, 45, 159-60
Collet, Joseph, 106-7
Communist Party of Indonesia, see PKI
Conrad, Joseph, 276

Cook, Captain James, 118, 276
Coomaraswamy, Ananda, 177
Courthope, Nathaniel, 258-61, 264
Covarrubias, Miguel, 220, 224, 235
Curup, Bengkulu, 102
Cut Nyak Dien, 21

Daendels, Marshall Willem, 159, 160
Dar-ul-Islam 25, 133, 243
Dekker, Edward Douwes, 137-8, 159, 182, 229-30
Dekker, E. F. E. Douwes, 169
Deli, North Sumatra, 30-3, 43, 45, 61
Demak, Central Java, 132, 138, 200-1
Denpasar, Bali, 137, 219, 224
Dewa Manggis Disasteria VI & VII of Gianyar, 216
Dias, Thomas, 85
Dilli, East Timor, 236, 239
Diponegoro, Prince, 193, 266
Drake, Sir Francis, 171
Dunlop, Dr Weary, 164
Dutch, see Netherlands
Dutch Reformed Church, 27, 36

East India Company, English (EIC), 8, 12, 18, 66, 85,
    105-8, 118, 129-30, 258, 266-7
East India Company, Dutch (VOC), 81, 118, 129-30
East Indonesia State, see *Negara Indonesia Timur* (NIT)
East Timor, 2, 135, 152, 236, 239-40
Equator, 79, 88

Fakfak, Irian Jaya, 210, 249
Flores, 108, 233, 251
Freeport Indonesia, 274
Fretilin, 239-40

Gedong Songo, Central Java, 179
Geertz, Clifford, 154, 180, 186, 216
GESTAPU, 50, 145-52, 176, 221-2, 239, 245, 251
Gianyar, Bali, 216, 222
Gili Islands, Lombok, 232
Gold, 81
Gomo, Nias, 73
Gorontalo, Sulawesi, 249
Gowa, Sulawesi, 242-3
Gresik, East Java, 202
Gunung Agung, Bali, 232
Gunung Api, Banda, 254, 257, 259

Habibie, Dr Jusuf, 168
Halmahera, 272
Hamengkubuwono, Sultans of Jogja, 185-9, 192-5
Haruku, 251, 272
Hasanuddin, Sultan of Gowa, 132
Hatta, Dr Mohammed, 93, 94, 96-7, 122, 194, 251, 264-
    5
Havelaar, Max, see Dekker, E. D.
Herbert, A.P., 229, 230
Hidayatulla, Sharif, 132
Hinduism, 27, 47, 104-5, 139, 176-80, 186-8, 213, 245
HMAS *Perth*, 126-8, 171
Hollandia, see Jayapura
Hurgronje, Dr Snouck, 22
Huria Kristen Batak Protestan, (Batak Protestant Christian
    Church), 48-9, 55-6

Ide Anak Agung Gde Agung, Dr, 216-9, 225-7, 231, 265
Imam Bonjol, Tuanku, 89-90
Imam, Teuku, 20-1
Independence struggle, 22, 80, 93, 108, 140, 161-3, 194-
    5, 203-8, 221, 226-7, 237, 252
Indian influences, 38-41, 177
'Indonesia', 229-30, 233-4
Indonesia Handbook, 13, 37, 62, 250
Indonesian Armed Forces, see ABRI
Indonesian Railways, 98, 153-8, 171
'Insulinde', 230
Irian Jaya, 2, 10, 135, 139, 209, 230, 233, 237-8, 272-3,
    274-8
Iskander Muda, Sultan of Aceh, 18, 21, 27, 41
Islam, 13, 22, 25, 27-8, 41, 49-50, 89-91, 92, 104, 132-
    3, 198, 200-1, 236, 243

Jack, Dr William, 66, 72, 112
Jacobs, Dr Julius, 218
Jakarta, 2, 14, 38, 50, 93, 116, 130, 138-52, 153-5, 207,
    253, see also Batavia, Sunda Kelapa
Jakarta Post, 48, 49, 156, 206
Jambi, 40, 79
Japanese Occupation, 22, 37-8, 83, 96, 122-9, 163-4,
    199, 204, 226-7, 251, 265, 277-8
Java, 4, 14, 30, 32, 34, 49, 85, 96, 110, 115, 121, 123,
    212-3, see also Jakarta, Surabaya, Bandung, Jogjakarta
    etc.
Java Sea, Battle of, 124-5, 128
Java War (1825-30), 193
Jayapura, 139, 210, 276-9
Jogjakarta, 40, 93, 122, 173-89, 192-5, 207
Johore, 7, 41, 244
Joyoboyo, 122-3

K'tut Tantri ('Surabaya Sue'), 37, 153-4, 163, 202-3,
    205-8, 225-7
Kalimantan, see Borneo
Kalinga Kingdom, 39
Kediri Kingdom, 40, 123, 181, 195
Kei archipelago, 250
Keli Mutu, Flores, 236
Ki Hadjar Dewantoro, 230
Klungkung, Bali, 220
Komodo, 102, 236
Konfrontasi, 146, 238-9
Krakatau, 1, 20, 118-22, 146
Kudus, Central Java, 138, 201
Kupang, West Timor, 236
Kuta, Bali, 226

Lagundri, Nias, 67, 69-70
Lampung, 79, 121
Lancaster, James, 8, 12, 118
Langkat, North Sumatra, 30
Lawrence, D. H., 137
Lebak, West Java, 137, 138
Leiden, John, 43
Lembar, Lombok, 231-2, 235
Lombok, 4, 210, 215, 218-9, 231-2, 235-6, 245-6
Lubang Buaya, Jakarta, 142-4
Lubuklinggau, South Sumatra, 101
Luwu, Sulawesi, 242-3
Luwuk, Sulawesi, 249

MacArthur, General Douglas, 277-8
MacKays of Medan, 33
Mackenzie, Colin, 177-8
MacLeod, Captain and Mrs Rudolph, 33-7, see also 'Mata Hari'
Madiun, East Java, 195, 265
Madura, 196
Mahabharata, 180, 183, 184
Majapahit kingdom, 40, 181, 188, 195, 200, 215
Makassar, 121, 151, 200, 233, 234, 240-44, (see also Ujung Pandang)
Malacca, 30, 32, 118
Malacca Strait, 5, 18, 39, 110, 118
Malay language, 41, 91
Malay peoples, 4, 42-3, 47, 81-2, 86
Malaysia, 18, 39, 97, 238-9, see also *Konfrontasi*
Mallaby, Brigadier A. W. S., 203-4
Maluku, see Moluccas
Manado, Sulawesi, 27, 97, 249
Manokwari, Irian Jaya, 249
'Manx, Miss', see K'tut Tantri
Marco Polo, 39, 43, 58
Marsden, William, 18, 43, 49, 53, 65, 81, 107, 117, 123, 201
'Mata Hari', 33-7, 180, 227
Mataram kingdoms, 40, 121, 172, 173-89, 192-5
Matulessy, Thomas 'Pattimura', 267-8
Maumere, Flores, 236
Max Havelaar, 137, see also Dekker, E. D.
Mead, Margaret (Bateson), 213, 223-4, 278
Medan, 10, 29-44, 48, 56, 61, 62, 79, 96, 151
Melanesian peoples, 4, 209-10, 230
Melayu, 40, 82
Merah-putih, 5, 123, 203
Merak, West Java, 117, 120, 121, 126-7, 128, 129
Merapi, Central Java, 121, 180
Merauke, Irian Jaya, 10, 265, 276, 278
Meulaboh, Aceh, 11, 21, 24
Minangkabau, 31, 65, 80-94, 95-7, 110, 141, 244
Modigliani, Elio, 67, 76
Moluccas, 30, 235, 237, 250-69, 271-3
Morotai, Moluccas, 250, 277
Mossman, James, 95
Mountbatten, Lord Louis, 10, 165
Muhammadiya movement, 91, 109, 194
Muntok, Bangka, 83
Musi River, 39, 116

Napoleon Buonaparte, 110
NASAKOM, 145, 147, 193, 195
Nasution, Gen Abdul Haris, 6, 50, 140, 147-52, 195
Negara Indonesia Timur (NIT), 231, 233, 237, 244, 267
Nehru, Jawaharlal, 165-6, 215, 221
Netherlands, The, see also East India Company, Dutch Colonial Army (KNIL), 27, 90, 219-21, 267-8
    Colonial Rule, 3, 17-22, 61, 67, 81, 94, 123, 137, 160, 164, 206, 218-19, 258-61
New Guinea, see Irian Jaya, Papua New Guinea etc.
Ngurah Rai, 221
Nias, Pulau, 47, 62, 64-77, 110, 212
Nicobar Islands, 8, 12
Nienhuys, Jacobus, 31, 33
Nommensen, Ludwig, 48
Nusa Penida, Bali, 232

'Nusantara', 230
Nusa-tengara, 233, 236
Nutmegs, see Spice Trade, Banda

Padang, West Sumatra, 23, 80, 84, 85, 90, 96-7, 118
Padang Bai, Bali, 231
Paderi movement, 89-91, 92
Pagarruyung, West Sumatra, 87, 90
Paisir, 141, 196-202
Pajajaran kingdom, 137, 188
Palembang, 31, 39, 82, 83, 116, 137
Palu, Sulawesi, 249
Pancasila, 145, 246
Papua New Guinea, 278
Parangtritis, Central Java, 189
Parapat, North Sumatra, 61-2
Parkin, Ray, 126
Parr, Thomas, 107-8
'Pasundan', 140, see also Sunda
'Pattimura', see Matulessy
Patty, A. J., 266, 268
Pelagic status, 1, 40-1, 195-6, 233-5, 241-2, 278
Pemacutan, Bali, 219
Pemuda, 203-4
Penang, 19, 30, 32
Pepper, 18, 19, 20, 30, 86, 107, 130, 257
PKI (Communist Party of Indonesia), 93, 96, 144, 147, 150-1, 200, 221-2, 230, 253
Polynesian peoples, 47, 76
Pontianak, Kalimantan, 249
Portuguese empire, 18, 81, 138, 231, 242, 267
Prambanam, 176-9
Pramoedya Ananta Toer, 6, 17, 252-4
Preanger, 157, 159-60
PRRI (1958), 95-7, 100, 144, 237
Puncak Jaya, 276

Qur'ān, Al, 28, 168-70

Raden Patah, 201
Raden Trenggana, 201
Raffles, Sophia, Lady, 85, 102, 110-12
Raffles, Sir Thomas Stamford, 5, 53, 66-7, 81-2, 84-8, 89, 102, 105, 109-13, 115, 128, 159, 174-5, 192, 209-10, 212
Rafflesia Arnoldi, 102
Ramayana, 39, 177, 186
Rantepao, Sulawesi, 249
Ratu Loro Kidul, 172, 188-9, 193
Rejang, 103
Republik Maluku Selatan (RMS), 268-9
Riau, 79
Ricklefs, M. C., 80, 192
Rinjani, Lombok, 232
Rockefeller, Michael, 277
Rubber, 31, 45
Run, Pulau, Banda, 250, 258-61, 263

Sabah (North Borneo), 238
Sabang, 10, 22, 277
Samosir, North Sumatra, 46, 58-9, 62
Sangaing Island, 124, 127
Sanskrit, 39-41, 47, 139
Sanur, Bali, 219, 224, 226

Saparua, 272
Sarawak, 238
Sartono, Dr, 40, 181, 184, 229
Sastroamidjojo, Ali, 167
Schnitger, F. M., 67, 71, 76
Semarang, 128, 196-200
Seram, 250, 268, 271-3
Serang, West Java, 129-30, 137
Serdang, Sumatra, 30
Siak, Sumatra, 30, 31
Siantar, North Sumatra, 33, 45, 49
Siberut, 70
Sibolga, North Sumatra, 63-4, 88
Siliwangi, 139
Simaleue, 70
Simbolon, Colonel, 96
Singapore, 5-7, 19, 30, 41, 66, 111, 124, 127
Singaraja, Bali, 216
Singosari kingdom, 34
Sisingamangaraja, 43-4, 48, 55
Sjahrir, Sutan, 93, 231, 251, 264-6
Sjarifuddin, Amir, 93, 227
Smithies, Prof. Michael, 175
Soekmono, Dr, 6, 175-6, 178-9
South East Asia Command (SEAC), 10, 129
South Moluccan Republic, see *Republik Maluku Selatan*
   (RMS)
South Pacific, 2, 213
Spice Islands, 233, see also Moluccas
Spice Trade, 138, 215, 235, 243, 257-63
Spies, Walter, 224, 225, 226
Srivijaya, 39-41, 82
SS *Nisero*, 17, 20-21
Sudirman, General, 204
Suharto, President, 139, 141, 144-5, 146, 149-52, 159,
   168, 239, 251
Sukarno, President, 2, 10, 17, 93, 96-7, 108-9, 122, 139,
   141, 145-52, 154, 165-6, 167-8, 169, 204, 218, 221,
   231, 237, 251
Sukarno, Dewi, 146, 153
Sukarnoputeri, Megawatti, 181
Sukuh, Candi, 179, 180
Sulawesi, 4, 96, 97, 193, 230, 233, 237, 241-7, 249, see
   also Makassar etc.
Sumatra, 4, 8-10, 79-80, 86, 115-6, see also Aceh,
   Medan, Toba, Bukittinggi, Bengkulu etc
Sumba, 236
Sumbawa, 121, 232, 233
Sunan Kalijaga, 201
Sunda (West Java), 137-40, 159-60
Sunda Islands, 118, 122, see also Sumatra, Java, Bali,
   Lombok, Flores etc.
Sunda Kelapa, 138, see also Batavia, Jakarta
Sunda Strait, Battle of, 124-7
Sunda Straits, 39, 110, 115-29
Surabaya, 124, 128, 137, 154, 161, 192, 195, 202-8,
   209-10, 227
Surabaya, Battle of, 202-8
'Surabaya Sue', see K'tut Tantri
Surakarta (Solo), 177, 179, 185, 192, 194

Suranadi, Lombok, 236
Sutomo ('Bung Tomo'), 203, 204-5, 207
Szekely, Laszlo, 32-3, 41, 43, 56

Tabanan, Bali, 214, 219, 220
Tambora, Sumbawa, 121, 122, 232
Tan Malaka, 93, 169
Tanahtoraja, see Torajaland
Tanimbar, 250
Tanjung Balai, North Sumatra, 33
Tanjung Priok, Jakarta, 126
Tapanuli Bay, 63
Tarakan, Kalimantan, 249
Tarumanegara kingdom, 138
Tarutung, North Sumatra, 63
'Tavip', 'The Year of Living Dangerously', see
   GESTAPU
Tebingtinggi, North Sumatra, 33
Teluk Betung, Lampung, 121
Teluk Dalam, Nias, 69-72
Tempagapura, Irian Jaya, 274-5
Tengger, East Java, 136
Ternate, 233, 257
Timor, 215, 230, 235, see also East Timor, West Timor
Toba, Lake, 38, 46-59, 121
Tobacco, 31-3
Tomok, North Sumatra, 50-1, 56, 57
Toraja, 47, 244-7
Torajaland, 244-7, 273
Torres Strait, 276
Transmigrasi, 103, 195-7, 274-5
Trowulan, East Java, 195
Tuban, East Java, 201
Tumpang, East Java, 34

Ubud, Bali, 224
Ujung Pandang, 233, 241, 244, 249, see also Makassar
Umar, Teuku, 20-22, 27
United States of Indonesia (USI), 231, 237
USN *Houston*, 126

Van der Post, Laurens, 128-9, 131, 161-5, 191, 251
Van der Tuuk, H. N., 218
Vlekke, B. H. M., 115

Wahab, Muhammad ibn Abd al-, 89
Wallace, Alfred Russel, 232-3, 249-50
Wallace Line, 4, 232-3
Watson, Captain, 118-20
Wayang kulit, 182-3, 188
Weh, North Sumatra, 10
West Timor, 135
Westerling, Captain 'Turk', 243
Woodhouse, Captain, 17

Yamin, Mohammed, 93
Yani, Gen. Ahmad, 97, 141, 143-5, 148-9, 185, 266
Year of Living Dangerously, The, 2, 145-6, 199

Zheng-Ho, 198